Moving the AEC
Beyond 2015

The **ISEAS–Yusof Ishak Institute** (formerly Institute of Southeast Asian Studies) was established as an autonomous organization in 1968. It is a regional centre dedicated to the study of socio-political, security and economic trends and developments in Southeast Asia and its wider geostrategic and economic environment. The Institute's research programmes are the Regional Economic Studies (RES, including ASEAN and APEC), Regional Strategic and Political Studies (RSPS), and Regional Social and Cultural Studies (RSCS).

ISEAS Publishing, an established academic press, has issued more than 2,000 books and journals. It is the largest scholarly publisher of research about Southeast Asia from within the region. ISEAS Publishing works with many other academic and trade publishers and distributors to disseminate important research and analyses from and about Southeast Asia to the rest of the world.

Moving the AEC Beyond 2015

MANAGING DOMESTIC CONSENSUS
FOR COMMUNITY-BUILDING

EDITED BY

THAM SIEW YEAN   SANCHITA BASU DAS

 YUSOF ISHAK
INSTITUTE

First published in Singapore in 2016 by
ISEAS Publishing
30 Heng Mui Keng Terrace
Singapore 119614

E-mail: publish@iseas.edu.sg
Website: <http://bookshop.iseas.edu.sg>

The responsibility for facts and opinions in this publication rests exclusively with the author and his interpretations do not necessarily reflect the views or the policy of the publisher or its supporters.

ISEAS Library Cataloguing-in-Publication Data

Moving the AEC Beyond 2015 : Managing Domestic Consensus for Community-Building / editors, Tham Siew Yean and Sanchita Basu Das.
1. ASEAN.
2. Regionalism—Southeast Asia.
3. Southeast Asia—Economic integration.
4. Southeast Asia—Economic conditions.
5. Southeast Asia—Foreign economic relations.
I. Tham, Siew Yean.
II. Basu Das, Sanchita.
HC441 M93   2016

ISBN 978-981-4695-51-0 (soft cover)
ISBN 978-981-4695-52-7 (e-book, PDF)

Typeset by Superskill Graphics Pte Ltd
Printed in Singapore by Markono Print Media Pte Ltd

CONTENTS

FOREWORD

As we draw to the end of 2015 and the date of completion of the ASEAN Economic Community (AEC), there is a lot of analysis regarding what happens post 2015. Most analysis involve a review of the achievements and progress measured against the AEC Blueprint and then make recommendations on the way forward. Most of the recommendations are made up of completing the unfinished business of AEC 2015 and then go on to outline how to widen and deepen AEC 2015 so ASEAN can be an integrated production base and market. Only a few try to understand the root causes of the slower than desired progress towards this end goal. This book fills the gap by exploring how domestic conflicts at the level of each ASEAN country have impacted on each country's AEC commitments.

Therefore, the editors of this volume and ISEAS–Yusof Ishak Institute should be congratulated on choosing such a topic in a timely way. This publication is a very welcome publication because it attempts to get at the root causes of domestic constraints on the commitments that each ASEAN economy can make. Despite the acceptance of the vision at the very top level and the long-term process of development in ASEAN, it is a fact that the lack of appreciation for the ASEAN process in a country and that the benefits are not directly felt in the country, means that there has been lack of support domestically. Furthermore, despite the fact that the AEC has four pillars including an equitable ASEAN, there is not much in terms of commitments and concrete actions in this pillar. Most of the AEC commitments and actions have been in the first pillar of a single production base and market, which involves liberalization and facilitation.

In 2011 when Indonesia was the Chair of ASEAN, it was recognized that without strengthening of the equitable pillar it would be hard to have the confidence to progress on the first pillar and other pillars related to a competitive ASEAN and the way ASEAN engages externally. Without addressing the inequitable development due to economic integration within and between ASEAN countries, it was difficult to get more support to speed up opening up and integration. At the time it was thought that part of the answer to addressing the imbalances within and between countries was infrastructure, and the ASEAN Infrastructure Fund came about, as well as attempts to address the financial inclusion agenda. However, concrete actions have not really come through on this count with the exception of attempts to create funding for infrastructure such as the ASEAN Infrastructure Fund, whose effectiveness is still to be tested.

Given the more recent developments with the push back against globalization playing out in many countries, not just in ASEAN, the reality is that without domestic support and buy in, it would be difficult to move forward on greater opening up. More importantly, the situation has changed in most of the ASEAN countries with democracy and greater transparency, so that as one of the themes emphasized in the book, state-led economic integration with limited ownership of domestic stakeholders can no longer be the norm.

The papers in this volume will help us better understand the domestic issues faced by each country and will hopefully be useful as to how to best ensure that the AEC vision beyond 2015 will be able to be delivered with greater ownership by the people of ASEAN. As indicated in the papers in this volume, this is not an easy task but we should not be discouraged. Greater understanding of the issues is still better than pretending that we can go on with the task of greater regional integration without more collective domestic support.

The papers show that the nature and type of domestic conflicts vary between the ASEAN countries depending on the economic structure of the country, the degree of openness and its long-term development goals. The nature of the conflicts also range from the broad macro level to the micro level of firm level and public perceptions of the net benefits or costs of economic integration.

The various types of domestic conflicts, which emerge from these country studies, are not surprising. The various conflicts include firstly sectoral vested interests and interests of sectors dominated by certain state-owned companies. There is also the expected conflict between losers and gainers from any opening up and economic integration.

Secondly "water" in the commitments or that unilateral liberalization policy is much more open than the offered regional AEC commitments is the reality of negotiation processes. Negotiators are not going to give too much away in terms of binding commitments if they are negotiating bilaterally and multilaterally. In a way this is a good example of the importance of making progress on multilateral commitments to frame and ensure progress on commitments under preferential agreements. The Agreement on the Framework on Services is basically GATS plus which is based on the Uruguay Round of negotiations, which ended in 1994. With no movement on services negotiations multilaterally, WTO plus still means GATS plus and not much more binding commitments are forthcoming.

Thirdly is the lack of internal consultation process with all stakeholders. While this varies between countries, the reasons for lack of wide consultations often have to do with the limitations on the number and representation of stakeholders, and lack of transparency in the consultancy process. There is also a seemingly glaring outcome that the low utilization of the lower tariff under CEPT in surveys, show that firms and the wider public do not have a good understanding of the benefits of the AEC.

The findings of the chapters of this book are not new, but should make us ponder about what needs to be done to ensure there is confidence to move forward with the AEC beyond 2015. This book also provides recommendations to address these domestic sources of conflict such as aligning domestic policies with liberalization commitments, broaden stakeholder consultations, better public education and dissemination, and assistance/training programmes to mitigate any negative impact from liberalization.

In conclusion, I hope that many policymakers and the wider public will read this book and find it useful to explore how the recommendations can be enacted upon in each ASEAN country. Because without addressing these domestic conflicts, there will be no confidence to realize the current AEC 2015 Blueprint, let alone think of AEC 2015 and beyond.

Dr Mari Pangestu
Professor of International Economics, Faculty of Economics,
University of Indonesia
Minister for Trade, Indonesia (2004–11)
Minister for Tourism and Creative Economy, Indonesia (2011–14)

PREFACE

As ASEAN reached its milestone of December 2015, there is immense debate on the state of regional integration. While member countries have made commitments to the regional goals and targets of an ASEAN Economic Community (AEC), they continue to face hurdles in the effective implementation of their commitments in their respective domestic economies. This slows down the entire process of ASEAN Community-Building, thereby limiting the realization of the full potential of the ASEAN Leaders' vision, envisaged in 1997, of "a stable, prosperous and highly competitive ASEAN economic region in which there is a free flow of goods, services, investment and freer flow of capital, equitable economic development and reduced poverty and socioeconomic disparities".

Given this scenario, we thought it is important and useful to undertake a study that can illuminate the academics, policymakers and ordinary citizens on implementation issues in member countries. Our reading of the literature and discussions with fellow researchers and domestic stakeholders in different countries led us to conjecture that domestic conflict may be an important source of implementation problems. We found that these domestic conflicts can take several forms in ASEAN countries ranging from macro-level policy-making to firm-level perception of winners and losers from the establishment of AEC. As ASEAN members are very different from each other, the nature of domestic conflicts also varies depending on the economic structure of the country, its stage of development, degree of openness to the global economy and its development goals and priorities. It is important to understand the nature of conflict and identify the winners and losers so that the member economies can formulate appropriate domestic policies for deeper economic integration in ASEAN beyond 2015.

In order to meet the objective of the study, we gathered Southeast Asian experts to discuss about six selected countries of ASEAN — Indonesia, Malaysia, the Philippines, Singapore, Thailand and Vietnam. We also thought it is important to incorporate some discussions at the regional level to foster an understanding of the overall perspective and how it is determined as this will provide a backdrop to the country studies.

It should be noted that part of this book volume is already published as a journal issue — *Journal of Southeast Asian Economies* (JSEAE), vol. 32, no. 2. Special Focus on "Moving the AEC Beyond 2015: Managing Domestic Consensus for Community-Building" — in August 2015. The articles of the journal issue and a few more constitute this volume's chapters. It begins with an overview chapter that covers the literature on regionalism, an evaluation on the state of AEC and summarizes important observations from the subsequent chapters. The chapter concludes with a summary of the recommendations made in the regional and country chapters of the book. The introductory chapter is followed by a regional chapter and six country chapters by experts both on regional integration and country economic studies.

We hope this book will help ASEAN stakeholders and other interested public members in understanding the current state of AEC and domestic conflicts arising out of it. We hope that the policy recommendations can provide food for thought for policymakers in the region.

ACKNOWLEDGEMENTS

It is a pleasure here to thank the many hands that have assisted and guided us along this journey. First, we would like to thank the ISEAS–Yusof Ishak Institute (ISEAS) for providing us with a platform to undertake research on ASEAN studies. In particular, we would like to thank Mr Tan Chin Tiong, Director of the Institute, for extending his kind support and frequent words of encouragement throughout the journey. We are also grateful to Dr Ooi Kee Beng, Deputy Director of ISEAS and Mr Rodolfo C. Severino, Head of ASEAN Studies Centre, for their interest in this project as well as their confidence in us — it served to inspire us to do our best. Special thanks to Mr Severino for sharing his invaluable insights on ASEAN economic integration in this book. Dr Francis Hutchinson, Coordinator of Regional Economics Studies Programme, and Dr Cassey Lee, both Senior Fellows at ISEAS, shared with us their precious time to provide counsel and constructive comments throughout the process. We were also assisted by Ms Reema Bhagwan Jagtiani, research officer at ISEAS, at critical junctures of the project and we especially would like to thank her for going beyond the normal call of duty. Our sincere thanks to the staff of the ISEAS Publishing, especially Mr Ng Kok Kiong, Head, and Ms Rahilah Yusuf, Senior Editor, for their professionalism in getting this book published. We are especially grateful to Dr Mari Pangestu, the former Trade Minister of Indonesia (2004–11) as well as a renowned trade economist who has contributed significantly to the development of ASEAN policies, for kindly writing the foreword in this book. Last but not least, we are indebted to our chapter writers and anonymous reviewers of the volume and we thank them from the bottom of our hearts as they are the ones who made the project a success and this publication possible.

LIST OF ABBREVIATIONS

AA	ASEAN Architects
AAF	ASEAN Automotive Federation
ACCP	ASEAN Committee on Consumer Protection
ACD	ASEAN Cosmetics Directive
ACIA	ASEAN Comprehensive Investment Agreement
ACTLN	ASEAN Cosmetic Testing Laboratory Network
ACTR	ASEAN Common Technical Requirements
ADB	Asian Development Bank
ADBI	Asian Development Bank Institute
AEC	ASEAN Economic Community
AEM	ASEAN Economic Ministers
AEMM	ASEAN Economic Ministers Meeting
AEO	Authorized Economic Operators
AFAFGIT	ASEAN Framework Agreement on the Facilitation of Goods in Transit
AFAFIST	ASEAN Framework Agreement on the Facilitation of Inter-State Transport
AFAMT	ASEAN Framework Agreement on Multimodal Transport
AFAS	ASEAN Free Trade Agreement on Services
AFC	Asian Financial Crisis
AFMM+3	ASEAN Plus Three Finance Ministers Meeting
AFTA	ASEAN Free Trade Area
AHEEERR	ASEAN Harmonized Electrical and Electronic Equipment Regulatory Regime
AHTN	ASEAN Harmonized Tariff Nomenclature
AIA	ASEAN Investment Area
AIF	ASEAN Infrastructure Fund

AIGA	ASEAN Investment Guarantee Agreement
AIIB	Asian Infrastructure Investment Bank
AIJV	ASEAN Industrial Joint Venture
AIP	ASEAN Industrial Projects
AJCEP	ASEAN-Japan Comprehensive Economic Partnership Agreement
AKFTA	ASEAN-Korea FTA
AMDD	ASEAN Medical Device Directive
AMM	ASEAN Ministerial Meeting
AMRO	ASEAN+3 Macroeconomic Research Office
APEC	Asia Pacific Economic Cooperation
APSC	ASEAN Political-Security Community
ARTNeT	Asia-Pacific Research and Training Network
ASC	ASEAN Security Community
ASCC	ASEAN Socio-cultural Community
ASEAN	Association of Southeast Asian Nations
ASEAN OS/SAM	ASEAN Open Skies/Single Aviation Market
ASPs	Application Services Providers
ASW	ASEAN Single Window
ATIGA	ASEAN Trade in Goods Agreement
ATISA	ASEAN Trade in Services Agreement
ATR	ASEAN Trade Repository
BAI	Bureau of Animal Industry
BCIC	Bumiputera Commercial and Industrial Community
BFAR	Bureau of Fisheries and Aquatic Resources
BIR	Bureau of Internal Revenue
BIS	Bureau of Import Service
BKPM	Badan Koordinasi Penanaman Modal (Investment Coordinating Board)
BOC	Bureau of Customs
BOI	Board of Investment
BOQ	Bureau of Quarantine
BOT	Build-Operate-Transfer
BPI	Bureau of Plant Industry
BPOM	Badan Pengawas Obat dan Makanan (Food and Drug Control Agency)
BPS	Bureau of Product Standards

BSN	Badan Standardisasi Nasional (National Standardization Agency)
CAAP	Civil Aviation Authority of the Philippines
CABs	Conformity Assessment Bodies
CARS	Comprehensive Automotive Resurgence Strategy
CBU	Completely Built-Up
CDC	Clark Development Cooperation
CDP	Car Development Programme
CEISA	Customs-Excise Information System and Automation
CEP	Comprehensive Economic Partnership
CEPA	Comprehensive Economic Partnership Agreement
CEPEA	Comprehensive Economic Partnership for East Asia
CEPT	Common Effective Preferential Tariffs
CGN	Chula Global Network
CITS	Centre for International Trade Studies
CLMV	Cambodia, Laos, Myanmar, Vietnam
CMI	Chiang Mai Initiative
CMIM	Chiang Mai Initiative Multi-lateralization
CVDP	Commercial Vehicle Development Programme
DB	Designating Body
DDB	Dangerous Drugs Board
DOH	Department of Health
DTI	Department of Trade and Industry
DTN	Department of Trade Negotiation
EAFTA	East Asia Free Trade Area
EEE	Electrical and Electronic Equipment
EMB	Environment Management Bureau
EPAs	Economic Partnership Agreements
EPU	Economic Planning Unit
EU	European Union
FDA	Food and Drug Administration
FDI	Foreign Direct Investment
FEO	Firearms Explosives Office
FIC	Foreign Investment Committee
FMS	Forest Management Service
FPA	Fertilizer and Pesticides Authority
FTA	Free Trade Agreement

FTAAP	Free Trade Agreement for the Asia-Pacific
GATS	General Agreement on Trade in Services
GCC	Gulf Cooperation Council
GCI	Global Competitiveness Index
GDP	Gross Domestic Product
GFC	Global Financial Crisis
GLCs	Government-linked Companies
GLIC	Government-linked Investment Companies
GMS	Greater Mekong Subregion
GVCs	Global Value Chains
HDI	Human Development Index
HDMF	Home Development Mutual Fund
HKTDC	Hong Kong Trade Development Council
HO	Heckscher-Ohlin
HS	Harmonized System
IAI	Initiative for ASEAN Integration
IC	Integrated Circuit
ICT	Information and Communication Technology
IECPS	Integrated Enhanced Customs Processing System
IGA	Investment Guarantee Agreement
IMF	International Monetary Fund
IMP	Industrial Master Plan
IMP3	Third Industrial Master Plan
IMT-GT	Indonesia-Malaysia-Thailand Growth Triangle
INSW	Indonesia National Single Window
INTR	Indonesia's National Trade Repository
IPRs	Intellectual Property Rights
ITA	Information Technology Agreement
ITD	Institute for Trade and Development
KAN	Komite Akreditasi Nasional (National Accreditation Committee)
LPI	Logistics Performance Index
LSPs	Logistic Service Providers
MAAS	Multilateral Agreement on Air Services
MAFLPAS	Multilateral Agreement for the Full Liberalization of Passenger Air Services
MALIAT	Multilateral Agreement for the Liberalization of Air Transport
MARINA	Maritime Industry Authority

MCMC	Malaysian Communications and Multimedia Commission
MCMCA	Malaysian Communications and Multimedia Act
MDTCC	Ministry of Domestic Trade, Cooperatives and Consumerism
MERCOSUR	Mercado Común del Sur (Common Market of the South)
MIDA	Malaysian Industrial Authority
MITI	Ministry of International Trade and Industry
MNCs	Multinational Companies
MNP	Movement of Natural Persons
MoA	Ministry of Agriculture
MoI	Ministry of Industry
MoT	Ministry of Trade
MPAC	Master Plan on ASEAN Connectivity
MRA	Mutual Recognition Agreement
MSC	Multimedia Super Corridor
NDG	Narrowing the Development Gap
NDP	National Development Policy
NEP	New Economic Policy
NFA	National Food Authority
NGOs	Non-Governmental Organizations
NMIS	National Meat Inspection Service
NSWs	National Single Windows
NTBs	Non-Tariff Barriers
NTC	National Telecommunications Commission
NTMs	Non-Tariff Measures
NTR	National Trade Repository
NTT	New Trade Theory
OECD	Organization for Economic Co-operation and Development
OEM	Original Equipment Manufacturers
OMB	Optical Media Board
OSS	One Stop Service
P4	Brunei Darussalam, Chile, New Zealand and Singapore
PBR	Philippine Business Registry
PC	Personal Computers

PCA	Post Clearance Audit
PCA	Philippine Coconut Authority
PCG	Putrajaya Committee on GLC High Performance
PCMP	Progressive Car Manufacturing Program
PCP	People's Car Program
PDEA	Philippine Drug Enforcement Agency
PEZA	Philippine Economic Zone Authority
PEZA	The Philippine Export Processing Zone Authority
PhilHealth	Philippine Health Insurance Cooperation
PMET	Professionals, Managers, Engineers and Technicians
PNPS	National Programme for Standard Development
PNRI	Philippine Nuclear Research Institute
PNSW	Philippine National Single Window
PSCC	Philippine Standard Commodity Classification
PTA	Preferential Trade Arrangement
PTMP	Progressive Truck Manufacturing Programme
QAB	Qualified ASEAN Banks
R&D	Research and Development
RA	Republic Act
RCEP	Regional Comprehensive Economic Partnership
RIATS	Roadmap for Integration of Air Travel Sector
ROK	Republic of Korea
ROOs	Rules of Origin
RTAs	Regional Trading Arrangements
SBMA	Subic Bay Metropolitan Authority
SCP	Singapore Cooperation Programme
SEC	Securities and Exchange Commission
SET	Stock Exchange of Thailand
SFM	Specific Factors Model
SIA	Singapore Airlines
SMEs	Small and Medium Enterprises
SNI	Standard National Indonesia (Indonesian National Standards)
SRA	Sugar Regulatory Administration
SSS	Social Security System
TCs	Technical Committees
TEL	Temporary Exclusion List

TM	Telekom Malaysia
TPA	Trade Promotion Authority
TPP	Trans-Pacific Partnership
WCO	World Customs Union
WTO	World Trade Organization

ABOUT THE CONTRIBUTORS

Myrna S. Austria is Full Professor at the School of Economics, De La Salle University, Manila. She earned both her Masters in Development Economics and Doctor of Philosophy in Economics at The Australian National University in Canberra, Australia. Her areas of specialization include: trade, investment and industrial policy, development economics, competition policy, and regional economic integration. She has published journal articles, monographs, books and chapters in books along these areas. She has done consultancy work with international development agencies such as the World Bank (WB), Asian Development Bank (ADB), International Development Research Centre (IDRC-Canada), U.S. Agency for International Development (USAID), APEC Business Advisory Council (ABAC), and the ASEAN Secretariat.

Sanchita Basu Das is Fellow and Lead Researcher (Economics) at the ASEAN Studies Centre and the Coordinator of the Singapore APEC Study Centre, both based in the ISEAS–Yusof Ishak Institute, Singapore. She is also a co-editor of the *Journal of Southeast Asian Economies* (Economic Journal, formerly known as *ASEAN Economic Bulletin*). Prior to joining the Institute in 2005, she has worked in the private sector as an economist in India and Singapore. Sanchita has an MBA from the National University of Singapore (NUS) and an MA from the Delhi School of Economics (University of Delhi, India). She is the author/editor of seven books, special editor of three journal issues and author of numerous book chapters and policy papers. Her latest co-edited book publications include: *The ASEAN Economic Community: A Work in Progress* (ISEAS and ADB, 2013); *Asia and the Middle Income Trap* (Routledge, forthcoming). Sanchita's research interests include: Economic Integration in ASEAN and the Asia-Pacific Region; International Trade; Macro-economic Issues in Southeast Asia.

Chia Siow Yue is Senior Research Fellow at the Singapore Institute of International Affairs (SIIA). Prior to joining SIIA, she was the Director of the Institute of Southeast Asian Studies and Director at the Singapore APEC Study Centre Regional Coordinator, East Asian Development Network and former Professor of Economics at the National University of Singapore. Chia Siow Yue's research areas are international economics and development economics, particularly foreign direct investment, trade policy, and regional economic integration. She has authored, co-authored and edited more than 40 books and reports and published more than 100 papers and articles in academic books and journals. She serves as committee member and resource person on numerous international and regional organizations.

Suthiphand Chirathivat is Professor of Economics at Chulalongkorn University, Bangkok. He is also chairman of Chula Global Network and executive director of ASEAN Studies Center. He was Dean of Faculty of Economics, Chairman of the PhD Program in Economics, Chairman of Economics Research Center and Center for International Economics at Chulalongkorn University. His academic interests involve the issues related to international trade, investment, finance, regional integration and development, and emerging issues in Asia in relation to the global economy and society.

Yose Rizal Damuri is Head of the Department of Economics, Center for Strategic and International Studies, Jakarta. His research activities focus on international trade, regional integration initiatives and globalization of value chain. Yose also teaches International Economics courses at the Faculty of Economics and Business, University of Indonesia. He is active in several research and advisory networks both in Indonesia and in East Asia. He received his PhD in International Economics from the Graduate Institute of International Studies (HEI), Geneva, Switzerland.

Sineenat Sermcheep is currently the Director of Research Affairs at ASEAN Studies Center, Chulalongkorn University and Assistant Dean, Faculty of Economics, Chulalongkorn University, Bangkok. She has a PhD in Economics from the University of Utah. Sineenat Sermcheep mainly undertakes research related to foreign direct investment, economic integration and ASEAN. Her other areas of interests include trade in services and economic development.

Rodolfo C. Severino was the Head of the ASEAN Studies Centre at the ISEAS–Yusof Ishak Institute, Singapore from March 2008 till August 2015. He was the Centre's first Head. Prior to this appointment, Mr Severino was a Visiting Senior Research Fellow at the Institute. He continues to be affiliated to the Institute as an Associate Senior Fellow. He has authored four books, all published by ISEAS: *Southeast Asia in Search of an ASEAN Community* (2006), *ASEAN* (2008), *The ASEAN Regional Forum* (2009) and *Where in the World is the Philippines?* (2010). Mr Severino served as ASEAN Secretary-General from 1998 to 2002. Prior to that, Mr Severino was Undersecretary of Foreign Affairs of the Philippines, and Ambassador to Malaysia, among other duties. He twice served as ASEAN Senior Official for the Philippines.

Tham Siew Yean is Professor in International Trade and Deputy Director at the Institute of Malaysian and International Studies, Universiti Kebangsaan Malaysia. Her research and publications focus on trade, ASEAN, foreign direct investment, manufacturing and services developments. She is also a consultant for international agencies, such as World Bank, World Bank Institute, Asian Development Bank, Asian Development Bank Institute and Economic Research Institute for ASEAN and East Asia (ERIA). Her most recent publication includes co-editing with Sanchita Basu Das, a special issue of *Journal of Southeast Asian Economies (JSEAE)*, on "Managing Domestic Consensus For ASEAN Economic Community Beyond 2015", August 2015.

Moe Thuzar is Fellow and Lead Researcher (socio-cultural) at the ASEAN Studies Centre of the ISEAS-Yusof Ishak Institute, Singapore. Moe is also a member of the Institute's Myanmar Studies Programme, which she earlier coordinated from July 2012 to October 2013. Before Moe joined the Centre in May 2008, she headed the ASEAN Secretariat's Human Development Unit, which coordinated ASEAN cooperation in labour, youth, social welfare, education, women's affairs, poverty reduction and rural development, health, and civil service matters. Moe has co-authored with Pavin Chachavalpongpun, *Myanmar: Life After Nargis* (ISEAS, 2009), and has co-edited with Yap Kioe Sheng, *Urbanization in Southeast Asia: Issues and Impacts* (ISEAS, 2012). She has contributed to several compendia/volumes on ASEAN, and on Myanmar. Her research interests cover urbanization and environmental cooperation in ASEAN, ASEAN integration issues,

ASEAN's dialogue relations, as well as Myanmar's reforms. Moe was a Temasek scholar for the Master in Public Policy Programme at the National University of Singapore.

Vo Tri Thanh is currently the Vice-President of the Central Institute for Economic Management (CIEM). He holds a PhD degree in Economics from The Australian National University. Vo Tri Thanh mainly undertakes research and provides consultation on issues related to trade liberalization and international economic integration and macroeconomic policies. His other areas of interests include institutional reforms, financial system and economic development.

1

INTRODUCTION
The ASEAN Economic Community and Conflicting Domestic Interests

Tham Siew Yean and Sanchita Basu Das

1. INTRODUCTION

The prospect of an ASEAN Economic Community (AEC) has progressively raised interest on the state of economic integration among members of the Association of Southeast Asian Nations (ASEAN). Although the Chairman's Statement from the 26th ASEAN Summit (April 2015) indicated that the current rate of implementation of the 2007 AEC Blueprint ("the Blueprint") goals stands at 90.5 per cent (ASEAN Secretariat 2015), there are numerous studies that question the use of a scorecard approach as a monitoring mechanism. These implementation scores do not necessarily capture the actual extent of economic integration in the region. For instance, recent business surveys show that although tariffs have been reduced or eliminated among ASEAN countries, non-tariff barriers are still prevalent (Kawai and Wignaraja 2011; Hu 2013). These include non-automatic licensing schemes, technical regulations, benchmarked standards, administrative costs, which are attached to the use of preferential measures, and a lack of physical and institutional connectivity (ASEAN Secretariat and World Bank 2013). Similarly, ASEAN citizens can hardly attribute the rise in incomes or better job opportunities to the AEC initiatives (Chia 2011*a*). These caveats suggest that not all of the AEC targets can be achieved by the end of 2015. This deadline may well mark a milestone rather than the complete achievement of intended goals.

How then do we interpret the disparity between stated intentions, goals and targets of the AEC and its current state of achievements and implementation? The literature frequently attributes the lack of effective progress in ASEAN economic integration to a lack of political will. One possible explanation for the lack of political will is the fact that deep regional economic cooperation faces domestic opposition arising from various economic conflicts. For example, after the Treaty of Rome was signed, it took the European Economic Community nearly forty years to achieve its objective of a single market. The stalling Doha Development Agenda can also be attributed to domestic resistance and hostility from protectionist groups in participating economies that prevent member countries from achieving the required single undertaking rule. Likewise, for ASEAN, even though the AEC is a regional initiative, implementation is left to the individual member economies. Thus, regional cooperation might have to overcome domestic antagonism. In other words, while ASEAN's economic integration is a response by the region's respective governments to globalization, it may not be supported by some domestic interest groups.

This book surveys the developments in the past decade (2003–14) and argues that conflicting economic interests in each country is one of the possible reasons for the current fragmented state of community-building in the region. The objective of this introductory chapter is to explore this issue and to set the stage for the country studies featured in this publication. This chapter is organized as follows: the next section briefly synthesizes relevant literature on economic integration and contestations in trade policy formulation to provide an analytical framework for the featured country studies. Section 3 provides an account of the AEC and its progress since the Blueprint came into effect in 2008. Section 4 offers a preview of the country studies in this book and synthesizes the arguments on how conflicting domestic interests have affected the economic community building process in each of these countries. Finally, the last section summarizes the key findings of this chapter and provides some policy suggestions for deepening economic integration in ASEAN beyond 2015.

2. THE THEORETICAL LITERATURE ON ECONOMIC INTEGRATION AND CONFLICTING DOMESTIC INTERESTS

There are several definitions and interpretations of economic integration. Balassa (1961, p. 1) defines economic integration as "the abolition of discrimination within an area" and Kahnert et al. (1969) explain it as a process that is expected to progressively eliminate the discriminations that take place at national borders. Mutharika (1972), on the other hand, describes economic integration as the coordination of economic policies by states within a specific region so that they can meet the objectives of development. Subsequently, Panagariya (1998) argues that because economic integration may take many forms such as free trade agreements (FTAs), customs unions, common markets and economic unions, a more representative means of describing economic integration is to use the term preferential trade agreements (PTAs). A PTA is said to be an arrangement between two or more countries in which goods produced by those countries can be traded with fewer or lower barriers than goods produced by a country that is not a party to the arrangement (a non-member).

Mansfield and Milner (1999) argue that the theory of economic integration (or regionalism) has undergone four phases of evolution, each reflecting the policy concerns of its time. The first phase occurred during the second half of the nineteenth century and was largely concentrated in Europe. The second phase was during the inter-war period between World War I and II. The current economic integration is a post-World War II phenomenon spanning two phases: (i) from the late 1950s through the 1970s; and (ii) from the conclusion of the Cold War in the early 1990s, when there was a change in interstate power and security relations, to the present day.

The latest phase of economic integration from the early 1990s, also termed "new regionalism", is said to have emerged primarily as a state-led project in the face of global competition. Grugel (2004, p. 604) describes the latest form of regional integration as a "route through which states mediate the range of economic and social pressures generated by globalization". This is especially pertinent to smaller states that may lack the capacity to manage the pressures of globalization at a national level. It is argued that this is the period when the states felt competition in attracting foreign capital to support production, forcing them to collaborate in order to attain a larger market space (Mittelman 2000).

Economic integration within ASEAN is also part of "new regionalism". The ASEAN Free Trade Area (AFTA) was instituted in the early 1990s to provide new political purpose to the association/region after the end of the Cold War and the Cambodian crisis (Buszynski 1997). More than a decade later, when ASEAN decided to establish the AEC, several global forces had already pushed the ten small Southeast Asian economies to advance their economic integration process (Kawai 2005; Hew 2007). First, the 1997–98 Asian Financial Crisis (AFC) made the ASEAN countries realize the importance of a collective economic mechanism for regional stability and the prevention of future financial crises. Secondly, China's accession to the World Trade Organization (WTO) and its rapid growth as an attractive market and production base also pressurized ASEAN countries to cooperate in order to offer economies of scale. Lastly, the proliferation of regional trading arrangements (RTAs) by European nations and the United States raised concerns among ASEAN governments to develop mechanisms to remain competitive and relevant in multilateral negotiations.

Therefore, ASEAN's moves towards economic integration were motivated not just by economic reasons but also by political and strategic imperatives that pushed these ten economies to act coherently and manage their economic vulnerabilities. In light of this, ASEAN economic integration is often perceived as state-led or top-down integration (Sally 2006; Terada 2009). This form of state-led economic integration, with limited engagement of domestic stakeholders, can slow down the integration process in two ways. It can generate apathy from economic entities during the negotiation phase, and it may also generate domestic conflicts during implementation, as awareness of the implications of the commitments made sink into the minds of key stakeholders.

In international trade theory, economic conflicts are rooted in the distribution of gains and losses that emerge with trade liberalization. The two standard models used are the classic Heckscher-Ohlin (HO) and Ricardo-Viner models of trade. Factor endowments play a crucial role in determining patterns of trade in the Heckscher-Ohlin model. The related Stolper-Samuelson theorem in this model claims that returns to the owners of abundant resources will rise absolutely and disproportionately from trade, hence, trade liberalization benefits the owners of abundant factors while owners of scarce factors will lose out. Abundant factors of a country engaged in trade will be used intensively in the production of goods whose prices will rise from increasing exports, thereby increasing their returns. Conversely, the returns to owners of scarce resources will fall absolutely and proportionately, since their factors will be used intensively in the production of goods whose prices will fall from increasing imports. The model thus predicts conflicts between capital and labour over trade policy as shown in Table 1.1 (Peamsilpakulchorn 2006; Keohane and Milner 1996).

The Ricardo-Viner model (or Specific Factors Model — SFM), is often deemed to be a short-run model, as it assumes an immobile factor that cannot be shifted across two sectors that are producing two different goods. A return to the immobile factor (usually assumed to be capital) is inevitably tied to the fortunes of the industry where it is employed. Thus factors specific to export-oriented industries will favour liberalization, whereas the reverse will hold true for the factor that is fixed in import-competing industries. The mobile factor (usually assumed to be labour) will shift between sectors until its return is equalized across the two sectors. Conflicting economic interests are therefore inevitable between the export-oriented or competitive sector (free traders) and import-oriented or uncompetitive sectors (protectionists) (Table 1.1). The impact on the real income of the mobile factor is ambiguous as it depends on the consumption patterns of the two goods. Hence, trade policy preferences will depend on their respective consumption patterns.

These traditional models are more applicable to inter-industry trade. However, intra-industry trade has become more important as evidenced by trade between similar countries or countries with similar endowments. New trade theory (NTT), developed by Krugman (1979), attempts to use economies of scale to explain the specialization of production in countries — done mainly to take advantage of increasing returns. Other assumptions that have been used in NTT include market imperfections, strategic behaviour and new growth theory. Many of the models based on market imperfections and strategic behaviour justify the use of protection to nurture firms or industries (Deraniyagala and Fine, n.d.). Although this strand in the literature dominated the discourse in the 1980s, it has since fallen out of favour due to difficulties in empirically verifying these theories. Furthermore, policy recommendations for protection based on these theories have been refuted by alternative arguments such as the

TABLE 1.1
Key Models of Interest Group Competition over Trade Policy

	Heckscher-Ohlin (HO) Model	Specific Factors Model (SFM)	Heterogeneous Firms Model
Principal Actors	Factors of production	Industries or sectors	Firms which are heterogeneous
Mobility of Factors	Perfectly mobile across sectors	Immobile factors that are fixed in sectors (usually capital)	Mobile
Winners and Losers from Trade Liberalization	Winners: Abundant factors Losers: Scarce factors	Winners: Immobile factor in export-oriented sectors Losers: Immobile factor in import-competing sectors	Winners: Productive firms that export Losers: Less productive firms in import-competing industries
Conflicts	Capital vs. Labour	Export-oriented vs. import-oriented industries	Exporters vs. importers at the firm level

Source: Adapted and updated from Peamsilpakulchorn (2006).

predatory behaviour of governments. Hence, interventions aimed at remedying imperfect markets may lead to worse outcomes than those originally attributed to imperfect markets.

"New" trade theory shifts the unit of analysis from the country- or industry-level to the firm-level by assuming heterogeneity across firms rather than homogeneity, based on the Melitz model (Melitz 2003). In this class of models, different characteristics of firms have different implications on their trade policy preferences. For instance, productivity differences among firms can influence their respective trade policy preferences — highly productive firms are likely to be exporters while less productive firms are not. Thus in these models, less productive domestic firms lobby for higher tariffs whereas exporters favour liberalization to gain market access abroad. Another characteristic that can influence trade preferences is the size of a firm as larger firms tend to be pro-liberalization while smaller firms favour protection. Importantly, these firms may be operating in the same sector or industry and so political cleavages can occur within the same industry, unlike the class or sectoral cleavages analysed by the HO and SFM (Kim 2013). Therefore, regardless of whether the analysis is framed in terms of factors, sectors or firms, winners will press for liberalization and losers will resist, thereby setting the stage for economic conflicts from any liberalization efforts by an economy.

3. THE ASEAN ECONOMIC COMMUNITY

In December 1997, ASEAN leaders adopted the ASEAN Vision 2020 in order to give the region long-term direction. This plan envisioned the formation of an ASEAN community by 2020, comprising three pillars: ASEAN Security Community (ASC),[1] AEC and ASEAN Socio-cultural Community (ASCC). At the 2003 ASEAN Summit in Bali, Indonesia, ASEAN leaders declared the establishment of an AEC by 2020.[2] The objective of the AEC is "to create a stable, prosperous and highly competitive ASEAN economic region in which there is a free flow of goods, services, investment and a freer flow of capital, equitable economic development and reduced poverty and socio-economic disparities in year 2020". In January 2007, during the ASEAN Summit in Cebu, Philippines, the AEC deadline was brought forward by five years to the end of 2015 (ASEAN Secretariat 1997, 2003, 2007).

Subsequently, ASEAN achieved a major milestone at the November 2007 ASEAN Summit in Singapore when leaders embraced the 2007

AEC Blueprint, which lays out a roadmap for strengthening economic integration and realizing the AEC. The Blueprint is organized according to the AEC's four objectives: (i) a single market and production base; (ii) a highly competitive economic region; (iii) a region of equitable economic development; and (iv) a region that is fully integrated to the global economy, with 17 "core elements" and 176 "priority actions", to be undertaken within a strategic schedule of four implementation periods (2008–09; 2010–11; 2012–13; and 2014–15). The adoption of a blueprint showcased ASEAN members' willingness to approach the integration process with clearly defined goals and timelines. There seemed to be an eagerness among participating countries to achieve comprehensive and deeper economic integration and institutional development in the region.

Relevant ASEAN Ministers from each country as well as the ASEAN Secretariat were tasked with implementing the Blueprint and regularly reporting their progress to the Council of the AEC. This is when ASEAN came up with an AEC scorecard to track implementation. Since the Blueprint was adopted, the ASEAN Secretariat has released two official scorecards, one in 2010 and the other in 2012. The latter scorecard (published in March of 2012) states that ASEAN achieved 68.2 per cent of its targets for the 2008–11 period. The first scorecard (for 2008–09) reported an implementation rate of around 87.6 per cent of a total of 105 measures; the second scorecard (2010–11) reported a lower rate of 56.4 per cent of a total of 172 measures (ASEAN Secretariat 2010, 2012). Thereafter, official publication of scorecards was stopped, thereby generating concerns among the key stakeholders on the state of ASEAN integration. The only access to information is the Chairman's statement after the ASEAN Summits.

Indeed, ASEAN has achieved significant progress under its economic cooperation initiatives (Chia and Plummer 2013; Hill and Menon 2010; Basu Das 2012; ERIA 2012). The ASEAN-6 countries[3] have eliminated tariffs since 2010 and the CLMV countries (Cambodia, Laos, Myanmar and Vietnam) have lowered their intra-ASEAN tariffs from 7.3 per cent in 2000 to 1.8 per cent in 2013, as scheduled under ASEAN Trade in Goods Agreement (ATIGA)[4] (ASEAN Secretariat and World Bank 2013). The region is about to establish an ASEAN Single Window (ASW), which involves developing and interconnecting the National Single Windows (NSW) of ASEAN member countries.[5] The ASW will allow the ASEAN trading community to process the clearance of goods at the border through a one-time submission of data, which will then allow quick processing and decision-making. If it works, it is expected to save traders significant time and money.

In order to raise foreign direct investment (FDI) in the region, the ten nations put together the ASEAN Comprehensive Investment Agreement (ACIA) in April 2012, which consolidated provisions of the ASEAN Investment Area (AIA) and ASEAN Investment Guarantee Agreement (AIGA). ASEAN countries also allow flows of skilled professionals (Mode 4) to facilitate investment and the free flow of services. It provides for Mutual Recognition Arrangements (MRAs), wherein each country may recognize education and experience, and licences and certificates granted in another country. To date, ASEAN has concluded seven MRAs for: engineering and architecture; nursing; accountancy services; surveying services; and the medical and dental profession.

In order to benefit from the free flow of goods and services, ASEAN needs to reduce transportation and logistics costs between and within member countries. In 2010, ASEAN leaders adopted the Master Plan on ASEAN Connectivity, which is expected to link ASEAN countries by enhancing the development of physical infrastructure, institutional connectivity and people connectivity. The region has also established the ASEAN Infrastructure Fund (AIF) in collaboration with the Asian Development Bank (with a start-up capital of US$485.2 million); the fund actively promotes a public-private partnership approach to implementing key infrastructure projects in the region. This initiative also helps with the region's competitiveness vis-à-vis the rest of the world.

To address development gaps, ASEAN embarked on a programme known as the Initiative of ASEAN Integration (IAI), wherein more developed ASEAN members are expected to support less developed members. ASEAN has strived to plug itself into the global economy and has played the role of a "bridge builder" among countries in the greater Asian context. The ten nations as a whole have signed free trade agreements with China, India, South Korea, Japan and Australia-New Zealand.[6]

Nevertheless, despite its achievements, it is also widely accepted that ASEAN is unlikely to fulfil all of its stipulated integration measures by the end of 2015, and even those that have been met are yet to be effective for key stakeholders (Chia 2011b; Severino 2011; Basu Das 2013; Chia and Plummer 2013). Although tariffs have been reduced or eliminated in the region, there has been very little progress in identifying and eliminating non-tariff measures (NTMs), which affect both imports[7] and exports,[8] hindering greater intra-regional trade (ASEAN Secretariat and World Bank 2013). With regard to the ASW, ASEAN countries may be challenged by a lack of coordination between agencies or a lack of appropriate human resources. Currently, ASEAN suffers from a wide gap between members' logistics performance — while Singapore occupies the top position, Myanmar stands at the 129th spot out of 155 countries ranked in the 2012 World Bank Logistics Performance Index (LPI).[9]

ASEAN has also been negotiating its services sector liberalization agreement for the past fifteen years, but efforts thus far have resulted only in marginal liberalization (Nikomborirak and Jitdumrong 2013). It should be noted that the commitment under the services sector agreement does not aim for full integration as yet. For example, liberalization for mode 3 or commercial presence[10] envisions 70 per cent of ASEAN equity shares, while liberalization for mode 4 (movement of natural persons) is confined to the movement of professional workers only, with pre-agreed flexibilities and exceptions. Moreover, the MRAs governing the seven professions, except for engineering and architecture, do not contain any liberalization commitments. The MRAs mostly provide frameworks to promote the mobility of professionals between member states, on a voluntary basis. This generates flexibilities and allows member-states not to commit.

ASEAN's regional investment initiative, ACIA, came into effect in April 2012 and superseded the earlier agreement on investment, the ASEAN Investment Area (AIA). However, it has yet to be supplemented with supportive domestic investment policies and regulations, effectively rendering ASEAN into ten different markets rather than a single one (Bhaskaran 2013).

With regard to the association's integration with the global economy, despite the numerous ASEAN+1 FTA initiatives in the last decade, empirical evidence on the benefits accruing to ASEAN from these FTAs remains patchy and limited. Instead, there are concerns over the potential negative effects from these FTAs due to their complexity, inconsistent regulations, different rules of origin (ROOs) and the resulting "noodle bowl" effect (Kawai and Wignaraja 2011).

Hence, NTMs (with respect to the free flow of goods across ASEAN countries), high transaction costs (trade facilitation), entry barriers restricting the flow of services and FDI policies, concerns with ASEAN-led FTAs need to be addressed before ASEAN can be viewed as a single market and production base. This has also been noted by Severino and Menon (2013) who have stated that the year 2015 is not going to bring any significant changes to ASEAN; its nature, processes and member countries' interests will remain almost the same.

This book seeks to fill a gap in the literature on ASEAN by examining the impact of state-directed economic integration on domestic economic conflicts. Through selected country studies, this book also examines how these conflicts can affect a country's readiness to embrace the AEC. Specifically, it seeks to ascertain the type and nature of conflicts that have emerged in each of the countries studied. Identifying these conflicts is important for managing domestic consensus which, in turn, can pave the way for deeper economic integration in ASEAN. This is a very pertinent issue for ASEAN as it is standing at a critical juncture in 2015 whereby the credibility of its economic integration efforts is at stake. Member countries have to deliver on their past commitments whilst simultaneously aspiring for deeper cooperation in the future.

4. THEMES IN THIS BOOK

The rest of this introduction summarizes key findings on the causes and nature of domestic conflict from the regional and selected ASEAN country chapters in this book. The regional chapter by Severino and Thuzar provides a backdrop to the issues at hand by describing how ASEAN economic cooperation has been politically motivated from the very beginning. It further explores the political underpinnings of regional economic cooperation within ASEAN and the Asia-Pacific region. The authors note that the foreign policy of all sovereign states is driven by national interests, which in the case of the AEC is to enhance domestic competitiveness by creating a bigger economic space in the region for their firms. Nevertheless, there is misalignment in the domestic arena as this motivation encounters domestic contestations from businesses and sectors that are affected by the redistribution of power and resources due to the liberalization measures of the AEC. Similarly, regional consensus has to be negotiated, with flexibility given to less ready members through separate tracks. The other misalignment lies in the long-term goals of the AEC as envisaged by past leaders that had a longer term in office, while current leaders may be more short term in their thinking, due in part to the pressure from new media that also focusses more on short-term issues. The authors go on to assert that these misalignments will not only impede ASEAN's efforts of trying to achieve economic integration and the region's motto of "One Vision, One Identity, One Community" as enshrined in the ASEAN Charter, but they will also undermine regional solidarity. It may result in uneven progress and may deliver on a two- or three-tier ASEAN, thereby dividing the region by winners and losers.

The nature of domestic contestations raised in the regional chapter is discussed in each of the chapters on the national economies in this book — Indonesia, Malaysia, the Philippines, Singapore, Thailand and Vietnam. It is observed that the conflicts range from macro-level policy-making to firm-level perception of winners and losers. The nature of domestic conflicts varies depending on the economic structure of the country, its stage of development and degree of openness to the global economy as well as its long-term development goals.

An important source of conflict in member countries is competing demand for scarce resources as the implementation of the AEC commitments requires considerable technical, financial as well as human resources. Yose Rizal Damuri's chapter on Indonesia points this out clearly in his discussion on the country's challenges in the implementation of facilitation and harmonization measures. It is reiterated in Vo Tri Thanh's study on Vietnam where it is explained that the country did not/could not expend resources to implement some aspects of the AEC, such as mutual recognition and services liberalization, because they are scarce. The bulk of government resources were used for the drafting of major laws or reforms that are considered to be cross-cutting issues related to the country's trade liberalization efforts. Hence, the domestic conflicts observed in this book may not be due to liberalization efforts under the AEC alone. This is because ASEAN member countries are not only pursuing economic liberalization under the auspices of the AEC, but are also involved in multiple trade agreements at the bilateral, regional and multilateral levels. There are also unilateral liberalization initiatives in some countries, as observed in the case of Malaysia and Singapore. These multiple commitments imply that scarce resources are stretched to the limit in some countries in terms of their abilities and capacities to meet their commitments in the Blueprint targets.

Nevertheless even when resources are available, poor coordination further compounds implementation issues in the face of complex bureaucracy and decentralized decision-making as discussed by Damuri in his chapter on Indonesia. For example, a single product may well be regulated by several ministries. Frequent reshuffling of ministerial positions further compounds the problem as it sometimes leads to discontinuities in the implementation process. To overcome these problems, a Presidential directive is sometimes used to force ministerial cooperation, as illustrated in the case of investment facilitation.

State-led liberalization can also result in policy conflicts as illustrated in the Indonesian chapter when domestic policies favouring enhancing domestic competitiveness is prioritized over liberalization measures in general, including the AEC as these liberalization measures are deemed to facilitate import rather than exports. Thus inward-looking sentiments have led to less priority given for the implementation of AEC measures. This is amply illustrated in Damuri's example of the use of standards for protectionist intentions by promoting standards that differ from internationally accepted ones and Indonesia's less receptive response towards regulatory harmonization.

Policy conflicts also arise when domestic policies in a country are not aligned with these liberalization policies. Tham's country chapter on Malaysia highlights this. On the one hand, the services sector has been targeted as a new source of growth since the Third Industrial Master Plan (IMP3: 2006–20). Seven out of the twelve promoted sectors in the Tenth Malaysia Plan and the Economic Transformation Plan also belong to the services sector. However, this sector is relatively more protected by equity constraints as well as domestic regulations. In recognition of the need to liberalize this sector, the government has progressively initiated several unilateral liberalization initiatives. Nevertheless, Malaysia is cautious about making irreversible commitments under FTAs, including its commitments in the AEC. At the same time, the government is also liberalizing unilaterally resulting in a gap between commitments at the regional level and practise in the country as the latter is also guided by the unilateral liberalization efforts of the country. This cautious approach also affects the commitments as the horizontal measures that covers all sectors in Malaysia's commitments in services liberalization in ASEAN, also further strengthen the role of domestic regulations in the services sector, as illustrated in the author's case study of the wholesale and retail sector. The liberalization of services is also constrained by the extensive presence of government-linked companies (GLCs). These GLCs may be "sheltered" from liberalization by domestic regulations, which can serve as bureaucratic hurdles to foreign investment. Consequently, as in the case of the Philippines, liberalization commitments in the AEC can be thwarted by domestic policies that continue to protect domestic preferences and entities from the competitive forces of liberalization.

Austria's country study on the Philippines using the automotive sector as a case study clearly demonstrates that liberalization policies need to be accompanied by supportive domestic measures, such as improvements in administrative efficiencies as high administrative costs as well as high export and import costs can deter the FDI required for the country's industrial development. Another source of domestic conflict can be observed in the discord between trade and investment policies. Trade policies that prohibit the importation of second-hand motor vehicles and parts and components, except those made by returning residents and members of the diplomatic corps, are circumvented by the enactment of duty free zones and special economic zones that are used instead to import duty free second-hand vehicles and/or smuggle used vehicles. In contrast, these zones are not able to attract the needed investment into the automotive sector due to high production costs and the absence of a strong supplier base. The reduction of tariffs under AFTA has instead led to greater imports of vehicles and components and parts. The banking sector reveals further conflicting interests as local banks are also significant shareholders of the major auto multinationals in the country. Banks are therefore directing capital into auto loans instead of directing capital to low value-added production.

State-driven economic integration may also involve very limited consultation (or none at all) with relevant stakeholders, leading to a lack of domestic support in the implementation of the AEC measures. This is raised in country chapters such as Thailand and Vietnam. In particular, Vo's chapter on Vietnam highlights the importance of increasing stakeholder consultation, which has been carried out with respect to revisions of major laws in the country. The need for consultation in the redrafting of these laws has recently been formalized in 2008 even though some consultation processes were adopted before then. However, interestingly, the author also notes that the effectiveness of the consultation process appears to be limited for three main reasons. First, government consultation is confined mainly to traditional stakeholders such as government agencies, research and business communities while civil society and non-governmental organizations (NGOs) are seldom consulted except in some instances (the AEC and some major FTAs). Second, the output of the consultative process is not necessarily made public and this makes it difficult for the public to comment or to prepare adequately for the implementation of Vietnam's commitments. Given the low utilization rates of AFTA and other

ASEAN-related FTAs in the country as well as limited consultation, it is not surprising that the author notes that awareness of the AEC in Vietnam is limited and that there is a general lack of readiness or preparation for the country's effective participation in the AEC.

Conflicts may also emerge among stakeholders that may experience losses from the liberalization process such as the rural or working poor in Vietnam. Sineenat and Suthiphand's co-authored chapter on Thailand also shows that small farmers in the Thai agricultural sector are perceived to lose out as they lack the resources to compete with large businesses and multinationals in this sector. Moreover, both the Vietnam and Thailand country chapters show that small domestic enterprises may stand to lose from the liberalization measures in the Blueprint. In the case of Vietnam, this is attributed to their lack of capacity to understand the technicalities of liberalization and cooperation measures. In Thailand's case, the authors' examination of the logistics sector identifies size as an important factor in a firm's capacity to respond to the competitive challenges of the AEC-led liberalization measures. Small local logistics firms in Thailand are perceived to lose out as they do not have access to financial support and they cannot compete against the larger firms and multinationals in this sector in terms of developments in technology, management systems and marketing. Sineenat and Suthiphand therefore suggest that the main winners of the AEC will be the large exporters, large processing food companies and high-productivity farmers in the agricultural sector. Similarly, the potential winners of logistics liberalization in Thailand will be the large logistics companies, multinationals in the logistics business and other businesses that are customers of such services. Likewise, the Thai case study on the movement of natural persons (from the medical profession) suggests that hospitals that are engaged in medical tourism will be the main winners due to a shortage of medical personnel in the country. However, it is also feared that Thai medical staff may not be able to compete against inflows of medical personnel from other ASEAN countries who may have a greater advantage in terms of language abilities to communicate with international patients, including patients at border hospitals.

The country chapter on Singapore presents a unique situation. Given the absence of natural resources and an agricultural sector, the city-state has adopted the strategy of an open economy (with the rest of the world) since its independence. It has a high trade-to-GDP ratio of over 300 per cent and practises free trade in goods, except for the six tariff lines imposed on alcoholic beverages. ASEAN economies are viewed as natural hinterlands to the city-state, and liberalization in ASEAN is viewed as a means to gain market access to this hinterland. Unlike almost all other ASEAN economies, where liberalizing engenders strong domestic political-economy responses, thereby slowing down the AEC implementation, this has not been the case for Singapore as domestic pressures hindering such implementation have been weak. Chia and Basu Das, in their chapter, note that this is partly due to the small size of the city-state and its long exposure to the competitive forces of globalization and regionalization. It can also be attributed to the high trust of the local citizens in their political and economic system, high employment rates, and a low incidence of poverty. Hence, as the authors illustrate with their case studies of the electronics and aviation sectors, there is very little domestic pressure in Singapore, particularly against the AEC's liberalization process. The pressure tends to come from Singapore's general approach of using non-protectionist measures in order to manage global competition. In such an environment, the government's policy response is to restructure its economic activities and continuously upgrade its competitiveness to meet liberalization challenges.

5. CONCLUSION: ASEAN BEYOND 2015

ASEAN has come a long way since the inception of the ASEAN Free Trade Area (AFTA) in 1992. After liberalization initiatives in services trade and investment respectively through the ASEAN Framework of Services Agreements (AFAS) and the ASEAN Investment Area (AIA), ASEAN members have decided to adopt a more comprehensive form of economic integration, namely the ASEAN Economic Community (AEC) by the end of 2015. The member economies also adopted a blueprint that was binding in nature with clear action plans and timelines. However, as the deadline for establishing an AEC approaches, it is increasingly evident that ASEAN members will not be able to meet all its commitments as stipulated in the Blueprint. Many significant initiatives have to be carried forward to the next phase of ASEAN economic cooperation, beyond 2015.

However, the implementation of the AEC commitments since 2007 offers important insights and one such insight is the need for building domestic consensus. As can be seen from the country studies, most of the liberalization commitments under the AEC face domestic conflicts in terms of implementation, with the exception of Singapore. These conflicts may occur due to the domestic policies of a country or the lack of domestic support in the absence of effective consultation among key stakeholders in an economy. There may be a lack of resources too as the AEC measures go well beyond tariff liberalization and impinge upon more complex issues such as trade and investment facilitation measures including the ASEAN Single Window, ASEAN Trade Repository, and Mutual Recognition Agreements.

Hence, as ASEAN stands at a juncture with respect to the nature of economic cooperation and liberalization beyond 2015, one needs to understand domestic conflicts and the different ways of handle them so as to achieve deeper integration. The country studies in this chapter present several ways of addressing this issue.

Domestic policies need to be aligned with liberalization commitments for greater policy coherence. This is especially emphasized in the Indonesian, Philippines and Malaysian country chapters. For example, the Indonesian country study highlights the need to harmonize domestic standards with internationally accepted ones instead of creating different national standards. For the Philippines, conflicts in trade and investment policies need to be overcome through the harmonization of investment incentives as well as centralizing investment promotion and facilitation. It also includes enhancing coherence across legislation, policies and programmes as well as improving the coordination of policies. In the case of Malaysia, domestic aspirations that are at odds with liberalization commitments need to re-evaluated for liberalization measures to be effective. This includes a re-evaluation of the role of domestic regulations to assess whether they intentionally or unintentionally counter liberalization measures. The Vietnam chapter provides a positive recommendation of embedding action plans or programmes of liberalization, including the AEC commitments, within its socio-economic development plans to harmonize all its liberalization commitments, thereby simultaneously enhancing policy coherence.

Policy priorities need to be reviewed so that the implementation of the AEC commitments is prioritized in each country's agenda. Conflicting policy priorities can be seen in the case of Indonesia and Vietnam where the former prefers to prioritize domestic issues that can enhance the country's competitiveness and supply side capacity while the latter prioritizes domestic reforms that focus on broad laws such as Enterprise Law and Investment Law. Given the scarcity of resources, be it in terms of technical capabilities, financial or human resources, in both of these countries, policy priorities will determine how these resources will be used for policy implementation.

The Thai and Vietnamese country chapters also emphasize broadening stakeholder consultation and deepening stakeholder engagement so that they are made aware of the implications of the country's commitments. This will enable stakeholders to take the necessary actions to prepare themselves for greater competition as well as to take advantage of the opportunities that come with greater regional economic integration. In this regard, stakeholder consultation may entail giving out more detailed and timely information as well as providing resources for the government to better engage with those affected by the integration process. It should be noted that poor countries may not necessarily have the human and financial resources for this purpose. Stakeholder consultation should be encouraged not at the ASEAN-level alone but at all levels of liberalization (multilateral and bilateral).

Another policy suggestion raised by the Thai and Vietnamese country chapters is the need to mitigate the negative impact of liberalization measures on domestic stakeholders, such as the poor and small domestic producers, by initiating assistance programmes and/or enhancing social safety nets. In this regard, the Philippines chapter also suggests the use of government assistance for improving the capabilities of those negatively affected to help them compete and withstand competition from cheaper imports. The Thai country chapter warns that there is a need to monitor such assistance funds so that they will be as effective as was intended. Other measures include the consolidation of small firms to increase their size, especially when size is a constraint on their ability to compete (such as the logistics sector). The Philippines chapter also discusses the need to find niche products and markets as a means of facilitating the country's ability to compete in the automobile sector. In terms of workers' mobility, the Thai country chapter recommends skills development for local workers to help them work in a cross-cultural environment and to compete with foreign medical workers from other countries. Thus, preparing domestic producers and workers for the AEC is an important step for allowing a country to fully implement and access the benefits of the AEC's liberalization measures.

An important lesson can also be learnt from the Singapore experience in terms of a country's readiness to embrace liberalization. Given increasing globalization, protectionist measures are no longer a viable policy response.

ASEAN member countries have to consider ways and means to restructure or upgrade key strategic sectors so that they may benefit from greater liberalization. As the authors of the Singapore chapter demonstrate, the electronics sector in the city-state has undergone dramatic restructuring in response to changing comparative cost advantages and the emergence of competitive facilities in other ASEAN countries and in China. The Singapore policy response has been to fully support liberalizing trade in goods within the AEC while concurrently assisting affected businesses and workers; helping them upgrade and move resources into more competitive sectors and activities. Likewise, with respect to the aviation sector, and although it is facing significant competitive pressures, the government's policy response has been to develop and upgrade Changi airport into a more competitive air hub, and to enable Singapore Airlines (SIA) and its affiliates to be more competitive.

The policy suggestions from the chapters in this book, therefore, highlight the importance of stakeholder consultation as a means of increasing information flows for facilitating successful buy in and cooperation among implementing agencies and enhancing the capacity of the domestic sector to compete. The aforementioned are critical for promoting domestic consensus. The use of limited resources for the implementation of the AEC commitments can only be achieved through prioritizing these commitments in each country. Coordinating domestic policies, integrating actions undertaken by various implementing agencies and embedding these aims within a country's development strategies are also crucial for reducing policy conflicts as ASEAN member countries move towards deeper economic integration beyond 2015.

Notes

1. This pillar is now known as the ASEAN Political and Security Community (APSC).
2. This is known as the Declaration of ASEAN Concord II or the Bali Concord II.
3. The ASEAN-6 countries are Brunei, Indonesia, Malaysia, the Philippines, Singapore and Thailand.
4. ATIGA consolidated and streamlined all provisions in the Common Effective Preferential Tariff (CEPT) scheme under the ASEAN Free Trade Area (AFTA) and other protocols related to trade in goods into one single legal instrument. It entered into force in 2010 and superseded CEPT-AFTA.
5. Being a single point of information for trade and clearance of goods at the

border, it allows for more simplified trade processes, with fewer delays and lower costs.

6. The FTA between Australia and New Zealand is known as the Closer Economic Relation (CER).

7. Import restrictions have been adopted to meet the objectives of public health, infant industry protection or consumer health.

8. Most ASEAN member countries require export licences (except for the Philippines) or impose export taxes (except for Brunei, the Philippines and Singapore) for selected products, including goods within intra-ASEAN trade.

9. The LPI measures border control efficiency (customs), infrastructure quality, ease of arranging competitively priced shipments, competence of logistics services, ability to track and trace consignments, timeliness in shipments.

10. The 1994 General Agreement on Trade in Services (GATS) has identified four modes of supply: cross-border trade (Mode 1: when neither producer nor consumer move, but the service itself is traded, e.g. business or financial services provided by mail or telephone); consumption abroad (Mode 2: consumption abroad occurs when consumers move to the location of the service, such as tourism); commercial presence (Mode 3: when producers enter a host country via a long-term presence); and movement of suppliers (Mode 4: when producers enter a host country via a shorter-term movement of people, for example, a foreign IT-expert travelling to a site to implement a technology plan).

References

ASEAN Secretariat. *ASEAN Vision 2020.* Jakarta: ASEAN Secretariat, 15 December 1997.

———. *Declaration of ASEAN Concord II (Bali Concord II).* Bali: ASEAN Secretariat, 7 October 2003.

———. *Cebu Declaration on the Acceleration of the Establishment of an ASEAN Community by 2015.* Cebu: ASEAN Secretariat, 13 January 2007.

———. *Charting Progress towards Regional Economic Integration: ASEAN Economic Community Scorecard.* Jakarta: ASEAN Secretariat, 2010.

———. *ASEAN Economic Community Scorecard: Charting Progress towards Regional Economic Integration Phase I (2008–09) and Phase II (2010–11).* Jakarta: ASEAN Secretariat, 2012.

———. Chairman's Statement of the 26th ASEAN Summit, Malaysia, 27 April 2015. Available at <http://www.asean.org/images/2015/april/26th_asean_summit/Chairman%20Statement%2026th%20ASEAN%20Summit_final.pdf> (accessed 8 May 2015).

——— and World Bank. "ASEAN Integration Monitoring Report", 2013. Available at <http://documents.worldbank.org/curated/en/2013/01/18780456/

association-southeast-asian-nations-asean-integration-monitoring-report-joint-report-asean-secretariat-world-bank> (accessed 8 May 2015).

Balassa, Bela. *The Theory of Economic Integration*. Homewood, Illinois: Richard D. Irwin Inc., 1961.

Basu Das, Sanchita. "Assessing the Progress and Impediments Towards an ASEAN Economic Community". In *ASEAN Economic Community Scorecard: Performance and Perception*, edited by Sanchita Basu Das. Singapore: Institute of Southeast Asian Studies, 2013.

———. "Can the ASEAN Economic Community be Achieved by 2015?". *ISEAS Perspective*. Singapore: Institute of Southeast Asian Studies, 11 October 2012.

Bhaskaran, Manu. "The Investment Dimension of ASEAN". In *ASEAN Economic Community Scorecard: Performance and Perception*, edited by Sanchita Basu Das. Singapore: Institute of Southeast Asian Studies, 2013.

Buszynski, Leszek. "ASEAN's New Challenges". *Pacific Affairs* 70, no. 4 (1197): 555–77.

Chia, Siow Yue. "Free Flow of Skilled Labour in the AEC". In *Toward a Competitive ASEAN Single Market; Sectoral Analysis*, edited by Shujiro Urata and Misa Okabe. ERIA Research Project Report 2010-01, Jakarta: ERIA, 2011a.

———. "Association of Southeast Asian Nations Economic Integration: Developments and Challenges". *Asian Economic Policy Review* 6, no. 1 (2011b): 43–63.

——— and Michael Plummer. "ASEAN Economic Cooperation and Integration: Progress, Challenges and Future Direction". *Monograph for the NUS-CIL ASEAN Project*. Mimeographed, 2013.

Deraniyagala, Sonali and Ben Fine. "New Trade Theory versus Old Trade Policy: A Continuing Enigma". Undated. Available at <https://www.soas.ac.uk/economics/research/workingpapers/file28872.pdf> (accessed 20 September 2014).

ERIA. *Mid-Term Review of the Implementation of AEC Blueprint: Executive Summary*. Jakarta: Economic Research Institute for ASEAN and East Asia, 2012. Available at <http://www.eria.org/Mid-term%20Review%20of%20the%20Implementation%20of%20AEC%20Blue%20Print-Executve%20Summary.pdf> (accessed 8 May 2015).

Grugel, Jean B. "New Regionalism and Modes of Governance: Comparing US and EU Strategies in Latin America". *European Journal of International Relations* 10, no. 4 (2004): 603–26.

Hew, Denis. "Conclusion: Towards an ASEAN Economic Community by 2015". In *Brick by Brick: The Building of an ASEAN Economic Community*, edited by Denis Hew. Singapore: Institute of Southeast Asian Studies, 2007.

———. "Introduction: Brick by Brick: The Building of an ASEAN Economic

Community". In *Brick by Brick: The Building of an ASEAN Economic Community*, edited by Denis Hew. Singapore: Institute of Southeast Asian Studies, 2007.

Hill, Hal and Jayant Menon. "ASEAN Economic Integration: Features, Fulfilments, Failures and the Future". ADB Working Paper Series on Regional Economic Integration, no. 69, Asian Development Bank, Tokyo, 2010.

Hu, Albert. "ASEAN Economic Community Business Survey". In *The ASEAN Economic Community: A Work in Progress*, edited by Sanchita Basu Das, Jayant Menon, Omkar L. Shrestha and Rodolfo Severino. Singapore: Institute of Southeast Asian Studies, 2013.

Kahnert, F., P. Richards, E. Stoutjesdijk and P. Thomopoulos. *Economic Integration Among Developing Countries*. Paris: Development Center of the Organization for Economic Co-operation and Development (OECD), 1969.

Kawai, Masahiro. "East Asian Economic Regionalism: Progress and Challenges". *Journal of Asian Economies* 16, no. 1 (2005): 29–55.

——— and Ganesh Wignaraja. "Main Findings and Policy Recommendations". In *Asia's Free Trade Agreements: How is Business Responding?*, edited by Masahiro Kawai and Ganesh Wignaraja. Cheltenham and Northampton: Asian Development Bank Institute and Edward Elgar Publishing, 2011.

Keohane, Robert O. and Helen V. Milner, eds. *Internationalization and Domestic Politics*. Cambridge: Cambridge University Press, 1996.

Kim, In Song. "Political Cleavages within Industry: Firm Level Lobbying for Trade Liberalization", 7 October 2013. Available at <www.princeton.edu/~insong/research/exporters.pdf> (accessed 13 September 2014).

Krugman, Paul R. "Increasing Returns, Monopolistic Competition and International Trade". *Journal of International Economics* 9, no. 4 (1979): 469–79.

Mansfield, Edward D. and Helen Milner. "The New Wave of Regionalism". *International Organization* 53, no. 3 (1999): 589–627.

Melitz, Marc J. "The Impact of Trade on Intra-Industry Reallocations and Aggregate Industry Productivity". *Econometrica* 71, no. 6 (2003): 1695–725.

Mittelman, James H. *The Globalization Syndrome: Transformation and Resistance*. New Jersey: Princeton University Press, 2000.

Mutharika, B.W.T. *Towards Multinational Economic Cooperation in Africa*. New York: Praeger Publishers, 1972.

Nikomborirak, Deunden and Supunnavadee Jitdumrong. "ASEAN Trade in Services". In *The ASEAN Economic Community: A Work in Progress*, edited by Sanchita Basu Das, Jayant Menon, Omkar L. Shrestha and Rodolfo Severino. Singapore: Institute of Southeast Asian Studies, 2013.

Panagariya, Arvind. "The Regionalism Debate: An Overview", November 1998. Available at <http://www.columbia.edu/~ap2231/Policy%20Papers/overview-we%281%29.pdf> (accessed 8 May 2015).

Peamsilpakulchorn, Pajnapa. "The Domestic Politics of Thailand's Bilateral Free Trade Agreement Policy". *International Public Policy Review* 2, no. 1 (2006): 74–120.

Sally, Razeen. "Free Trade Agreements and the Prospects for Regional Integration in East Asia". *Asian Economic Policy Review* 1, no. 2 (2006): 306–21.

Severino, Rodolfo. "Politics of Association of Southeast Asian Nations". *Asian Economic Policy Review* 6, no. 1 (2011): 22–38.

——— and Jayant Menon. "Overview". In *The ASEAN Economic Community: A Work in Progress*, edited by Sanchita Basu Das, Jayant Menon, Omkar L. Shrestha and Rodolfo Severino. Singapore: Institute of Southeast Asian Studies, 2013.

Terada, Takashi. "Competitive Regionalism in Southeast Asia and Beyond: Role of Singapore and ASEAN". In *Competitive Regionalism: FTA Diffusion in the Pacific Rim*, edited by Mireya Solis, Barbara Stallings and Saori N. Katada. Hampshire, England: Palgrave Macmillan, 2009.

World Bank. "Logistics Performance Index 2012". Washington, D.C.: World Bank, 2012.

2

ASEAN ECONOMIC COOPERATION AND ITS POLITICAL REALITIES

Rodolfo C. Severino and Moe Thuzar

1. INTRODUCTION

The late Dr Goh Keng Swee, speaking in his capacity as then Minister for Finance of Singapore, made this insightful observation on regional economic cooperation in a speech delivered at the University of Singapore Society's annual dinner on 12 January 1970 (Goh 1995, pp. 104–11):

> when people talk about regional economic cooperation, they talk as if this is something new. The truth is that, by any reasonable definition of the term, regional cooperation has been going on for more than a century, ever since the European imperialists set foot in this part of the world and opened it for economic development. What we are now doing is, in part, the outcome and the continuation of this long historical process (p. 105).

He then went on to outline the practical underpinnings for the then ASEAN members to trade with each other, citing the very real "value for money" from trade in goods and services among the different economies in the region. However, Dr Goh also acknowledged that the "classical doctrine of international trade" and the notion of free trade are rarely observed in their entirety in the real world, "either in Southeast Asia or elsewhere" (Goh 1995, p. 105). Close to five decades later, this observation still finds relevance in the efforts being made by members of the Association of Southeast Asian Nations (ASEAN) to achieve the ASEAN Economic Community (AEC) that will bring down barriers to free movement of goods, services, capital, and skilled labour across sovereign borders in the region. With 91 per cent of the 506 AEC measures being accomplished,[1] member states are now faced with the challenge of addressing behind-the-border barriers, and negotiating a comprehensive regional trade arrangement with several of ASEAN's external partners (Goh 1995, p. 104).

Despite the hype and excitement over what will be ushered in by end-2015 as the first milestone of the AEC, which is part of a politically, economically and socially integrated ASEAN Community, there is a sense of déjà vu. The reality is that the deliberate and planned inter-governmental measures taken by sovereign governments to benefit from international trade, requires the will and capacity of all parties negotiating these agreements to commit to and implement these complex plans and arrangements. Thus, national-level follow-through is important to give effect to regional commitments.

This chapter explores the different interplays of national and regional capacities in pursuing ASEAN economic cooperation. It expands the analysis of an earlier paper on the politics of ASEAN economic cooperation (Severino 2011, pp. 22–38), which looked at the domestic political obstacles standing in the way for full implementation of ASEAN's stated commitments to integrate the region's economy. With the announcements of the ASEAN Community in 2015 and its next milestones, it is worth looking at the existing and emerging political realities that will continue to shape how ASEAN members go about implementing their regional commitments individually and collectively, within ASEAN as well as the wider East Asia and Pacific context of economic interactions. In an attempt to do so, the chapter looks first at the political underpinnings of regional economic cooperation in ASEAN's early years where experiments in preferential trading arrangements, and complementary industrial projects met with different fates and were ultimately superseded by the ASEAN Free Trade Area (AFTA). The chapter then goes on to look at the expansion of ASEAN's external economic relations while AFTA's own expansion continued. Different political realities in the ASEAN member states' interactions with external partners shaped how these external free trade agreements were negotiated and given effect. The chapter then looks at implications of wider regional partnerships — including those that are emerging — on ASEAN members, to assess how these developments will affect their domestic consensus-shaping on regional economic commitments, and offers some concluding thoughts on the broad realities of ASEAN economic cooperation.

2. PREFERENTIAL TRADING ARRANGEMENTS AND INDUSTRIAL PROJECTS: THE POLITICAL UNDERPINNINGS OF ECONOMIC COOPERATION

The ASEAN Declaration issued on 8 August 1967 had seven "aims and purposes", four of which had to do with economic, social and cultural development. In reality, however, the new association's objective had everything to do with political issues — to keep the Southeast Asian countries' disputes from turning violent and the region out of the violent rivalries of the big powers. It was not until February 1976, when the ASEAN heads of state/government held their first summit meeting that ASEAN's objectives were set down in greater detail. The Declaration of ASEAN Concord issued at the First ASEAN Summit outlined a programme of action for regional cooperation, established a central secretariat, and directed ASEAN's "economic ministers"[2] to meet in Kuala Lumpur in March 1976 to talk about specific steps for setting up "large-scale" industries and tariff preferential arrangements for the region (ASEAN Secretariat 1976). The latter directive set the basis for regional economic cooperation.

The origins of the ASEAN Free Trade Area can be found in the Preferential Trading Arrangement (PTA), approved by the Third ASEAN Economic Ministers Meeting (AEM) in January 1972. Covering among others, a list of goods negotiated and agreed on by the ASEAN member states, the PTA basically allowed "margins of preference" from normal tariffs on covered goods. The number of goods on the lists, the margins of preference and the cut-off import value were periodically increased until the PTA was superseded in 1992 by the Common Effective Preferential Tariffs for the ASEAN Free Trade Area (CEPT/AFTA). In the case of CEPT/ AFTA, all goods were included for the 0–5 per cent tariff reduction unless explicitly excluded. CEPT/AFTA thus went one step further than the PTA in providing for the lowering of intra-ASEAN tariffs until their abolition. The PTA, on the other hand, had excluded everything unless specifically included, and goods could be imported from other ASEAN countries only under the prevailing margins of preference. AFTA's beginnings in 1992 were in a way signaling the political intent of member states to open up the region for business with the world.

Another component of ASEAN economic cooperation at the beginning was the ASEAN Industrial Projects (AIP). At their March 1977 inaugural meeting in Kuala Lumpur, the AEM agreed to assign a urea fertilizer plant each to Indonesia and Malaysia, a similar factory to the Philippines, diesel engines to Singapore, and a soda ash plant to Thailand. However, the AIP scheme soon ran aground on the shoals of projected national and/or personal interests. The ASEAN member states did not refrain from setting up industries competing with an AIP. They unilaterally decided to replace the industries assigned to them. They also did not commit themselves to purchasing the AIP products. The result has been that only the two urea fertilizer plants, in Sarawak and Aceh, have survived. The AIP scheme serves as a reminder of the competing attitudes and policies of individual governments in the region pursuing largely similar paths to industrialization through import substitution. This posed the main obstacle to the notion of a complementary regionwide collaboration. Yet, faced with the challenges and recognizing the opportunities of a liberalizing global economy, the ASEAN countries realized that they had to transform their economic orientations and business mind-sets from being largely state-guided to being market-driven, from import substitution to being export-led, from regional cooperation to integration (Severino 2011, p. 24).

What was the reality behind this logic? The Fourth ASEAN Summit's decision in 1992 to conclude the CEPT/AFTA agreement; the Fifth ASEAN Summit's agreement in 1995 to achieve by 2003 (instead of the originally scheduled 2008) the reduction of tariffs on intra-ASEAN trade; and the AEM's decision, in response to the 1997–98 crisis, to abolish all tariffs on the ASEAN-6[3] trade with one another by 2010, were all motivated by the need to integrate regional economies to:

> overcome the vulnerabilities inherent in operating as small, fragmented economies in a globalizing and regionalizing world. Politically, the region's governments wished to be seen as responding to the global trend toward globalization and free trade and to the challenges that it raised, as well as to attract investments from Japan and others through an integrated regional market.... However, ... economic integration entailed more than the reduction or elimination of tariffs on intraregional trade. It could even be said, without denying their symbolic and, in certain cases, actual

importance, that tariffs are of less importance in integrating a regional economy than the lowering of non-tariff barriers to trade, the efficient and honest application of customs regulations, the harmonization of product standards, the liberalization of trade in services, and seamless transportation and communication linkages (Severino 2011, p. 25).

In 2007, ASEAN's fortieth anniversary year, the Twelfth ASEAN Summit held at Cebu, Philippines in February 2007, issued the Cebu Declaration on the Acceleration of the Establishment of an ASEAN Community by 2015. The Declaration's preamble referred to the "proposal made at the 11th ASEAN Summit in Kuala Lumpur in December 2005, on accelerating the establishment of an ASEAN Community, as well as the exchange of views at the 39th ASEAN Ministerial Meeting in July 2006 in Kuala Lumpur and the recommendation from the 38th ASEAN Economic Ministers Meeting in August 2006".[4] This was a clear statement of ASEAN's political intent to accomplish its ASEAN Community objective sooner rather than later. The Cebu Declaration also acknowledged that some ASEAN members were in a better state of preparedness than others, by the statement in the Declaration's preamble section that "different levels of development within ASEAN require some flexibility as ASEAN moves towards a more integrated and interconnected future".[5] Closer to the realization date for the ASEAN Community, however, analysts and experts now feel obliged to qualify the political aspiration by more realistic assessments of the achievability of the ASEAN Community. Severino (2014b) asserts that:

> ASEAN is still far from being economically integrated as a region. And there is little prospect that it will be fully integrated, as envisioned, in the near future, much less by 2015. But ... the plan to realize the AEC by 2015 should be looked at as a reaffirmation of the ASEAN leaders' aspiration for, and commitment to, efficiency in trading, market openness and links with the international community. The year 2015 should be considered not as a hard-and-fast target, in which ASEAN, its objectives and the way it conducts business are suddenly transformed. Rather, it should be regarded as a benchmark to help measure ASEAN's progress toward regional economic integration.

3. EXPANSION OF ASEAN'S EXTERNAL ECONOMIC RELATIONS

With the AFTA becoming a reality in the six ASEAN member states by January 2003, ASEAN turned its attention to expanding its economic cooperation with several of its Dialogue Partners, notably China, Japan, the Republic of Korea, Australia and New Zealand, and India. The economic agreements that ASEAN as a group concluded with an external partner generally covers trade in goods (tariff preferences, rules of origin and the reduction of non-tariff barriers as protectionist measures), trade in services, trade facilitation in goods or services, investments, and help to Cambodia, Laos and Myanmar on human resource development ostensibly to enable them to take advantage of the benefits of regional economic integration.

The first economic agreement proposed for ASEAN with an external partner was actually one with Australia and New Zealand, in 1999. Although one of the ASEAN countries blocked its formal conclusion, the process of cooperation did not stop. In lieu thereof, ASEAN and Australia/ New Zealand signed a Comprehensive Economic Partnership (CEP) that avoided trade and investment liberalization and concentrated instead on technical cooperation, trade and investment facilitation, business competitiveness, transparency of regulations, technical and other non-tariff barriers to free trade, standards and conformity assessment, e-commerce, small and medium enterprises, and capacity-building.[6]

Although India signed an FTA framework agreement with ASEAN as early as October 2003, the country did not conclude a trade-in-goods agreement until August 2009, or almost six years later. The services and investments components are still being negotiated. Batra (2009) has critiqued the protracted negotiation process for the ASEAN-India Trade in Goods Agreement, listing, among others, India's contradictory stand on criteria for the Rules of Origin, and on the size and composition of the negative list.

The Chinese beat everyone else to recognizing FTA or similar agreements as a strategic asset. In November 2002, the leaders of ASEAN and China signed an agreement expressing their desire "to adopt a Framework Agreement on Comprehensive Economic Co-operation" (Batra 2009) that was so full of "flexibilities" as to render it ineffective for the lobbies which usually whisper in the ears of policy- and/or decision-makers, many of them on behalf of the sectors or companies that employ them. They concluded the agreement on trade in goods and adopted the ASEAN Rules of Origin in November 2004, and established a dispute-settlement mechanism for the Framework and associated agreements. China signed with ASEAN a trade-in-services agreement in January 2007 and one on investments in August 2009.[7] Above all, the Chinese managed to have each ASEAN member recognize China as a full market economy at a time (in 2004) when the United States and the European Union (EU) were refusing to do so, presumably for trade and other economic reasons, as well as political ones. By February 2010, the ASEAN-China agreements on investments and on trades in goods (implemented July 2005) and services (entered into force July 2007) had been concluded.[8]

By way of comparison, it was not until November 2004 that ASEAN and the Republic of Korea (ROK) jointly announced their intention to negotiate a free-trade agreement between them, and it was not until 2005 (December), 2006 (August), 2007 (November), and 2009 (June) that the ROK and ASEAN signed a framework on an FTA, trade-in-goods, trade-in-services, and investment agreements, respectively.

Japan had a different approach. Japan's bureaucracy concluded a general agreement with ASEAN that involved all ASEAN member countries as one of the outcomes of the ASEAN-Japan Commemorative Summit (for thirty years of dialogue relations) in 2014. It was the only way the Japanese and the ASEAN bureaucrats could agree to have the ASEAN leaders gather, for the first time, outside Southeast Asia for such an event. The Japanese leadership was convinced that Tokyo had to be perceived as having strong ties with Southeast Asia. Accordingly, the leaders of Japan and ASEAN signed a framework in Bali in October 2003, pledging their "maximum efforts to commence the negotiations on the Comprehensive Economic Partnership Agreement (CEPA) between Japan and ASEAN as a whole" at the beginning of 2005 and emphasizing that the proposed CEPA would include "elements of a possible free trade area".[9]

In the meantime, Japan negotiated and signed individual Economic Partnership Agreements (EPAs) with the ASEAN-6: Singapore (2002); Malaysia (2003); the Philippines (2006); Thailand (April 2007); Brunei Darussalam (June 2007); and Indonesia (August 2007). Japan concluded an EPA with Vietnam in December 2008, bringing to seven the number of EPAs that Japan has concluded with individual ASEAN members. The CEPA with ASEAN as a whole entered into force in December 2008.[10] This is in contrast to China's approach, as Japan opted to work first on bilateral EPAs with countries that were ready and prepared to do so. In Japan's view, starting with high-level bilateral EPAs would eventually lead to a higher level regional agreement. Otsuji and Shinoda (2014) have observed that this approach reduced the risk of negotiating a low-level regional agreement that merely paid lip service to the highest common factors.

Of the Dialogue Partners that consider themselves as having strategic interests by virtue of geography or history or both in East Asia, only the United States has no FTA agreement with ASEAN as a group. But then it would not have been consistent with the American culture or political system for Washington, D.C. to conclude such a general and unenforceable agreement as an FTA that other leaders have blithely signed with those of ASEAN, if only for symbolic purposes. This symbolic commitment will however find expression in the announcement of the Regional Comprehensive Economic Partnership (RCEP), which ASEAN aims to complete concurrently with the AEC by end-2015. ASEAN Dialogue Partners joining ASEAN members in the RCEP include all those that have signed an FTA with ASEAN: Australia and New Zealand, China, India, Japan, and ROK. Some analysts observe that the RCEP is another illustration of ASEAN side-stepping political exigencies. A proposal in 2001 — initiated by China — to establish an ASEAN Plus Three East Asia Free Trade Area (EAFTA), and Japan's proposal in 2006 for a Comprehensive Economic Partnership for East Asia (CEPEA) which would also include Australia, India and New Zealand in addition to the Southeast and Northeast Asian countries under the ASEAN Plus Three process, led to a flurry of study groups recommending the merits of each. In 2009, the heads of state/ government attending the Fourth East Asian Summit that their officials consider the recommendations of respective study groups on the EAFTA and CEPEA. The back and forth ended with ASEAN's compromise proposal in 2011 to establish a regionwide FTA with all its FTA partners, and with ASEAN at the centre. Negotiations for the RCEP were formally launched the following year at the Seventh East Asia Summit.[11]

ASEAN Plus Three and Financial Cooperation

The most active forum for ASEAN's economic relations, however, seems to be in the area of financial cooperation. The ASEAN Plus Three process, comprising the ten ASEAN members and the three Northeast Asian countries of the China, Japan, and the ROK, has its centrepiece the Chiang Mai Initiative (CMI) on financial cooperation.

The CMI was originally conceived in response to the 1997–98 Asian Financial Crisis (AFC). It was established after the United States, the International Monetary Fund (IMF) and China shot down the proposal for an Asian Monetary Fund set forth by Eisuke Sakakibara, then Japan's

Vice-Minister of Finance. Severino (2014a) assesses that while Japan "gained points in East Asian eyes" with the proposal for an Asian Monetary Fund, the withdrawal of this proposal caused it to lose "goodwill and esteem"; at the same time, China "won points and goodwill" with its agreement not to engage in "competitive devaluations" with the East Asian economies that were experiencing the brunt of the financial crisis. Nevertheless, Japan regained a lead role of sorts in the formulation of the CMI.

Because of the CMI's small size, the 1997–98 AFC prompted Thailand, ROK and Indonesia to turn to the IMF for assistance in tackling the impact of the financial crisis, rather than to their fellow East Asians, though many of them had large international reserves. The CMI had been based on bilateral currency swap arrangements, including the extension of the 1977 ASEAN Swap Arrangement to the economically powerful Northeast Asian countries. It had a considerable portion (about 90 per cent) subject to IMF conditionalities. It was also involved in the Sino-Japanese rivalry for dominance in East Asia.

In the face of all this, finance ministers and central bank governors (or their deputies) from the thirteen countries gathered as the ASEAN Plus Three Finance Ministers Meeting (AFMM+3) in Madrid in 2008, and Bali in 2009 for their twice-yearly meetings, plus Hong Kong. Hong Kong, though technically part of the Chinese delegation, also represented the interests of Hong Kong as an autonomous economy in its own right. The meetings increased the total pool of funds available to economies in need from the initial amount of US$36.5 billion in 2001 to US$80 billion in 2007. Following the decisions of the 2008 Madrid and 2009 Bali meetings, the pool was further increased to US$120 billion and US$240 billion respectively. These meetings also expanded the percentage of loans delinked from IMF conditionalities to 30 per cent. Perhaps most importantly, the thirteen economies agreed to multilateralize the system. This entailed adding to the available funds from existing bilateral currency swap arrangements the pool of currency reserves. This led to renaming the scheme as Chiang Mai Initiative Multi-lateralization (CMIM). The latest expansions took effect in July 2014. While some still view the pool as "insignificant",[12] the very existence of CMIM, backed as it is by foreign-exchange-rich countries, has helped prevent a repetition of AFC in East Asia, since 1997–98, and weathered the fallout from the global financial and economic crisis of 2008–09. Nevertheless, the complex interconnectedness of geopolitics and geoeconomics may well lend to a speculation that the

CMIM may only offer a partial answer to the complex causes of financial and economic crises.[13]

Although the CMIM was not and is not an ASEAN endeavour, all ASEAN member states take part in its major decisions and approve them by consensus. The CMIM retains its ASEAN character not only through the continued existence and extension to ASEAN+3 of the 1977 ASEAN Swap Arrangement[14] but also through the modified adoption of the "ASEAN Way" of decision-making.[15]

The CMIM has a small office in Singapore unprepossessingly named the ASEAN+3 Macroeconomic Research Office, or AMRO. As the surveillance unit of the CMIM, AMRO was set up in 2011 to monitor and analyse regional economies and to contribute to early detection of risks, ensure the swift implementation of remedial actions and assist in the effective decision-making of the CMIM.[16] However, there were at least two implementation problems, both of them having to do with the then-incipient rivalry between China and Japan for leadership in the Asia-Pacific. The first issue was who would be the first AMRO Director, a Chinese or a Japanese official, and for how long a term? The second issue had to do with which country would have the biggest contribution to the enlarged and more-independent CMIM, China or Japan? AMRO resolved these problems through a form of the ASEAN Way, that is, its informal and legally unenforceable nature, with its enforceability depending on peer pressure and friendly negotiations.

To address the first, Wei Benhua, a former senior official of the Asia Development Bank (ADB) and of China's Ministry of Finance, was appointed as the first Director of AMRO, but for only two years, 2011–12. In this way, he was able to recruit the first set of AMRO officials and also put the Chinese stamp on its operations. Japan's Yoichi Nemoto, a former senior official of AMRO and, before that, in Japan's Ministry of Finance, succeeded him in 2012 for a regular three-year term.[17]

The second concern was addressed in a similarly clever way. Japan already had the perennial presidency of the ADB. On the other hand, China was not yet in the major-power game. The question of the size of contributions to the CMIM, among other initiatives, had been meant to narrow this gap. Without Hong Kong's 3.5 per cent contribution, Japan would have the largest share of the CMIM. With Hong Kong's contribution counted as part of China's, the Chinese share would amount to 32 per cent, exactly the same as Japan's. This is a matter of at least symbolic importance for the two rivals for regional supremacy, although the governments of the two countries regularly deny the existence of such a rivalry.

4. WIDER REGIONAL PARTNERSHIPS

While the AEC is the centrepiece of ASEAN's economic integration, ASEAN's outward-looking nature does not preclude its members from participating in economic or other initiatives led by countries outside the region.

Trans-Pacific Partnership and the U.S.'s Trade Promotion Authority

Amid this flurry of activities between ASEAN, China and Japan, U.S. officials had not been idle. Early in 2008 or in 2009, depending on how one defines "join" and "lead", they joined and took over the leadership of the four-member (Brunei Darussalam, Chile, New Zealand and Singapore) Trans-Pacific Strategic Partnership Agreement of 2005, or P4 for short. They called the process the Trans-Pacific Partnership, or TPP. There are now eleven countries[18] negotiating with the United States on what the Obama administration has called the "Crown Jewel" of its trade policy and a twenty-first-century trade agreement. Because it embraces intellectual property rights, environmental protection, labour rights, government procurement, and other non-trade issues with politically powerful constituencies in the United States, some in the office of the American president, the State Department, academia and the media, think of the TPP as another weapon in the U.S. arsenal to contain China.

While the Obama administration, with the U.S. Trade Representative in the lead, continues to deny the political motives behind the TPP, Chinese officials are split between those who ask, perhaps disingenuously, whom to approach for an invitation to the TPP negotiations; and those who insist that China is not ready to make the concessions required by the United States on intellectual property and labour rights.

This lack of readiness on the part of state decision-makers is precisely the reason why the ASEAN member states (other than Brunei, Malaysia, Singapore and Vietnam) have so far opted out of joining the negotiations on the TPP. Yet, it is the non-trade issues, many of them pushed by the organized constituents of Democratic members of the U.S. Congress, that give the TPP a chance of gaining the Trade Promotion Authority (TPA) that seems to be a requisite for the TPP. The last TPA expired in 2007. It is the so-called "fast-track" authority that would compel the U.S. Congress, which, according to the U.S. Constitution, has the power to approve the TPP or any other foreign trade agreement, to take a Yes or No vote, without any amendments, and thus assure America's foreign interlocutors that whatever concessions they extract from the American negotiators would not somehow be taken back by the United States. Some U.S. officials had earlier estimated November 2014 as the time for the approval of both TPA and TPP. Yet, November 2014 has come and gone, and the TPP's fate was first dealt a blow with the U.S. Congress's rejection on 13 June 2015 of President Obama's bid for fast-track authority (Bloomberg Politics, 13 June 2015), then given a reprieve two weeks later with the Republican-dominated Senate approving the TPA in a "rare Republican-White House collaboration" (BBC, 25 June 2015). This gives a glimpse into the partisan interests in the United States, where Republican support for freer markets and lower trade barriers often collide with the Democrats' positions on labour and environmental standards.

Indeed, China and some of its neighbours prefer the RCEP agreement, which includes the ten ASEAN member states and those that have concluded FTAs with ASEAN as a group. This would exclude the United States, the EU and Russia, but includes China, Japan, ROK, India, Australia and New Zealand. Presumably, Brunei, Malaysia, Singapore and Vietnam would be in both the TPP and the RCEP. Presumably, too, the RCEP agreement would be devoid of those non-trade issues that would not be possible to resolve or even negotiate without the requisite internal domestic reforms on the part of China and of at least some of the ASEAN member-states.

Washington has been applying pressure on its allies like Japan, Taiwan, the Philippines, Thailand to join the TPP negotiations, and has succeeded in the case of Japan. Inasmuch as the TPP is seen as a U.S.-led initiative that Beijing views as a possible threat to the Chinese economy (He 2015) a particular country's attitude towards the TPP will be determined by its overall relationship with both Washington and Beijing.[19]

At the 2014 Summit of the Asia Pacific Economic Cooperation (APEC) under China's chairmanship, China pushed for the conclusion of a Free Trade Agreement for the Asia-Pacific (FTAAP). The United States shot down that idea, although it was among one of the FTAAP's first proponents, apparently preferring to push the TPP instead. Nevertheless, FTAAP remains on the APEC agenda.[20] Seven of the ASEAN members (Brunei, Indonesia, Malaysia, Singapore, the Philippines, Thailand and Vietnam) are APEC member economies.

Thus, several ASEAN members have numerous economic relations under other regional/multilateral frameworks, or bilateral arrangements, with multiple partners outside the region. For ASEAN's own regional economic arrangements, however, the priority is on achieving the AEC and RCEP. The discussions above highlight to a certain extent that despite the slow pace of progress of the various regional trade arrangements such as the TPP, FTAAP and even the RCEP, ASEAN's own AEC appears to be plodding along. It is targeted to come into reality at the end of 2015 though some of the stated objectives will remain a work-in-progress. Since all these regional arrangements are meant to be WTO-consistent, their eventual coming into fruition should add to the benefits of regional integration. While ASEAN centrality remains a key goal of ASEAN policymakers, it is likely that events surrounding the success or failure of the wider regional arrangements will be shaped by other more powerful influences beyond ASEAN.

Investing in Asian Infrastructure — the Asian Infrastructure Investment Bank

As a political counterweight to what is increasingly perceived as heavy American influence on the decisions of the World Bank and the IMF, and similar domination by Japan of ADB decisions, China has proposed an Asian Infrastructure Investment Bank (AIIB). Despite the initial misgivings of Washington, which had cautioned its allies to see how the proposed bank would operate before applying to become founding members, Washington now seems to have somewhat softened its stance towards the AIIB.

The AIIB website lists as "Prospective Founding Members" all ten ASEAN member states and EU members such as Austria, Denmark, Finland, France, Germany, Italy, Luxembourg, the Netherlands, and the United Kingdom. Other prospective founding members include Australia, Brazil, India, Kuwait, Mongolia, Nepal, New Zealand, Pakistan, Qatar, Russia, Saudi Arabia, South Korea, Sri Lanka, Switzerland, Turkey and the United Arab Emirates. About ten other countries, including Egypt, Israel and Norway have sent in their applications. Taiwan's application has been rejected. There are reports of China rejecting North Korea's application.

In October and November 2014, as a mark of the AIIB's Asian character, twenty-one Asian countries, including China and the ten ASEAN states, signed the Memorandum of Understanding in Beijing and met at the level of "chief negotiators" in Kunming, plus Hong Kong representatives who sat in as part of China's delegation, officially to set up the AIIB. A "Second Chief Negotiators' Meeting" took place in Mumbai in January 2015.[21]

All this adds up to astute political calculations on the part of China. It represents a public commitment to regional economic integration, since such integration simply cannot take place without the infrastructure that is supposed to be financed by the AIIB. A joint study by the ADB in Manila and the ADB Institute in Tokyo "estimates that Asia needs to invest approximately $8 trillion in overall national infrastructure and about $290 billion in specific regional infrastructure projects between 2010 and 2020" (ADB and ADBI 2009).

Physical infrastructure in the form of roads, bridges, sea ports and airports is absolutely needed for the integration, connectivity, and community-building that ASEAN and China keep talking about. Moreover, such things as roads and bridges, sea ports and airports could serve as monuments to political leaders. In any case, they are highly visible and usually are considered helpful for politicians' futures. By emphasizing the proposed bank's Asian character, China evidently hopes to keep the United States from poking around the affairs of Asia.

Finally, there is a growing trend in both the World Bank and the ADB to demand reforms in recipients' governance, intellectual property rights, environmental protection and labour rights on the ground that, without such reforms, loans from rich countries would benefit only the big corporations rather than the poor. The AIIB loans, at least the aspiring needy countries hope, would carry no such demands for reforms, with which, in any case, some political leaders in the putative recipient countries are extremely uncomfortable. Letting in EU members and others who hold values similar to those of Europeans even as prospective founding members may be a double-edged sword for China; it may reinforce the AIIB's legitimacy in Western eyes, but allow countries like Australia, Britain, Denmark, France, Germany, Italy and other EU countries to influence AIIB decisions.

The AIIB provides the ASEAN members with significant infrastructure requirements with an additional source of funds — perhaps with less stringent conditions than those set by the international financial institutions. Yet, the AIIB, coupled with China's recently announced "One Belt One Road" strategy for regional economic development and connectivity spanning Asia to Europe, and with maritime routes through to Africa, may bring ASEAN member states further into China's embrace. This, with the significance economic bilateral interactions that several ASEAN member states have with China, brings its own set of concerns for ASEAN members. ASEAN has consistently highlighted the importance of prioritizing ASEAN's interest above national interests, in matters that affect (or threaten) ASEAN's unity of purpose. This is usually played out in the arena of political-security cooperation. The failure to issue the annual Joint Communiqué of the ASEAN Foreign Ministers in July 2012 over disagreement on the wording to be used on competing claims by ASEAN and China in the South China Sea serves as a reminder of how political realities — often times national concerns — can affect regional priorities.

5. ALIGNING REGIONAL AND NATIONAL INTERESTS

Misalignments will not only impede ASEAN's efforts of trying to achieve economic integration and region's motto of "One Vision, One Identity, One Community" enshrined in the ASEAN Charter, but will also undermine regional solidarity, as uneven progress will continue to entrench a two-tier ASEAN where sentiments may be divided between those who are perceived as either winners or losers.

Every sovereign state's foreign policy is driven by national interest — primarily to survive. Survival is also at the core of ASEAN's collective interest to come together in the politically turbulent times of the Cold War era, and the need for economic competitiveness drove ASEAN's first action for regional economic cooperation. Even so, the need for looser, more flexible arrangements to pursue economic cooperation highlights the realities that the governments of each ASEAN member state face domestically in making the case for the practice of economic growth. In the same way that the consent of member states is required for the implementation of trade liberalization and other measures, so too is domestic consent required for governments to justify the course they chart for national development (and that of the people). In the same way that regional consensus has to be negotiated either jointly among all member states, or along concurrent separate tracks at the sub-regional level, so too is domestic consensus dependent on negotiating a compromise among the different communities and stakeholders involved in, and affected by, implementing economic agreements. ASEAN's regional policy — and that of its respective members — thus depends on the alignment of national interests with broader regional concerns as well as those that exist (or are emerging) at the global level.

This is easier said than done. An informal survey carried out by the ISEAS–Yusof Ishak Institute's ASEAN Studies Centre in 2012 found that business communities in several of the ASEAN member states were largely unaware or unprepared for the AEC, and mainly relied on the Internet as an information source rather than from the relevant government focal point in the country, or even from trade associations and other business networks/contacts. As the AEC priorities continue with implementation, business lobbies in some ASEAN countries are seeking protection from what they perceive will be a deluge of foreign investors and professionals entering the country with freer movement of goods, services, labour and capital.[22] Even without business lobbies, these concerns exist across ASEAN countries — whether their economies are integrated into the global economy or still emerging from former cocoons.

The primacy of domestic political economy in realizing the AEC is also examined in depth by Jones (2015), who posits that domestic sectors will resist regulatory changes arising from the AEC's economic liberalization agreements, mainly because sectoral interests are affected with the changes that may "radically redistribute power and resources". Certainly, the economic agreements negotiated and entered into by the ministers responsible for trade and industry representing each ASEAN member state at the ASEAN Economic Ministers meetings need consent from other key economic sectors, particularly finance, as well as sectors such as labour and education whose domestic policies will be affected by these economic agreements. Additionally, as Jones has highlighted, "the AEC agenda frequently collides with protectionist impulses arising from alliances between political and business elites, … and the broader imperatives of avoiding socio-political unrest that could accompany the structural adjustments required by the AEC" (Jones 2015, p. 4).

6. CONCLUSION

From the foregoing discussions it is possible to draw certain tentative conclusions on the political underpinnings of ASEAN economic co-operations and other potential economic initiatives in the region.

First, ASEAN agreements, declarations, and other statements, are seldom self-executory. While most of them may be drafted and negotiated by well-meaning bureaucrats and other technicians, who may have at heart the interests of the nation and of the economy and society as a whole, as well as the fates of their political masters, they need to be implemented by political leaders, who are invariably motivated by their own political, if not physical, survival; by the financial support of special interests; and/ or by the preservation of the lives and lifestyles of their families and friends (cronies).

Second, the ASEAN Community has to be seen as one integrated whole, encompassing the political and security, economic, and socio-cultural spheres. This takes time. The days of the long-serving visionary leaders are gone; the region is unlikely to see the likes of Lee Kuan Yew, Mahathir Mohamad, Suharto, Ferdinand Marcos, and Prem Tinsulanonda again. Instead, largely because of the broadening and flattening of information and its access via new media platforms, more and more people now have influence on the formulation and execution of policy, and these people have short, and narrow, attention spans. The more vocal and influential ones usually represent no one but themselves or the elites or special interest groups whom they serve. Is this democracy? In a certain sense, yes. In others, probably not. This provides an insight into why it may not be possible to give a narrow interpretation of the ASEAN Community as an integrated whole. The ideal long-term vision for the ASEAN Community lies beyond the more immediate political interests of elected politicians in various ASEAN nations. Thus, ASEAN objectives are bureaucratic in their origin, having being formulated in rounds of negotiations by senior officials, but their implementation takes on a political dimension. Therefore, the longer term goals of economic integration as previously envisaged by past leaders of ASEAN, may likely need to be revisited in light of the new conditions on the ground, where new media has an increasing voice in affecting the political discourse; including performance legitimacy of political leaders.

Geopolitics also affects the implementation of ASEAN's economic commitments, whether at regional or national levels. As the discussions on CMIM, TPP and AIIB in the sections above highlight, the dynamics of all these processes are contingent on many uncertainties, especially those that occur domestically in the countries leading these processes.

Finally, ASEAN's supreme achievement lies not in the region's economic integration — although the more it is economically integrated the greater its influence in today's world — but in the sensitive realm of political and security cooperation and in the cultivation of a regional identity. Without the mutual trust engendered by political-security cooperation and a regional identity, genuine economic integration would not be possible. Will these last? Only time, and the eventual outcomes of today's major-power rivalries, will tell.

Notes

1. Secretary-General of ASEAN Mr Le Luong Minh mentioned this in a keynote statement made at the Asia House Conference on "ASEAN Strategy — Seizing the New Regional Opportunity" jointly organized by Asia House and KPMG on 12 June 2015 <http://asiahouse.org/asean-secretary-general-regional-economic-integration-target/>, accessed 19 July 2015.
2. The term "economic ministers" was used, although there was no such position in any of the five founding ASEAN members then attending the first ASEAN Summit, precisely because in each of their respective political systems, more than one minister was in charge of the economy, including the then highly relevant issue of protective tariffs. The AEM later became dominated by trade (and industry) ministers.
3. The ASEAN-6 constitute the five founding members of ASEAN and Brunei Darussalam.
4. <http://www.asean.org/component/zoo/item/about-asean-overview-cebu-declaration-on-the-acceleration-of-the-establishment-of-an-asean-community-by-2015>.
5. Ibid.
6. *The Angkor Agenda*.
7. The texts of these agreements, in English and in Chinese, can be found in the China FTA Network website, as approved by China's Ministry of Commerce and "supported" by China International Electronic Commerce Centre, accessed 21 March 2015.
8. Ibid., accessed 20 March 2015.
9. The text of the CEP "framework" as signed is on the website of the Ministry of Foreign Affairs of Japan, accessed 21 March 2015.
10. <http://www.asean.org>, accessed 20 March 2015.
11. <http://dfat.gov.au/trade/agreements/rcep/Documents/rcep-background-paper-background.pdf>, accessed 20 June 2015.
12. Observation by Anwar Nasution, former deputy governor of Indonesia's Central Bank. I am indebted to Anwar Nasution, former Deputy Governor of Bank Indonesia and now Economics Professor at the University of Indonesia, for his extensive discussion of the Chiang Mai Initiative and CMI Multilateralised, particularly his chapter in the book on the early thinking on ASEAN economic

integration jointly published by the Institute of Southeast Asian Studies and the Asian Development Bank. However, for any errors of fact or judgement, I should be held responsible and not Mr Nasution.
13. Authors' insights from different discussions and interviews.
14. Full details of the 1977 ASEAN Swap Arrangement and its subsequent protocols are compiled at the National University of Singapore's Centre for International Law database on ASEAN agreements <http://cil.nus.edu.sg/1977/1977-memorandum-of-understanding-on-the-asean-swap-arrangements-signed-on-5-august-1977-in-kuala-lumpur-malaysia-by-the-central-bank-governors/>.
15. It is modified in the sense that the Executive-Level Decision-Making Body (ELDMB), usually made up of the deputy finance ministers and deputy Central Bank governors of the ASEAN+3 countries, approves its decisions on lending, renewal and default by a two-thirds majority-vote rather than by consensus. Each member has a vote of 1.6 plus a number equal to its contribution.
16. The AMRO website, accessed 28 February 2015.
17. This is derived from personal discussions with respective officials concerned.
18. Australia, Brunei Darussalam, Canada, Chile, Japan, Malaysia, Mexico, New Zealand, Peru, Singapore and Vietnam.
19. Lead author's insight derived from his personal discussions with experts and policymakers.
20. <http://www.apec.org>, accessed 12 April 2015.
21. <http://www.aiibank.org>, accessed 15 April 2015.
22. Personal interviews, including with past and present Secretaries-General of ASEAN.

References

ASEAN Secretariat. *Declaration of ASEAN Concord*, Bali, Indonesia, 24 February 1976. <http://www.asean.org/news/item/declaration-of-asean-concord-indonesia-24-february-1976>.
Asian Development Bank and Asian Development Bank Institute. *Infrastructure for a Seamless Asia*. Tokyo: Asian Development Bank Institute, 2009.
BBC online. "'Fast-Track' Trade Bill Passes US Senate and Awaits Obama Nod", 25 June 2015. <http://www.bbc.com/news/world-us-canada-33265241>.
Batra, Amita. "India-ASEAN FTA: A Critique". *IPCS Issue Brief*, no. 116 (September 2009). New Delhi: Institute of Peace and Conflict Studies, 2009 <http://www.ipcs.org/pdf_file/issue/IB116-SEARP-BatraFTA.pdf> (accessed 19 July 2015).
Bloomberg Politics. "House Fast Track Rejection a Blow to Global Trade Negotiations", 13 June 2015 <http://www.bloomberg.com/politics/articles/2015-06-12/house-fast-track-rejection-a-blow-to-global-trade-negotiations> (accessed 13 June 2015).

Goh, Keng Swee. "Regional Co-operation in Southeast Asia". In *The Economics of Modernisation*, pp. 104–11. Singapore: Federal Publications, 1995.

He, Laura. "China Getting Panicky over U.S. led Pacific Trade Deal". *MarketWatch*, 26 May 2015 <http://www.marketwatch.com/story/china-very-worried-about-us-led-pacific-trade-deal-2015-05-21> (accessed 19 July 2015).

Jones, Lee. "Explaining the Failure of the ASEAN Economic Community: The Primacy of Domestic Political Economy". *Pacific Review*. Routledge: Taylor and Francis, 2015 <http://dx.doi.org,/10.1080/09512748.2015.1022593> (accessed 1 July 2015).

Otsuji, Yoshihiro and Kunihiko Shinoda. "Evolution of Institutions and Policies for Economic Integration in East Asia: The Rise of China and Changes in the Regional Order". In *ASEAN-Japan Relations*, edited by Takashi Shiraishi and Takaaki Kojima. Singapore: Institute of Southeast Asian Studies, 2014.

Severino, Rodolfo. "The Politics of Association of Southeast Asian Nations Economic Cooperation". *Asian Economic Policy Review* 6, no. 1 (2011): 22–38.

———. "Japan's Relations with ASEAN". In *ASEAN-Japan Relations*, edited by Takashi Shiraishi and Takaaki Kojima. Singapore: Institute of Southeast Asian Studies, 2014a.

———. "Let's be Honest about What ASEAN Can and Cannot Do". *East Asia Forum*, 31 January 2014b <http://www.eastasiaforum.org/2014/01/31/lets-be-honest-about-what-asean-can-and-cannot-do/>.

3

INDONESIA'S IMPLEMENTATION OF FACILITATION AND HARMONIZATION MEASURES UNDER THE AEC

Yose Rizal Damuri

1. INTRODUCTION

The date 31 December 2015 will mark the formal establishment of the ASEAN Economic Community (AEC), and the commitments behind it. While it is generally understood that the AEC is likely to liberalize the region to create a single market, most often people forget to look at other aspects of the AEC: the creation of a competitive economic region; equitable economic development; and integration with a global economy. The other three pillars of this community depend upon the commitments of member countries to facilitate economic activities and conduct regulatory harmonization instead of simply liberalizing their markets.

The facilitation and harmonization aspects of the AEC Blueprint ("the Blueprint") are often overlooked and difficult to implement as they require changes or revisions to behind-the-border measures. For example, the implementation of the ASEAN Single Window (ASW) has been delayed due to incomplete related national initiatives. While the AEC Scorecard indicates that progress within Pillar I (measures for Single Market and Production Base) and II (measures for Competitive Economic Region) has reached 75 per cent and 86 per cent respectively in Phase III of implementation (2008–13), many of the reform measures under both these Pillars have yet to result in concrete positive outcomes.[1] Nevertheless, they are critical for enabling member countries to gain from the AEC and to ensure greater coverage of such gains.

There are many factors behind the difficulties in implementing the facilitation and harmonization measures. These range from technical and human resource capacity to political willingness and a reluctance to undertake reforms. Some countries in ASEAN face additional challenges as they have a large population and land area as well as a relatively dispersed decision making system, as in the case of Indonesia and the Philippines. It is harder for these countries to implement behind-the-border commitments and to align domestic policy with international practices due to a decentralized governance system and a fragmented political situation.

This chapter discusses the challenges that Indonesia faces in implementing the AEC's behind-the-border commitments. The current state of implementation is highlighted to provide some background to the situation. This chapter then examines several factors behind the country's readiness (or lack of it), taking into account political economy issues and perceptions towards the AEC and economic integration in general. This chapter also presents some lessons that can be drawn from the case of Indonesia and provides various options in handling similar issues for further integration in the region beyond 2015.

2. ASEAN INITIATIVES IN FACILITATION AND HARMONIZATION MEASURES

While the initiatives to create an AEC emphasize on liberalization efforts, the ASEAN member states also realize that liberalization alone is not enough to support the desired economic integration. Even in the area of trade in goods, full liberalization may increase trade, but it may also raise transaction costs for some economies that are less developed or landlocked in nature as well as for many small producers. Trade facilitation is needed, not only to make trade activities efficient and faster, but also to ensure that the process benefits all economic entities. Similarly, investment liberalization itself would not lead to higher investment unless and until bureaucratic procedures, and the investment environment, are also supportive of foreign investments. As for the services sector, unreasonable and often contradictory regulations lead to higher entry barriers, while it is also difficult for foreign suppliers to adapt to regulations that are very different from those implemented internationally.[2]

In the AEC Blueprint, the ASEAN member states propose various efforts to facilitate liberalization initiatives and to harmonize some regulatory frameworks in order to achieve the free flow of goods, services as well as a freer flow of capital and skilled labour. A few of these efforts are outlined below:

i.   Trade facilitation. Since the ASEAN-6 (Brunei Darussalam, Indonesia, Malaysia, Philippines, Singapore and Thailand) have managed to eliminate import duties on around 99 per cent of their traded tariff lines in 2010, most of the benefits of economic integration would come mainly from facilitating trade and the removal of non-tariff barriers (NTBs). Trade facilitation among ASEAN countries comprises, among others, the simplification of procedures, including the modernization of custom procedures as well as the development of an ASEAN Single Window. ASEAN has also launched an initiative, the ASEAN Non-Tariff Measures Database, to identify all measures in trade that have the potential to harm trade activities (Fukunaga 2015). By carefully identifying NTBs, trade policy can be directed towards the elimination of such barriers.

ii. In addition to the removal of core NTBs, some efforts have also been directed towards the harmonization of standards and technical regulations, as well as mutual recognition on conformity assessment systems among ASEAN countries. Greater harmonization of technical regulations is expected to reduce trade costs and increase extensive trade among the ASEAN member states and also with the rest of the world. Mutual recognition agreements (MRAs) on product conformity assessments enable products to be tested in the producing countries and to enter the importing country directly without having to undergo similar assessment procedures. This agreement helps to avoid the duplication of testing and approval procedures, which, in turn, reduces trade costs.

iii. Investment facilitation, promotion and protection. The ASEAN

Comprehensive Investment Agreement (ACIA) aims to provide transparent, consistent and predictable investment rules, policies and procedures. The ASEAN member states agreed to harmonize investment policies while at the same time promote best practices in supporting foreign investment. The ACIA provides enhanced protection to all investors and their investments, including various provisions that are common in bilateral investment treaties.

iv. ASEAN has no concrete plan to discuss regulatory coherence and harmonization in the services sector. Currently, the ASEAN Free Trade Agreement on Services (AFAS) does not specify how the members are supposed to deal with diversity and the differences in the regulatory frameworks of services (Damuri 2014). Most of the efforts towards regulatory cooperation are conducted through mutual recognition agreements that focus on eight professional fields: medicine; nursing; dentistry; architecture; engineering; land surveying; accounting; and tourism. These MRAs are intended to facilitate the intra-ASEAN movement of skilled labour by allowing for the mutual recognition of qualifications of professional services. While this facilitates the exchange of skilled labour at the regional level, it is not yet clear how the required domestic reforms within the services sector, to support such a regional initiative, will be formulated in the ASEAN member states.

The implementation of the above initiatives in each ASEAN member state determines how economic activities and relations between countries in the region can be deepened while simultaneously increasing the competitiveness of the region as a whole. However, facilitation measures cannot be implemented easily, even more so in the case of harmonization measures.

3. IMPLEMENTATION OF ASEAN'S TRADE FACILITATION MEASURES IN INDONESIA

There are three major initiatives that provide trade facilitation among ASEAN member states. The first, and perhaps the most important one, is the development of the ASW, which is expected to provide an integrated platform for cooperation and the exchange of information among government agencies and related end-users on the trade activities of different countries in the region. The second initiative is the modernization of customs procedures. The third is the establishment of the ASEAN Trade Repository (ATR), where traders and other relevant parties can access information about trade-related measures that they need to comply with for cross-border trade in the region.

3.1 Indonesia's National Single Window

As part of the ASW initiative, each AMS is required to establish their respective National Single Windows (NSWs) that has to be subsequently connected at the regional level. The ASEAN-6 countries were scheduled to activate their NSWs no later than 2008. However, they are still being developed in order to be connected at the ASEAN level.

In the case of Indonesia, by early 2015, seventeen major ports, accounting for more than 98 per cent of Indonesia's foreign trade has been said to have been connected to the Indonesia National Single Window (INSW) system. While the Directorate General of Customs (DG Customs) of the Ministry of Finance is the main agency responsible for trade facilitation and the implementation of the INSW, there are eighteen other agencies involved in goods clearance, such as the Ministry of Trade, Quarantine Agencies and the Ministry of Defence. For most agencies, the INSW is already fully automated. The only exceptions are those agencies that have limited authority to provide trade permits and licences such as the National Police and the Ministry of Defence. Since these agencies are only involved in the export and import procedures of a limited number of products (arms and ammunition), they do not have a full automation interface for efficiency reasons.

The INSW currently works as a multi-window interface; integrates information from all agencies and redirects users from the INSW portal to those agencies' system interfaces before once again returning users to the INSW portal.[3] There is a plan to improve the system to enable users to use a single, integrated online portal. However, this would require more than just technical improvements.

An integrated portal requires greater coordination and, to a certain extent, the transfer of authorization from the different agencies to the DG Custom. There are various reasons why it is difficult to achieve this. These eighteen agencies have different responsibilities in supervising trade procedures that require different technicalities and abilities. It would therefore take some time and intensive exchanges between the agencies to allow better understanding for the development of an integrated portal.

An integrated system also requires certain regulatory frameworks that allow for better communication for the purpose of work sharing. Presidential Regulation 76/2014 provides the legal basis for the formation of a committee on INSW Portal Management to manage and to develop the system. The complexity of the INSW has made it difficult to be managed by the current ad hoc team from several agencies. The regulation also stipulates the establishment of INSW Governance Board comprising several ministerial level officials such as the Minister for Finance and Minister for Trade to formulate all necessary future policy and regulations.[4] However, it does not describe in detail how the communication and transfer of authorities between different agencies should be performed by the managing committee.

In addition there is also reluctance between the agencies to give up part of their authority as it may hamper their effectiveness in performing their tasks or reduce their control over the procedures. Hence, the INSW Portal Management has yet to be formed as of June 2015, although almost a year has passed since the promulgation of Presidential Regulation 76/2014. This highlights the organizational difficulties in forming a more effective INSW.

Besides challenges to making the INSW facilitate trade more effectively, Indonesia and other ASEAN members are also facing problems with meeting the deadline for an integrated ASW. It is technically challenging to connect ten national-level systems that were developed and work separately without a central system (Nathan Associate 2013). Moreover, the ASW is expected to be operationalized at the same time as the deadline of the AEC — 31 December 2015. Indonesia is currently preparing itself to join the regional single window. A major challenge is providing a legal framework for cross-border data exchange, which would help to prevent the illegal trade of goods across countries. A second challenge is convincing all ASEAN member states to support and agree on a legal framework for such a cross-border data exchange, since some member countries still feel that the creation of such an exchange is against their national interests.

3.2 Trade Repository

Indonesia's National Trade Repository (INTR) has been operating since 2012 under the supervision of the Preparation Team for NSW. The information in this facility includes: HS Codes and tariff information; national customs rules and regulations; import-export prohibitions and restrictions; regulations on licensing applications and processing; rules of origin; manifest information and requirements; exchange rates; trade simulation; and excise tax information.

While the INTR provides very useful trade-related information, most of the information has yet to be translated into English for the use of foreign traders and investors. Finding and allocating necessary resources for this translation process is going to be an urgent agenda in the future. It is going to need greater involvement from the Indonesian government since the Preparation Team for INSW is running out of capacity to handle the workload, while the INSW Portal Management has not been established.

Another problem with INTR is the lag in content updates from related ministries and other government agencies while some crucial information, such as the payment system, is still not provided in the INTR. This limits the ability of the INTR to act as a single-reference integrated information system at the national level. Part of the problem is due to the absence of a coordinating agency to collect and request trade-related information on a continual basis from all related agencies.

The establishment of INSW Portal Management is expected to improve the effectiveness of INSW and INTR and increase coordination among agencies. However, the fact that it has taken four years after the establishment of the INSW for the Indonesian government to come up with a proper regulatory framework, and more than a year to set up the portal management, indicates the extent of problems in Indonesia's implementation of trade facilitation measures. The reluctance of various related government agencies to transfer part of their responsibilities and functions has made it difficult for the government to come up with the required regulatory framework.

Moreover, the government might not see trade facilitation measures as its priority such that it should be handled at higher level to provide better coordination. Experience from the establishment of Investment One Stop Services indicates that instructions and monitoring should come from a very high level in order to come up with better coordination; in this case it was from the President himself (see subsection 3.5 on Investment Facilitation in Indonesia). Even with the establishment of the INSW Portal Management agency, the issue of coordination may persist as this new agency will work under the Ministry of Finance, and has less authority to coordinate with other agencies.

3.3 Customs Modernization in Indonesia

Indonesia has implemented various modern custom techniques and procedures based on international standards. As mentioned above, some measures that have been fully established include the use of: HS Codes classifications; tariff management systems; valuation systems and databases; manifest processing systems; goods declaration processing systems; risk management systems; inspection management systems; bonded warehouse management systems; cargo release notification systems; and post-clearance audit (PCA) systems (see Table 3.1).

Indonesia has relatively few problems in implementing custom modernization commitments as most of the measures have been part of the Customs Reform implemented since 2003. The reform comprises the modernization and automation of customs procedures through the utilization of telecommunication technology and the application of risk-based management through the control system (Damuri 2006). Few coordination problems have arisen since most of the measures can be implemented directly by the DG Customs. Some issues on modernization process may be due to the lack of a systematic process at the ASEAN level.

One example is Indonesian DG Customs' initiative to implement the Authorized Economic Operators (AEO) programme from the World Customs Union (WCO). Under this programme, a business entity that have met predetermined security and business standards will be accredited as AEOs, and enjoy appropriate customs facilitation, including simpler and reduced customs inspection. This programme is completed and was tested in 2015 and has already awarded AEO status to five companies. In order to provide greater facilitation, the country's AEO programme has to be supplemented by Mutual Recognition Agreements (MRAs) with trading partners for the AEOs to enjoy substantial and comparable facilitation as at home. Despite ASEAN's commitment to implement the AEO programme, little has been done to form MRAs among member countries. Indonesia is currently considering MRAs with five countries, but none of them are ASEAN members.

3.4 Harmonization of Standard and Conformance Measures in ASEAN

The ASEAN member states have agreed to proceed with greater harmonization of standards and technical regulations in eight sectors. These sectors are automotive, cosmetics, electrical and electronic

TABLE 3.1
Customs Modernization Process in Indonesia

Measures and Activities	Description	Remarks
Standardize HS Code	Using HS code based on World Customs Organization or ASEAN Harmonized Tariff Nomenclature (AHTN)	
Tariff management system	Implementation of tariff management that ensures provision of tariff data based on a legal text spread across diverse government agencies and facilities trading while maintaining legal compliance	
Valuation system	Implementation of a valuation system, that is customs procedure applied to determine the customs value of imported goods	Using transaction value methods but do not use any third party valuation database
Advance manifest processing system	It requires the party that is responsible for the cargo to submit information before the actual arrival of the cargo. The key component is that it specifies a time limit or cut-off time for the submission of the advance information	EDI and physical submission with support by IT system
Risk management systems	Systematic application of management procedures and practices providing customs with the necessary information to address risks, including risk identification, risk record and assessment, selection and treatment, risk review and monitoring	Using random system for inspection and implementation of company rating
Inspection management systems	Implementation of inspection management that encompasses various activities performed in order to optimize inspection resources and ensure the technical integrity of the asset	Conduct risk-based inspection using non-intrusive techniques
Bonded-warehouse management	Enables the suspension of import duty and/or VAT, for imported goods by storing them in premises or under an inventory system authorized by customs, e.g. a bonded warehouse in customs area	
Post clearance audit system	Enables the checking and auditing to be made by the customs based on relevance documents, e.g. account books, account vouchers, customs declaration forms, to verify the authenticity and legality of the import and export activities of the person being audited	Customs also conducts pre-arrival clearance and IT support; but do not release from clearance
Authorized Economic Operators	AEO is a party involved in the international movement of goods in whatever function that has been approved by or on behalf of a national customs administration as complying with WCO or equivalent supply chain security standards.	Will be released on a national scale this year
MRA of AEO	Implementation of AEO mutual recognition	Not yet implemented
Information system	On line information system. On line resource system on customs issuances, processes, policies, guidelines and other related information	Customs-Excise Information System and Automation (CEISA)

equipment (EEE), medical devices, rubber-based products, pharmaceutical products, prepared foodstuffs and traditional medicines. Harmonization of these sectors includes a review and revision of standards and technical requirements so as to ensure alignment with the agreed international standards or benchmarks, or harmonization at the regional level. The harmonization is followed by MRAs in these eight sectors to facilitate acceptance or recognition of results of conformity assessment procedures, produced by the Conformity Assessment Bodies in other ASEAN countries.

Before looking at the implementation of these commitments, it is useful to briefly discuss how standards and technical regulations are formulated in Indonesia. Badan Standardisasi Nasional (BSN or National Standardization Agency) is the government institution in charge of coordinating and facilitating standardization activities, while all technical regulations are under the relevant authorities (Table 3.2). The process of formulation of standard starts by proposal submissions by the Technical Committees (TCs) to BSN based on its stakeholders' needs. Once it has been reviewed and revised by other committees, the proposed standard is put on the National Programme for Standard Development (PNPS), which is then introduced as part of Standard National Indonesia (SNI; Indonesian National Standards).

Although the law on Standardization rules by SNIs is voluntary in nature, it becomes mandatory if it is related to requirements of national security, the protection of human health or safety, animal or plant life or health and the environment. As of April 2014, 9,817 standards have been developed by SNIs, of which 270 are mandatory for all products (both local and imported products) distributed in Indonesia.

For conformity assessment procedures, BSN is assisted by Komite Akreditasi Nasional (KAN or National Accreditation Committee), which is supposed to assure the quality of laboratories, inspection and certification bodies. The Committee is a member of regional and international MRAs such as the Asia Pacific Laboratory Accreditation Cooperation, Pacific Accreditation Cooperation, International Laboratory Accreditation Cooperation and International Accreditation Forum.

The ASEAN MRA of goods was ratified by Indonesia in 2002 through Presidential Decree No. 82/2002. While BSN has been named the Designating Body (DB), it has, in turn, appointed laboratories and certification bodies that have to be listed under ASEAN Conformity

TABLE 3.2
Technical Ministries and Their Responsibilities

Technical Ministries or Agencies	Responsibility and Industrial Domain
Ministry of Trade (MoT)	Labelling, registration of imports and exports
Ministry of Industry (MoI)	Food and beverages, forest and plantation products, furniture, automotive, machinery, electronic and electrical equipment, textiles, etc.
Ministry of Agriculture (MoA)	Fresh foods, plant origin registration, livestock
Food and Drug Control Agency (BPOM)	Processed foods, contaminants, food additives, drugs, cosmetics
Ministry of Marine and Fishery	Fishery products and processed fisheries products
Ministry of Forest	Raw materials from forest, timber and plywood
Ministry of Transport	Vehicles
Ministry of Manpower	Professionals, foreign workers
Ministry of Environment	Waste water, air emission, hazardous waste

Source: Compiled from DFC SAU (2010).

Assessment Bodies (CABs). There are currently five testing labs and three certification bodies that are listed under ASEAN CABs.

Among the priority integration sectors, cosmetics is the most advanced in implementing commitments for standards harmonization. Indonesia has completely aligned its national laws, legislation and regulation to the ASEAN Harmonized Cosmetic Regulatory Scheme since 2011, ensuring that the regulations are in line with the five harmonized aspects laid out in the ASEAN Cosmetics Directive (ACD). These include, among others, the implementation of a product notification system that replaces pre-market approval to post-marketing surveillance, which reduces requirements at the introduction phase of a product and reduces the initial costs of marketing. As the terms of reference of the ASEAN Cosmetic Testing Laboratory Network (ACTLN) has not been agreed upon, the MRA on cosmetic products has not been fully implemented.

Indonesia has also advanced in adopting ASEAN standards on Electronics and Electrical Equipment (EEE). Eighty-five per cent of national standards are in line with the identified international standards or international benchmarks. In terms of the harmonization of technical regulations, Indonesia ratified the ASEAN Harmonized Electrical and Electronic Equipment Regulatory Regime (AHEEERR) in 2010 and has also changed some regulations to align it with the given regional provisions. With regard to the implementation of conformity assessment procedures, the ASEAN Guidelines to Determine the Type of Conformity Assessment Regime Based on Risk Assessment for EEE has not yet been adopted at the national level. This could be due to the fact that there is no ASEAN-wide agreement on the kind of products that has to adhere to the guideline. Thus, further adoption will have to wait till a regionwide agreement has been reached.

In the case of pharmaceutical products, Indonesia has completed almost all the necessary infrastructure for the implementation of the AEC measures for standards and conformance. The country has successfully transposed the regional technical guidelines under the ASEAN Common Technical Requirements (ACTR) into applicable national regulations since 2011. The National Agency of Drug and Food Control (BPOM) has been recognized internationally as a competent drug regulatory authority, which makes it easier for Indonesia's conformity assessment bodies to be recognized as ASEAN Listed CABs. However, listing of the CABs submitted by other ASEAN member states often faces difficulties in the evaluation and assessment stage of the proposals mainly due to technical issues and limited resources.

The situation is a little different in the case of automotive products. Out of all fifty-one standards that have been agreed upon at ASEAN level, only nineteen have been adopted with some modifications. The rest of the thirty-two standards are still in the process of being adopted and harmonized, and it is difficult to complete these by the end of 2015. As of now, the ASEAN MRA for Type Approval of Automotive Products has not yet been signed or ratified. Although it is likely to be finalized and signed in 2015, it is not clear how the MRA will be ratified and implemented fully before the AEC kick-starts on 31 December 2015. The harmonization of standards and technical regulations in prepared foodstuff products also face similar difficulties since no substantial agreement has been reached.

The pace of the implementation of standard harmonization is affected by the Indonesian government's perception on how harmonization will be beneficial for its industrial development. In the case of the automotive sector, there is concern that the adoption of higher standards will place a greater burden on the industry, in particular, the domestic parts and components industry. The number of Indonesia's auto parts suppliers remains small with around 550 companies, one-third of Thailand's suppliers, of which only few are domestic companies (Kobayashi 2013). A higher standard is not perceived as supporting the development of the automotive parts industry. This differs from the cosmetics industry since the industry is relatively developed with the potential for exports. Hence, the government and stakeholders see the harmonization in cosmetics to be more favourable for the industry's development.

3.5 Investment Facilitation in Indonesia

Investment promotion and facilitation is implemented by Badan Koordinasi Penanaman Modal (BKPM or Investment Coordinating Board), which is an autonomous government agency reporting to the President, and it is responsible for coordinating investment policy and procedures. The investment promotion and facilitation strategic plan that has been approved by the government contains the country's vision for investment, its priority sectors, possible FDI segments as well as a blueprint for the organizational structure to implement these priorities and to meet its objectives. Although BKPM is tasked to facilitate the issuance of investment permits and licences, the real authority lies with several technical government agencies and local government, which are often poorly coordinated with each other. This has become a hindrance for investment facilitation in Indonesia and it has not been rectified sufficiently.

Nevertheless, BKPM has been quite successful in providing investment-related information. The board's website provides adequate information on the country and economy, investment laws, rules, and so on. It also contains information on the process of setting up businesses in the country, priority industries, and clusters as well as success stories highlighting country's strengths and potential. The information is available in English and can be accessed easily, although there may be some time lag for the translation of some regulations and legislations.

The Indonesian government has also adopted principles of prior notification and consultation with stakeholders as well as building constructive relationships with them. Most government agencies, especially BKPM, provide prior notification of intended changes in investment laws, regulations and policies, and allow interested stakeholders to provide written comments. In addition, the government undertakes face-to-face consultations with a broad cross-section of stakeholders, which are held on an ad hoc basis, and the results are publicly released. This was demonstrated during the formulation of the new 2014's investment negative list.

However, BKPM has not delivered good investment servicing practices. Since November 2014, under the direction of President Jokowi himself, the agency launched some big initiatives to facilitate the issuance of investment permits and licences under the One Stop Service (OSS) programme. The programme has introduced online investment application form that allows potential investors to submit applications electronically. It was followed by the launch of one stop integrated services in January. There are twenty-two related agencies that have to hand over part of their authority in dealing with investment permits to BKPM, or place their officers in the agency. Under this system, investors would get all necessary licences at one agency, i.e., BKPM, including almost all sectoral licences. The integrated service is expected to significantly reduce the time required to obtain investment permits and facilitate investment in Indonesia.

The new integrated system, however, only deals with investment permits at the national level, while acquiring licences from local government is also a part of Indonesia's investment problem. The government plans to set up similar integrated service at the district and provincial levels. But it is still not clear how these separate services will be connected to each other.

3.6 Progress of MRAs in Services

The ASEAN member states have agreed on MRAs to facilitate the movement of skilled labour in the region in order to support trade in services and investment. The agreement enables the qualifications of professional services to be mutually recognized by a signatory ASEAN member state. So far, there have been agreements on eight professional services: engineering; nursing; architecture; land surveying; medical practitioners; dental practitioners; accountancy and tourism professionals.

However, there are several approaches to how these MRAs are to be implemented. MRAs for architectural and engineering services have clearly laid out their terms. The agreements are equipped with guidelines on criteria and procedures to getting recognized as an ASEAN Chartered Engineer/ Architect. The agreements also specify the establishment of committees at regional level that coordinate and monitor its implementation. MRAs on nursing services and tourism professionals also describe actions needed to develop the core competencies that would be needed to be evaluated later by regional committees. Other than these, there are MRAs for the dental and medical professionals that, and although they describe the recognition of foreign professionals, also state that they need to be in compliance with the host country's requirements and necessary assessments. Others require the ASEAN member states to conduct bilateral or multilateral agreements to advance the movement of professionals.

Indonesia has implemented MRAs in engineering services and architecture by establishing the Indonesia Monitoring Committees — the body responsible for developing, processing and maintaining registrations for ASEAN chartered engineers and architects. Despite reasonable implementation of the MRAs on these two services, the agreements seem to be unsuccessful in attracting professionals to apply for regionally recognized certifications. In architecture, there are only 129 domestic applicants who have undergone the screening process, and only 51 have been selected and registered as the ASEAN Architects (AA) by the ASEAN Architect Council. In engineering services, the situation is the same: only 211 domestic applicants have undergone the screening process, while 154 domestic applicants have been selected and registered.

Being registered as an ASEAN Professionals, however, does not mean that foreign workers can automatically work in Indonesia. Foreign architects, for example, must also be registered with the Ministry of Manpower as foreign workers, as described in Decree of the Minister of Manpower and Immigration No. 12/2013 concerning Guidelines for Recruiting Foreign Workers and Law No. 6/2011 concerning Immigration. However, foreign architects face little urgency to get registered since the regulations do not appear to be binding, while they can still practise as consultants or corporate employees without the foreign architect status.

Indonesia has also been successful in aligning its regulations to support the implementation of an MRA in nursing services, especially in order to create an official framework within which foreign nurses can work as registered nurses in Indonesia. The registration process for foreign nurses working in Indonesia is very similar to that of native nurses, although the permits for foreign nurses expire much sooner. However, despite all the facilitation, there are officially no foreign nurses currently working in Indonesia, although it has been recognized that many have entered the country as consultants, and are therefore not registered through the ASEAN MRA.

As for the other MRAs of medical and dental professionals, it is difficult to implement these as they do not provide specific details on how the movement of the professionals should be facilitated. There are some efforts for harmonization of regulations to ensure that they support and do not contradict MRA implementation, although the scale is very limited. There are also activities for dissemination of MRA-related information through websites, but the language barrier remains an issue in the provision of sufficient information.

4. LESSONS LEARNT FROM THE IMPLEMENTATION OF FACILITATION AND HARMONIZATION MEASURES IN INDONESIA

4.1 Technical Issues

While facilitation and harmonization are believed to bring about significant benefits for the creation of an integrated region and, hence, for economic growth, their implementation requires greater financial, technical and human resources. A lack of resources often slows down the implementation process and delays it beyond the targeted deadlines. The difficulties are even more prevalent for a large country such as Indonesia, which is simultaneously undertaking a decentralized form of administration. One area where such problem is starkly evident is the country's development of its national single window (NSW).

Indonesia started the development of its NSW in 2007. While a trial run of the programme was done in November 2007 in Tanjung Priok Port, the largest and busiest port in Indonesia, the same can only be repeated for other ports after several years. By 2010, the INSW had been developed and implemented in only five major ports with the plan to connect other thirteen smaller ports by 2015. One key reason for such slow implementation is the lack of sufficient infrastructure as well as financial resources, coupled with a shortage of skilled professionals, who have the technical know-how and other types of human resources as well.

Even for ports where the NSW have been fully implemented, the system has yet to run smoothly. This is mainly because of technical issues. The first impediment is in substandard IT infrastructure which lacks the capability to quickly adopt changes and improvements in the INSW system. As a result, a number of ports use the INSW system for their custom clearance system only. The second impediment arises from inadequate supporting infrastructure such as electricity. Due to frequent power outages in the port areas and lack of availability of power generators in eighteen institutions that are connected to the INSW of major ports, there are periods when the INSW system is not available, thereby forcing the custom clearance to return to paper-based procedures. The third impediment arises from smaller ports which may not be ready to support the huge network of eighteen government agencies. This is because the single window system still works as an online gateway, instead of an integrated services portal. Moreover, for smaller ports in Indonesia the presence of important institutions, such as health-related agencies or quarantine bodies, are rather limited.

Similar problems in technical issues, albeit on a smaller scale, also appear in several other facilitation and harmonization initiatives. To implement commitments on standard and conformance, the national Designating Bodies (DB) for conformity assessment are often constrained by limited resources and lack of technical understanding. This leads to several cases where Indonesia has denied test reports or certification licenses to Listed CAB from other ASEAN member states. Similarly, there are cases where certifications from Indonesia based on CAB are rejected on the grounds that they have failed to abide by requirements set by the national regulating agencies.

In addition, the relevant government agencies often find themselves with inadequate resources to disseminate relevant information related to harmonization of standards and to carry out capacity-building both for the regulators and industry players. This becomes a crucial problem for small- and medium-scale enterprises as they often do not have sufficient access to information and have limited capacity to understand the issues and related regulations.

4.2 Coordination Problems

Poor coordination is another factor that substantially holds back the implementation of facilitation and harmonization measures. Even with the support of sufficient resources combined with the supporting regulatory framework, the implementation might be slow due to the reluctance of related agencies to implement necessary measures. Indonesia's NSW, for example, and although it manages to connect eighteen different institutions, remains a gateway of different windows, each representing its own institutions, rather than a single portal that integrate all necessary functions. It took more than five years to get the current system to function. Even now, a handful of less relevant agencies are not fully connected to the system.

In the harmonization of standards and technical regulations, national standards and regulations need to be reviewed and often modified to adopt the agreed principles laid in regional agreements. These standards can be adopted through a series of processes which require the coordination of different agencies. The review process for adopting a new national standard requires several steps and a significant amount of time. A single product is often regulated by different ministries. While some are not focused on finishing the necessary work to amend the rules, others are not aware of the work that needs to be done, as they were not present during discussions on these issues. Frequent reshuffling of ministerial positions also slows down the process. Changes in government's interests also result in the disappearance of a harmonization process from the priority list, or even from its budgetary allocation. Hence, in order to improve the process, the bureaucracy needs to be made more efficient, and ministries need to be made more aware of the urgency in meeting their commitments in the AEC.

The problem of investment facilitation in Indonesia is another classic example on how the bureaucratic structure, coupled with poor coordination, has resulted in ineffective and slow implementation of the AEC measures, in particular those related to facilitation and harmonization. It requires the President's direct instructions, combined with clear assignments to a specific institution, to move investment facilitation forward to an integrated service. Since streamlining and simplifying investment procedures have become a focus of the new administration under President Jokowi, the current administration has ordered around twenty-two ministries to work together for this process. The BKPM is also tasked to coordinate and to become the entry point of investment procedure. Within a relatively short time, these efforts have led to substantial improvement in investment facilitation. In the case of permits for construction of power plants, for example, the required days for processing the permits have been reduced from 923 days to 256 days. The programme has also reduced the number of permits for investment, such as the reduction of 101 required permits for coal mining to only 71 permits.

4.3 Political Will and the Regulatory Framework

The lack of political will can be observed as a factor behind slow progress in many harmonization efforts as well as in trade facilitation. It stems from the practice that it was the Ministry of Trade (MoT) who made the deal to conform to regional agreements, while it is other technical ministries that are responsible and have the authority to implement regulatory reform and harmonization. However, there are some ministries that have not agreed to conform to regional agreements as they may not share the same interest and have less priority on the integration agenda. In addition, coordination between the high-level officials and the lower level public officials, who are responsible for the more technical aspects, do not function properly.

As discussed earlier, the Indonesian government seems to be less enthusiastic about implementing trade facilitation measures, in particular INSW and INTR and, hence, it has not placed these initiatives in its priority programme. One main reason behind this is that Indonesia may not see the benefits of having more efficient trade procedures and facilitation. The common perception is that Indonesia's trade problem lies in its competitiveness and supply side capacity. Thus it is perceived that the country will still have difficulties improving its trade performance even with greater market access in the destination market as well as simpler and efficient trade procedures. According to this argument, Indonesia should focus on dealing with domestic issues that improve the country's competitiveness before taking trade integration further (Damuri and Day 2015). Trade facilitation is not perceived to be a priority since it may not benefit Indonesia's exports, rather it only facilitates imports that can further exacerbate trade balance. This inward-looking perception has held back Indonesia not only its implementation of the AEC goals, but also from pursuing other integration plans.

In other areas of harmonization, the inward-looking sentiment is intensified with protectionist measures. While the Law on National Standards clearly defines that the standards and technical regulations that are intended to provide protection for consumers, environment, and society in general, there is a common perception among officials in technical agencies to use standards as protectionist measures towards imported goods. In doing so, they tend to promote standards that are different from internationally accepted ones, and are not really enthusiastic with the idea of regulatory harmonization.[5] Some regulations on professional services also tend to erect barriers towards foreign professionals and it therefore makes the efforts for facilitating greater labour mobility more difficult.

The lack of political will is also a factor that hinders more elaborate action plans on the implementation of these facilitation and harmonization measures. Some MRAs need more concrete guidelines and action plans to function properly, while others may even need agreements at a bilateral level. Once again, the lack of political support and the weak coordination between negotiators and regulatory authorities can lead to lengthy and complicated processes.

Regulatory frameworks incompatible with the regionally agreed principles also pose implementation challenges. Indonesia signed several agreements that have not been ratified and incorporated into the country's regulatory system. As a result, applicable legislation and regulations have not been aligned to its provisions. Indonesia, for example, signed the ASEAN Medical Device Directive (AMDD) to harmonize standards and technical regulation on medical devices. Indonesia's current regulatory framework identifies only three types of risk classifications, while the AMDD requires four types of risk classifications. In order to align with the AMDD, Indonesia would need to change its regulations to acknowledge this fourth class of risk.

But it is quite difficult to incorporate such risk principles as they are embedded in several high-level regulations, including the draft law on Medical Equipments. The problem of alignment between regional policies and domestic regulation in Indonesia is very common. This is especially because the process or amending laws in Indonesia is quite lengthy besides being a complicated political process as many stakeholders need to be involved, and sometimes it may require approval from the parliament.

5. CONCLUSION: THINKING AHEAD ON FACILITATION AND HARMONIZATION

Despite its importance, it is difficult to implement the regional commitments on facilitation and harmonization. The bottleneck may arise from either the regional and national level, or a combination of the two. Looking at Indonesia's experience, there are some lessons that can be drawn to successfully implement some of these measures.

At the regional level, the ASEAN member states should speed up some unfinished business in formulating guidelines and applicable directives on the harmonization of standards and MRAs. It seems that the ASEAN member states only manage to come up with applicable guidelines on products and services that are less sensitive and attract less interest from the countries in the region. Standard harmonization efforts on cosmetics are among the most advanced initiatives. However, only less than 15 per cent of cosmetic companies operating in Indonesia are originated from or supply products from other ASEAN member states. In the automotive sector, where the ASEAN market is growing faster due to the strong presence of the production networks, the initiative's progress is quite slow. The ASEAN member states need to harmonize and facilitate integration in the more sensitive industries. This may be done by setting agreements that do not require the approval of all the member states, but can instead be carried out by countries that are ready, although with a condition that others need to join later.

Capacity-building initiatives at the ASEAN level may also help the implementation of harmonization and facilitation measures. Since new standards and regulations need to be adopted in line with regional commitments, technical assistance from other more advanced ASEAN member states will help to speed up the process. Technical assistance and capacity building may also support the conclusion of pending agreements. One of the reasons behind the delay in the agreement on standards harmonization within the automotive industry in Indonesia is its concern over the readiness of supporting industries to supply components and spare parts that meet agreed standards.

This indicates that capacity-building is needed in order to speed up the supply chain and help mitigate the inability of some supporting industries to supply the needs of other industries. But in order to provide enough capacity-building and technical assistance, the ASEAN member states need to devote greater resources at regional level, rather than only at national level. More advanced countries in the region, such as Singapore, Malaysia and Indonesia, should provide such assistance for less developed ones in order to support greater integration.

ASEAN members should also come up with more tangible commitments in facilitation and harmonization. Some cases in professional services show that even when the agreement is fully implemented, there can still be questions on the effectiveness of these MRAs. The movement of skilled labour has been occurring long before the MRA scheme came into conception. Manning and Bhatnagar (2004) estimated that skilled and professional workers account for 5 per cent of around 2 million migrant workers in Southeast Asia in the early 2000s, 60 to 70 per cent of this group originate from within the region. Therefore, the implementation of an MRA can sometimes be viewed as adding more steps and processes rather than facilitating integration. If the ASEAN member states are serious in facilitating labour movement across the region, they should expand the MRAs into substantial market access agreements, including labour regulations and the removal of domestic requirements from professional associations, as for example, in the case of language requirements.

At the national level, governments of the ASEAN member states should realize that having greater facilitation and more coherent regulations will have a positive impact on their competitiveness. Harmonization of standards and conformance measures to internationally accepted ones will allow domestic producers to increase their capacity for the global market or to participate in global value chains. Instead of creating national standards that are too different from international ones, the governments should provide supporting infrastructures and facilities, such as laboratories, technical assistance and information related to technical regulations. This will help not only big businesses in the region, but would also assist small- and medium-scale producers with entering the international market.

The government agencies should also put the implementation of commitments into their priority list. Greater political will and coordination support should come from top-level government officials in order to address the gaps in implementation. Without good intention to carry out the commitments in facilitation and harmonization measures, the AEC will not deliver benefits from regional integration to a greater number of stakeholders and this may impede the momentum to proceed with further economic integration.

Notes

1. There is no official report on AEC blueprint implementation for Phase III, but a presentation from the ASEAN Secretariat available at <http://www. slideshare.net/naythiha/session-4-aec-scorecard-ntp-ann?qid> outlines the progress of implementation till 2012. Indonesia's overall implementation of its commitments reached 83 per cent by March 2013 (Saputra and Trilaksana 2014).
2. Differences in services regulations among ASEAN countries can be observed in many important sectors such as financial services and telecommunication.

In banking, many prudential regulations, e.g. minimum capital requirements and bank accounting standards, differ quite greatly from country to another. While these regulations may have important objectives to ensure the quality of services, their differences pose difficulties to foreign services providers.
3. The INSW portal is found here: http://www.insw.go.id/. To access this portal, users need to register first before getting approval from relevant agencies.
4. This new agency, however, will operate under the authority of the Ministry of Finance and will report to the Ministry of Finance.
5. Many local standards are often defined differently from international ones. They also require additional sampling, testing, labelling and import documentation by a certified laboratory. One example are toys that include additional limits of certain chemical elements. The additional requirements may not be difficult to comply but require additional testing on a per-shipment basis for imported goods, while additional testing is only required every six months for locally produced toys (USTR 2015).

References

Damuri, Y.R. "An Evaluation of the Need for Selected Trade Facilitation Measures in Indonesia: Implications for the WTO Negotiations on Trade Facilitation". In *An Exploration of the Need for and Cost of Selected Trade Facilitation Measures in Asia and the Pacific in the Context of the WTO Negotiations*, edited by UNESCAP. Bangkok: United Nations Economic and Social Commission for Asia and the Pacific, 2006.
———. "Services Sector Development and Improving Production Network in ASEAN. CSIS Working Paper ECON 01-2014. Jakarta: Centre for Strategic and International Studies, 2014.
——— and C. Day. "Survey of Recent Development". *Bulletin of Indonesian Economic Studies* 51, no. 1 (2015).
DFC SAU. "Indonesia's Export Quality Infrastructure". A Report prepared for the European Union, 2010. <http://eeas.europa.eu/delegations/indonesia/documents/eu_indonesia/indonesia_s_export_quality_infrastructure_en.pdf> (accessed 22 June 2015).
Fukunaga, Yoshifumi. "ASEAN's Leadership in the Regional Comprehensive Economic Partnership". *Asia & the Pacific Policy Studies* 2, no. 1 (2015): 103–15.
Kobayashi, H. "Current State and Issues of the Automobile and Auto Parts Industries in ASEAN". In *Automobile and Auto Components Industries in ASEAN: Current State and Issues*, edited by Waseda University. ERIA Research Project Report 2013-7. Jakarta: Economic Research Institute for ASEAN and East Asia, 2013 <http:/www.eria.org/RPR_FY2013_No.7_Chapter_2.pdf>.

Manning, C. and P. Bhatnagar. "The Movement of Natural Persons in Southeast Asia: How Natural". Working Papers in Trade and Development, Research School of Pacific and Asian Studies. Canberra: Australian National University, 2004.

Nathan Associates. "ASEAN Single Window Task Order: Final Report". ASEAN Single Window Pilot Project. Bangkok: USAID/Regional Development Mission for Asia, 2013.

Saputra, W. and A.C. Trilaksana. "Toward ASEAN Economic Community: Revitalising Indonesia's Position in Financial and Customs Cooperation". Paper presented at the 12th Indonesian Regional Science Association (IRSA) Conference, 2–3 June 2014.

Setiati, I., W. Mugijayani, D. Rafitrandy and S. Indasari. "Study to Further Improve ASEAN Economic Scorecard (AEC) Phase Two: Toward a More Effective AEC Scorecard Monitoring System and Mechanism". Mimeo. Jakarta: Centre for Strategic and International Studies, 2012.

USTR. "2015 National Trade Estimate Report on Foreign Trade Barriers". <https://ustr.gov/sites/default/files/2015%20NTE%20Combined.pdf> (accessed 22 June 2015).

4

THE AEC AND DOMESTIC CHALLENGES IN MALAYSIA
Examining the Liberalization of Services in AFAS

Tham Siew Yean

1. INTRODUCTION

Services currently account for more than two-thirds of the world's GDP (63 per cent in 2013) although its share in total trade remains below 20 per cent (WTO 2014*a*). It should, however, be noted that traditional trade statistics, which measure gross trade flows rather than value-added at various stages of production, may strongly underestimate the contribution of services to international trade as shown by recent research on production through global value chains (GVCs). These GVCs make extensive use of services such as information and communication technology (ICT), logistics, transport, distribution and business services (United Nations 2014). Almost half (46 per cent) of value-added in exports is contributed by service-sector activities. This share is higher in developed countries (50 per cent) than in developing countries (38 per cent). This fact confirms that greater value-added tends to be captured by developed countries, in which many transnational corporations are headquartered, largely through services activities. More importantly, two-thirds of global foreign direct investment (FDI) stock concentrates on services, underscoring the importance of openness to FDI in services, especially for developing countries where the services sector tends to be more protected than manufacturing.

In Malaysia, the service sector has also grown considerably over time. In 1990, it contributed towards 44.5 per cent of the country's GDP and 53.5 per cent of its total employment. By 2014, its contribution to GDP was 55.3 per cent while the share to employment was 59.4 per cent (Ministry of Finance, Malaysia 2014).[1] Its importance for the country in terms of complementing growth in manufacturing was first recognized in the Second Industrial Master Plan (IMP2: 1996–2005) that introduced the idea of developing supporting services under its "Manufacturing ++" strategy, or the cluster-based development strategy. Nevertheless, no specific service sectors were targeted for development. In contrast, the Third Industrial Master Plan (IMP3: 2006–20) not only reiterates the importance of the service sector as an important intermediary for supporting the development of businesses and trade in all sectors, but it further targets eight service sub-sectors for development. These are business and professional services, distributive trade, construction, education and training, healthcare services, tourism services, ICT services and logistics. The contribution of these sub-sectors as new sources of growth for the country includes their potential to provide linkages and spill-overs between sectors. In the Tenth Malaysia Plan and Economic Transformation Plan unveiled in 2010, seven out of the twelve promoted sectors are services sectors. These are namely financial services, wholesale and retail trade, tourism, education services, business services, communications content and infrastructure and private healthcare.

Nevertheless, given the limited size of the domestic economy and the importance of trade to the country, the potential of these sectors to be new sources of growth for the country is inevitably dependent on their export potential. Consequently, it is important to assess the extent of liberalization in these sectors as well as the barriers to trade that are constraining their export potential. The objectives of this chapter are twofold. First, it seeks to examine Malaysia's commitments in the ASEAN Framework Agreement on Services (AFAS) as well as review the gap between commitments and practice in Malaysia. Second, it also aims to examine domestic conflicts that may constrain Malaysia's liberalization efforts in ASEAN. A key question considered in the analysis is the source or sources of these conflicts. Is the conflict confined to the private sector or is the government conflicted from within in terms of services liberalization? The chapter is organized as follows. A brief summary of services liberalization under AFAS is presented in section 2. Malaysia's commitments in AFAS and the gap between commitment and practice are discussed in section 3. Section 4 analyses the conflicts between liberalization and the domestic agenda in services sector. The conclusion in section 5 summarizes the main findings of the chapter.

2. SERVICES LIBERALIZATION UNDER AFAS

The AFAS was signed on 15 December 1995, based closely on the provisions of the General Agreement on Trade in Services (GATS), which is the first multilateral agreement on services that was concluded under the Uruguay Round of multilateral trade negotiations in 1994.

When the proposal to establish an ASEAN Community was accepted at the Bali Summit in 2003, the ASEAN Economic Community (AEC) became one of the three pillars in the aspired Community. It is envisaged that the AEC would be a single market and production base, with a free flow of goods, services, investments, capital and skilled labour by the end of 2015. The AEC thus provides a comprehensive framework to build on the existing ASEAN integration programmes, such as ASEAN Free Trade Area (AFTA), AFAS and the ASEAN Investment Area (AIA). The old agreements are therefore galvanized and housed under a new concept, which is the AEC as a new form of regional institutionalization. In 2007, the lofty goals of the AEC were translated into action when the ASEAN Leaders issued the Declaration on the AEC Blueprint. The Blueprint is essentially a master plan formulated for guiding the achievement of an AEC by the end of 2015 by means of detailing economic integration measures, commitments, targets and timelines for their implementation into four pillars, namely, a single market and production base, a competitive economic region, equitable economic development and full integration into the global economy.

Since the free flow of services is one of the key components in the first pillar, the Blueprint aims to substantially reduce restrictions on ASEAN services suppliers in providing services and in establishing companies across national borders within the region, subject to domestic regulations. AFAS also aims to progressively liberalize trade beyond the measures undertaken in GATS, and to provide mutual recognition of qualifications and experience through mutual recognition agreements (MRAs). Eight packages of liberalization have been signed by the ASEAN Economic Ministers since 1997.[2] It should be noted that although the eighth package was signed in October 2010, the ninth package has yet to be signed as at January 2015, indicating a stalling in the liberalization agenda.[3] It would also mean that the last two packages of liberalization will have to be signed before the end of 2015 for ASEAN to be able to meet some of its stated Blueprint goals.

AFAS aims to liberalize 128 sub-sectors by 2015, based on 12 broad sectors[4] identified in the World Trade Organization (WTO) Services Sectoral Classification List (W120) and covering the four modes of supply. The four modes refer to: cross-border supply such as distance education, where neither consumer or producer is required to cross borders as the service is provided through telecommunications or mail (mode 1); consumption abroad, where the consumer moves across borders, as for example, in tourists travelling to other countries (mode 2); commercial presence, or where the producer in the form of the juridical person moves across borders to establish a territorial presence to provide a service, such as domestic subsidiaries of foreign insurance companies or hotel chains (mode 3); and presence of natural person, which refers to producers moving across borders in the form of the natural person as in the case of movement lecturers or professionals travelling abroad to teach or render professional services (mode 4).

However, ASEAN allows for 15 per cent flexibility[5] on sub-sectors that may be of national sensitivity and/or may not comply with agreed parameters. Besides expanding the number of sectors committed, the liberalization agenda includes the removal of limitations in market access and national treatment on service delivery via mode 1 (cross-border trade) and mode 2 (consumption abroad), except where there are bona fide reasons such as public safety. In the case of mode 3 (commercial presence), foreign (ASEAN) equity participation is progressively increased in each sector, to be no less than 70 per cent in the four priority sectors by 2013, and to be no less than 51 per cent by 2010 and 70 per cent in all other sectors by 2015 as shown in Table 4.1.[6]

TABLE 4.1
Targeted Timeline for Equity Liberalization under AFAS

Sectors	Targets
Priority sectors e-ASEAN,[a] healthcare, and tourism services	51% – 2008; 70% – 2010
Logistics	51% – 2010 70% – 2013
Others	51% – 2010 70% – 2015
Construction	51% – 2008 70% – 2015

Note: a. An initiative established in 2000, the e-ASEAN vision is threefold: to create a common market place of half a billion people for ICT products and services; to enhance the competitiveness of ASEAN through harnessing ICT in private and government sectors; and to enhance the living standards of ASEAN through ICT, by narrowing the digital divide. *Source*: MITI (2011).

3. MALAYSIA'S COMMITMENTS IN AFAS

3.1 Approach Towards Liberalization

It is important to understand the approach taken towards services liberalization as it explains the pace of Malaysia's commitments in AFAS. In general, Malaysia takes a cautious approach towards the liberalization of services. This is because modes 3 and 4 are affected by the New Economic Policy (NEP) that was introduced in 1970 to guide all socioeconomic planning in the country. The NEP has a two-pronged objective, namely poverty reduction and wealth redistribution, within the context of an expanding economy. The latter includes the redistribution of wealth to ensure an equitable distribution among the country's various ethnic groups. In order to achieve this, quantitative targets were set: by 1990, the *bumiputera* are targeted to hold 30 per cent of corporate equity while non-*bumiputera* and foreigners should hold 40 per cent and 30 per cent, respectively. In addition, 30 per cent of employment is also reserved for the *bumiputera*.

The enforcement mechanism for the NEP is a licensing system that was set up under the Industrial Coordination Act of 1975. This Act empowered the Ministry of International Trade and Industry (MITI) to impose any condition (including compliance with NEP targets) on the issuance and renewal of licences. The Malaysian Industrial Authority (MIDA), under MITI, is the agency that is in charge of the promotion and approval of foreign direct investment (FDI) in manufacturing activities. It also promotes FDI in services. In the case of services, the Foreign Investment Committee (FIC) was set up in 1974 for the approval of non-manufacturing activities.

Although the NEP officially ended in 1990 and was subsequently replaced by the National Development Policy (1991–2000), and the National Vision Policy (2001–10), the latter policies continued to embody the aims and the objectives of the NEP. However, since 2003, the equity ruling under the FIC has been changed as foreign investment in services in Malaysia may be up to 70 per cent while *bumiputera* citizens have to hold at least 30 per cent.

Subsequently, the 2008–09 Global Financial Crisis (GFC) prompted the government to "liberalize" its approval process for FDI for several reasons, namely the urgent need to revive private investment, including FDI which has dropped by half since the 1997–98 Asian Financial Crisis (AFC) (Tham 2013). In June 2009, the government announced the deregulation of the FIC guidelines, including the repeal of FIC's *bumiputera* participation requirement (WTO 2010). This simplifies the approval process as the FIC no longer processes any acquisitions, mergers or takeovers; nor does it impose any equity conditions, although sector specific regulators can still impose equity conditions. Since there are eighteen ministries and thirty-two government agencies overseeing the different service sub-sectors in the country, there is still a possibility for these ministries and government agencies to impose *bumiputera* requirements. Nevertheless, the former two-step approval process has been reduced to one step, thereby reducing some of the complexities in the approval process. However, there are still strategic sectors such as banking, telecommunications, energy and transport, that will not be liberalized. For companies seeking listing on the Malaysian stock exchange, the 30 per cent *bumiputera* equity requirement imposed by the FIC has been removed and replaced with a *bumiputera* equity condition of 12.5 per cent, which is half of the 25 per cent public spread required by the Malaysian Securities Commission (WTO 2010). There will be no requirement to maintain *bumiputera* equity conditions after initial public offerings (IPOs). Foreign investors will be allowed to own up to 70 per cent of stock-broking companies, compared with a previous 49 per cent limit, and foreign fund managers will be allowed to establish 100 per cent foreign-owned fund management companies.

3.2 Gap in Implementation: Compliance of Malaysia by the Time of AFAS 8

Although AFAS also covers the movement of natural persons, this section will focus primarily on the establishment of commercial presence as the Agreement on the Movement of Natural Persons (MNP) that was signed in 2012, is yet to be implemented across member states (Jurje and Lavenex 2015).[7] Moreover, the establishment of commercial presence is the most important mode of delivery in services due to the proximity burden in services.

Over time, Malaysia has progressively increased the number of sub-sectors scheduled in AFAS, reaching 96 sub-sectors by AFAS 8 or 75 per cent of the targeted 128 sub-sectors by 2015 (Table 4.2). This includes twenty-six sub-sectors in the priority integration sectors, with seven in logistics and sixty-three in others (MITI n.d.). Although the number of sub-sectors scheduled by Malaysia for liberalization is the second highest in ASEAN (after Thailand), its overall compliance in modes of supply is the third lowest in ASEAN, while it has exercised flexibility over twenty-one modes of supply, which is the third highest in ASEAN. Thus, it is most likely that Malaysia will be able to fulfil the liberalization goals of AFAS, in terms of number of sectors committed for liberalization by the end of 2015 (with flexibilities). This does not, however, imply that liberalization is in anyway substantial as there is a gap between commitments and practice as is explained in the following section.

3.3 Gap Between Commitments and Actual Practice

Dee (2013) has provided some evidence that commitments still lag behind actual practice in ASEAN. This is certainly the case for Malaysia for mode 3 as the government has progressively liberalized foreign equity restrictions in several selected service sub-sectors since 2009 and for specific purposes such as the targeted sectors under the ETP. In April 22 2009, the government announced that twenty-seven service sectors are exempted from the 30 per cent equity *bumiputera* ruling in an attempt to improve

TABLE 4.2
Malaysia's AFAS-8 Compliance Status Compared to Other ASEAN Member States

AFAS-8	B	C	I	L	MY	MM	P	S	T	V
Completed	Yes	Yes	Yes	Yes	Yes	Yes	Yes	Yes	Yes	Yes
Number of sub-sectors scheduled	79	87	86	89	96	79	89	84	104	88
Overall Compliance (in Modes of Supply) Minimum requirement is 204	222	240	218	223	219	226	222	240	240	213
Flexibility Exercised (in Modes of Supply): Shall not exceed 36	18	0	22	17	21	14	18	0	0	27
Balance sub-sectors to be achieved under 9th and 10th packages	49	41	42	39	32	49	39	44	24	40

Source: MITI (n.d.).

Malaysia's competitiveness in view of the global economic downturn that had emerged in 2008. The twenty-seven services listed for this purpose are found in ten out of the twelve broad sectors that are listed for liberalization,[8] namely computer and related services, health and social services, tourism services, sporting and other recreational services, business services, retail/ leasing services without operators, and supporting and auxillary transport services. Significantly, the government later clarified that liberalization in these sectors will not hurt local or *bumiputera* interest as there is little or no *bumiputera* and non-*bumiputera* participation in these sub-sectors (The Malaysian Insider, 13 May 2009 cited in Tham 2012). Furthermore, the liberalization in computer and related services is only an extension of the sectors opened to the Multimedia Super Corridor (MSC). In Table 4.3, it can be observed that although some subsectors in business services, especially in computer and related services are "liberalized" with 100 per cent foreign equity ownership, there were no ceilings prior to the market opening measures. Sub-sectors that have "real" liberalization in terms of an increase in foreign equity ownership permitted are promoted sectors such as private universities and hospitals.

In the second package of autonomous liberalization unveiled in October 2011, eighteen more sub-service sectors were added for liberalization.[9] Later in 2012, the government started to implement partial or complete lifting of foreign equity restrictions in seventeen services subsectors under six sectors (professional services, communications services, distribution services, educational services, environmental services, and health and social services) (WTO 2014*a*). In addition, it also formalized the market-access status quo in accountancy services where full foreign equity participation was already permitted. Based on autonomous liberalization, Table 4.3 shows several service sub-sectors that allow 100 per cent foreign equity ownership indicating a significant gap between AFAS commitments which is capped at 70 per cent at best (Table 4.1). Thus despite Malaysia's aim to shift to a service-oriented economy and the need for FDI in its economy, its liberalization efforts in AFAS is limited and falls short of the autonomous liberalization in the country for selected sectors. Hence in reality, there is greater liberalization in selected sectors compared to Malaysia's commitments in AFAS. It is therefore important to understand the policy conflicts that are affecting the liberalization of its services sector.

TABLE 4.3
Autonomous Services Liberalization, 2009–13

Services sub-sector	Market opening (date announced)	New foreign equity ownership ceiling (date of implementation)	Previous foreign ownership ceiling
BUSINESS SERVICES			
Professional Services			
• Accounting (including audit) and taxation	2011	100% (2012)	None
• Legal services	2011	Foreign equity ceiling not yet decided (not yet implemented)	Foreign ownership not previously allowed
• Architectural services	2011	100% (not yet implemented)	30%
• Engineering services	2011	100% (not yet implemented)	30%
• Quantity Surveying services	2011	100% (not yet implemented)	30%
Computer and Related Services			
• Consultancy services related to the installation of computer hardware	2008	100% (2009)	None
• Software implementation services	2008	100% (2009)	None
• Data processing services	2008	100% (2009)	None
• Database services	2008	100% (2009)	None
• Maintenance and repair services of computers	2008	100% (2009)	None
• Other services: data preparation services; training services; data recovery services; and development of creative content	2008	100% (2009)	None

continued on next page

TABLE 4.3 — *cont'd*

Services sub-sector	Market opening (date announced)	New foreign equity ownership ceiling (date of implementation)	Previous foreign ownership ceiling
Rental and Leasing Services without Operators			
• Rental/Leasing services of ships that excludes cabotage and offshore trades	2009	100% (2009)	30%
• Rental of cargo vessels without crew (bareboat charter) for international shipping	2009	100% (2009)	30%
Other business services			
• Regional distribution centres	2009	100% (2009)	None
• International procurement centres	2009	100% (2009)	None
• Technical testing and analytical services	2009	100% (2009)	70%
• Management consulting services	2009	100% (2009)	49%
COMMUNICATION SERVICES			
Courier Services			
• Courier services	2011	100% (2012)	n.a.
Telecommunication Services			
• Telecommunication licenses for application services providers (ASPs)	2011	100% (2012)	40%
• Telecommunication licenses for network service providers (ASPs)	2011	70% (2012)	30%

DISTRIBUTION SERVICES

• Departmental and specialty stores	2011	100% (2012)	70%

EDUCATIONAL SERVICES

• Technical and vocational schools	2011	100% (2012)	n.a.
• Technical and vocational schools for students with special needs	2011	100% (2012)	n.a.
• Skills training centres	2011	100% (2012)	—
• International schools	2011	100% (2012)	20%
• Private universities	2011	100% (2012)	51%

ENVIRONMENTAL SERVICES

• Incineration services	2011	100% (2012)	—

HEALTH RELATED AND SOCIAL SERVICES

• All veterinary services	2009	100% (2009)	Foreign ownership not previously allowed
• Welfare services delivered through residential institutions to the aged and handicapped	2009	100% (2009)	Foreign ownership not previously allowed
• Welfare services delivered through residential institutions to children	2009	100% (2009)	Foreign ownership not previously allowed
• Child day care services including day care services for the handicapped	2009	100% (2009)	Foreign ownership not previously allowed
• Vocational rehabilitation services for the handicapped	2009	100% (2009)	Foreign ownership not previously allowed
• Private hospitals	2011	100% (2012)	30%
• Medical specialist clinics	2011	100% (2012)	Foreign ownership not previously allowed
• Dental specialist clinics	2011	100% (2012)	Foreign ownership not previously allowed

continued on next page

TABLE 4.3 — *cont'd*

Services sub-sector	Market opening (date announced)	New foreign equity ownership ceiling (date of implementation)	Previous foreign ownership ceiling
TOURISM SERVICES			
• Theme park	2009	100% (2009)	49%
• Convention and exhibition centre (seating capacity of above 5,000)	2009	100% (2009)	49%
• Travel agencies and tour operators services (for inbound travel)	2009	100% (2009)	49%
• Hotel and restaurant services (for 4 and 5 star hotels)	2009	100% (2009)	49%
• Food serving services (for services provided in 4 and 5 star hotels)	2009	100% (2009)	49%
• Beverage serving services for consumption on the premises (for services provided in 4 and 5 star hotels)	2009	100% (2009)	49%
SPORTING AND OTHER RECREATIONAL SERVICES			
• Sporting services (sports event promotion and organization services)	2009	100% (2009)	None
TRANSPORTATION SERVICES			
• Class C freight transportation (Private carrier license in order to transport own goods)	2009	100% (2009)	None
Supporting and auxiliary transport services			
• Maritime agency services	2009	100% (2009)	30%
• Vessel salvage and re-floating services	2009	100% (2009)	30%

Notes: n.a. (not applicable); — (not available).
Source: WTO (2014*b*).

4. CONFLICTS BETWEEN LIBERALIZATION AND DOMESTIC AGENDAS

Bumiputera requirements affect liberalization through various channels, namely horizontal commitments, domestic regulations and practices, and through government-linked companies in the country.

4.1 Horizontal Commitments

In AFAS schedules, commitments are split into two sections: (i) "horizontal" commitments, which stipulate limitations that apply to all of the sectors included in the schedule; and (ii) sector-specific commitments. Any evaluation of sector-specific commitments must, therefore, take the horizontal entries into account. Horizontal commitments cover only modes 3 and 4 for both market access and national treatment (Appendix 1). These commitments have remained the same from AFAS 2 to AFAS 8, and are the same as the horizontal commitments made in GATS.

Under mode 3, the main concern for *market access* is the acquisition of assets or interests of Malaysian companies and businesses, mergers or takeovers. This requires approval and application in the case of: (i) the acquisition of the voting rights of a Malaysian corporation by any single foreign interest or associated group of 15 per cent or more, or an aggregate foreign interest of 30 per cent or more or exceeding RM5 million in value;[10] (ii) any proposed acquisition of any assets or interests by any means which will result in ownership or control passing to foreign interest; and (iii) the control of Malaysian corporations through any form of joint-venture agreement, technical assistance agreement or other arrangements. Mode 4 is unbound except for measures affecting the entry and temporary stay of natural persons which is mainly intra-corporate transferees and specialists or experts.

In the case of *national treatment*, there are limitations for land, property and real estate in mode 3 where approval can be denied for speculative, non-productive purposes or those that may conflict with the interests of the state. Incentives are limited to eligible Malaysian-owned corporations in service sectors promoted by the government. *Bumiputera* privileges under the NEP are unbound while corporations in which the government has an interest will give first consideration to service suppliers in which the government has an interest. As for mode 4, it remains unbound except for the categories of natural persons referred to under market access.

Since horizontal commitments apply across all sectors, foreign investors will still have to seek for approval from the respective sector regulators for establishing commercial presence in the country even when there are no limitations in the sector specific commitments. This merely serves to reinforce the role of domestic regulations and practices in the country's approval process for FDI.

4.2 Domestic Regulations and Practices

As noted by Dee (2013), governments often regulate services markets to correct market failures and/or to meet equity objectives. These regulatory measures may thwart liberalization measures as they may intentionally or unintentionally restrict the entry of both domestic as well as foreign service suppliers. In the case of Malaysia, the main service sectors are guided by their own set of legislations, of which a sample is shown in Table 4.4. The regulations shown have a broad spectrum of power, including awarding licences for the provision of services in the country for both domestic and foreign suppliers as well as the approval of fee structures. Establishing a foreign presence will require obtaining a licence to operate in the country, and this is where the different sectoral ministries have the power to determine entry.

The power of the regulator to impose *bumiputera* requirements can, for example, be seen in the wholesale and retail sector, which plays a crucial role in the economy as the government seeks to rebalance growth by boosting domestic consumption. The sector is also important as it contributed to over 68 per cent of Malaysia's GNI in 2013 (EPU 2013). It is interesting to note that although Malaysia is in general one of the most open economies in East Asia in terms of statutory restrictions on FDI, the country is considered to be restrictive when it comes to distributive services and telecommunications (HKTDC 2014). In fact, it was reported by the Hong Kong Trade Development Council (HKTDC) that the Organization for Economic Co-operation and Development (OECD) ranked Malaysia's retail sector as the fourth most restrictive in terms of regulatory restrictiveness out of fifty-eight selected economies, after Myanmar, Tunisia and Jordan. Moreover, the World Bank's services trade restrictiveness index shows that Malaysia's overall restrictiveness is higher than the ASEAN average, which excludes Singapore (Sauvé 2013).

TABLE 4.4
Selected Legislations Governing Services Sectors, 2013

Sector	Legislation
Private Health Care Services	• Fees Act 1951 (amended in 2003) • Medical Act 1971 • Dental Act 1971 • Standards of Malaysia Act 1996 • Malaysian Health Promotion Board Act 2006
Private Tertiary Education Services	• Immigration Act 1959 and 1963 • Employment (Restriction) Act 1968 (revised in 1988) • Universities and University Colleges Act 1971 • National Accreditation Act 1996 • National Council on Higher Education Act 1996 • Private Higher Educational Institutions Act 1996 (latest amendment 2014)
Telecommunications	• Communications and Multimedia Act, 1988 • Communications and Multimedia Commission Act, 1988
Tourism and Related Services	• Innkeepers Act 1952 • National Parks Act 1980 • Malaysia Tourism Promotion Board Act 1992 • Tourism Industry Act 1992 (latest amendment 1998) • Tourism Vehicles Licensing Act 1999

Source: WTO (2014b) and Mahani, Tham and Loke (2012).

The wholesale and retail sector is regulated by the Ministry of Domestic Trade, Cooperatives and Consumerism (MDTCC). Foreign companies are required to obtain approval from the MDTCC before investing in the retail business in Malaysia; these foreign companies are also required to be locally incorporated. The regulator issues guidelines on foreign participation in the distributive trade services in Malaysia. The 2010 guidelines came into effect retrospectively on 1 January 2010.

Under the previous 2004 guidelines, the MDTCC imposed a general condition that a locally incorporated company involved in distributive trade must have at least 30 per cent *bumiputera* equity (Tan 2010). This equity requirement has been relaxed to a certain extent under the 2010 guidelines, as currently only proposals for the setting up of hypermarkets in Malaysia that involve foreign participation are required to comply with this equity requirement. If this requirement is not met at the time of application, a grace period of three years for compliance may be given depending on the merits of each case and any extension thereafter is at the discretion of the MDTCC. Furthermore, this requirement also applies to operations established prior to the coming effect of the 2010 guidelines, and hypermarkets are not allowed to open a new branch unless the company has fulfilled this equity requirement. Foreign-owned department stores and specialty stores are allowed to be wholly foreign-owned, but this does not extend to supermarkets, mini markets and convenience stores.

Additional requirements for all distributive trade companies with foreign equity include the following (Tan 2010): (i) the appointment of one or more *bumiputera* directors; (ii) hiring personnel at all levels, including management to reflect the racial composition of the Malaysian population; (iii) utilizing local companies for legal and other professional services that are available in Malaysia; and (iv) allocating at least 30 per cent of shelf space in each outlet for products manufactured by *bumiputera*-owned small and medium enterprises (SMEs) within three years (only applicable to department stores, hypermarkets and superstores). These requirements were considered as a disincentive by some foreign store operators, with Carrefour reportedly having sold its Malaysian branches to AEON due to the introduction of these controls (Sharifah Mariam 2014).

The above regulations illustrate clearly how domestic regulations can be a disincentive to foreign investment, thereby negating any liberalization efforts in AFAS.

4.3 Government-linked Companies (GLCs)

Apart from the potential of domestic regulations to deter entry, Dee (2013) also pointed out the importance of having a regulator that is independent from industry. Government-linked companies (GLCs) can have substantial influence on the regulator, when regulators also sit on the board of companies such as GLCs (*The Malaysian Insider*, 10 June 2014). Besides, many GLCs were created to facilitate the redistributive objective of the NEP (Menon 2012). In addition, GLCs that are not governed by the procurement rules and regulations of the public sector are encouraged to purchase from locally owned businesses, including *bumiputera* enterprises. In 2014, the government reportedly directed GLCs to generate RM7 billion in business opportunities for *bumiputera* firms (*The Malaysian Insider*, 17 July 2014). GLCs' key performance indicators, developed by the Putrajaya Committee on GLC High Performance (PCG), were based on merit:[11] transparency; market-friendly; and being able to assist the *bumiputera* community with being competitive. GLCs' socio-political mandate thus includes the development of the Bumiputera Commercial and Industrial Community (BCIC) (Lee 2015). Menon estimates GLCs comprise 36 per cent of the Malaysian stock exchange capitalization and 54 per cent of the entities that make up the Kuala Lumpur Composite Index. Based on data from publicly listed companies, he found GLCs' presence (93 per cent) in utilities to be the highest compared to the other sectors in 2012.

In the case of utilities, the Malaysian Communications and Multimedia Commission (MCMC) was established as an independent regulatory body to regulate and licence telecommunications under the Malaysian Communications and Multimedia Act 1998 (MCMCA). Telecom services providers must obtain a licence from the Minister of Information, Communication and Culture (MICC) and the company must be locally incorporated. Licensing conditions are the same for local and foreign service suppliers. The equity cap on foreign investment was progressively liberalized after the AFC and under autonomous liberalization efforts after 2009. Thus, although the commitment made under AFAS permits only 70 per cent foreign equity, Malaysia began allowing 100 per cent foreign equity participation in Applications Service Providers in April 2012 (Table 4.3). However, liberalization of telecommunications services for Network Facilities Providers and Network Service Provider licenses has yet to be implemented and currently only 70 per cent foreign participation is permitted.

Despite progressive liberalization, the government still maintains a strong presence in the telecommunications sector through its GLCs. It is the majority shareholder of Telekom Malaysia, the former government division for telecommunication services (WTO 2014*b*). Telekom Malaysia was privatized in 1987 and sold its mobile division in 2008, which is now a separate GLC called Axiata. The fixed-line sector continues to be dominated by Telekom Malaysia (TM), with a market share of 95 per cent, indicating limited competition even though competition was introduced in the fixed-line sector in the early 1990s, when five additional licences were issued in line with the National Telecommunication Policy to encourage competition (WTO 2010). TIME dotcom Berhad (TIME), which is wholly owned by the government, provides wholesale bandwidth and operates the Cross Peninsular Cable System. Data from 2011 to 2013 from the MCMC (2014) indicate that 75 per cent of the country's telecommunication revenue accrues to Axiata, CELCOM, TM and TIME, while the remaining 35 per cent is divided between MAXIS and DiGi. Of these five companies, three of them (Axiata, TM and TIME) belong to the stable of companies under Khazanah Nasional, a government-linked investment company (GLIC), while CELCOM belongs to TM.

Despite commitments in AFAS and other trade agreements, the extensive presence of GLCs can crowd out private investment, including foreign investment due to their superior reserves and political connections (Lee 2015). In turn, the licensing process allows the government substantial discretionary power to award licences to either local or foreign suppliers. Since GLCs play an important role in generating profits for the GLICs as well as in meeting the social agenda of the country, it is difficult to have a level playing field for foreign suppliers in the country. Thus, despite the commitment to increase foreign equity shares in the telecommunication sector, bureaucratic practices and uncertainty in the licensing process can deter the entry of foreign as well as domestic providers, while favouring the incumbent and politically connected.

5. CONCLUSION

In terms of policy directions, Malaysia has clearly identified the services sector as a critical sector for upgrading its manufacturing sector since the implementation of its Second Industrial Master Plan. The sector has also been targeted as the next engine of growth for the country. Services continue to occupy policy attention — in 2012 the government commissioned the World Bank to formulate a Services Sector Blueprint, which will serve as an input into the Eleventh Malaysia Plan (2015–20) (WTO 2014b). Accordingly, the new Services Sector Blueprint is aimed at transforming the services sector and accelerating its growth, with a specific focus on the development of more knowledge-intensive and higher-value-added sectors through reforms of targeted services sub-sectors and an acceleration in the internationalization of service providers. A plan of action to implement the Services Blueprint has also been planned.

Despite these policy directions, there are other policy objectives in the domestic agenda that prevent real liberalization of this sector. In the domestic agenda, *bumiputera* preferences continue to frustrate liberalization efforts in the services sector by reaffirming the powerful role of domestic regulations and practices in the country. The extensive presence of GLCs is another deterrent to the entry of foreign investors, especially in services where privatized former-government monopolies continue to dominate the market in certain services sub-sectors. GLCs are also "sheltered" from liberalization by domestic regulations that can serve as bureaucratic hurdles to domestic and foreign investment. The importance of streamlining the regulatory regime to enhance efficiency is also shown by the commissioning of another study on domestic regulations for the services sector in 2012 (WTO 2014*b*). The focus, however, is only on specific promoted sectors such as healthcare travel, private higher education, technical and vocation education and training as well as environmental services.

The liberalization of the services sector is essential for attracting domestic and foreign investment as well as for improving the sector's efficiency, thereby permitting services to play a transformative role in industrial development. However, substantial liberalization of the services sector, save for selected promoted services, is unlikely unless policy conflicts within the country are resolved. With regard to these promoted services, the government has preferred autonomous liberalization over binding and irreversible commitments in trade agreements. By allowing flexibilities and countries to liberalize at its own pace AFAS, in particular, will not be able to extract substantial liberalization efforts from Malaysia in its services sector.

APPENDIX 1
Horizontal Commitments

INITIAL PACKAGE (1997)
Sector: All included in this schedule unless otherwise indicated
There is no change in horizontal commitments after the Second Package (1998).

Limitations on Market Access	*Limitations on National Treatment*
Mode	*Mode*
3 **Acquisition, Mergers and Takeovers** The acquisition of assets or interests of Malaysian companies and businesses, mergers or takeovers requires approval and apply to the following: a) Acquisition of the voting rights of a Malaysian corporation by any single foreign interest or associated group of 15 per cent or more, or an aggregate foreign interest of 30 per cent or more or exceeding RM5 million in value b) Any proposed acquisition of any assets or interests by any means which will result in ownership or control passing to foreign interest c) Control of Malaysian corporations through any form of joint-venture agreement, management agreement, technical assistance agreement or other arrangements. Approval is normally granted. However it may be denied in circumstances where the proposed investments conflicts with the interest of the State	3 **Land, Property and Real Estate** Approval may be denied in the acquisition, disposal or dealing of land or any interest in land, property and real estate is undertaken for speculative or non-productive purpose or for purposes which may conflict with the interest of the State. **Incentives/Preferences** Incentives are limited to eligible Malaysian-owned corporations engaged in service sectors promoted by the Government. Any measure and special preference granted to *bumiputera, bumiputera* status companies, trust companies and institutions set up to meet the objectives of the New Economic Policy (NEP) and the National Development Policy (NDP) shall be unbound. **Corporations in which the Government has an interest shall, in acquiring services, give first consideration to service suppliers in which the Government has an interest. This requirement does not prevent the acquisition of services from other service suppliers where their services are competitive in terms of price, quality and delivery. (Added in the 2nd Package)**

| 4 | Unbound expect for measures affecting the entry and temporary stay of natural persons defined below: | 4 | Unbound except for the categories of natural persons preferred to under market access. |

1. **Intra-corporate Transferees**
   a) Senior managers being persons within an organization having proprietary information of the organization and who exercise wide latitude in decision making relating to the establishment, control and operation of the organization being directly responsible to the CEO and receive only general supervision or direction from the board of directors or partners of the organization;
   b) Two specialists or experts per organization being persons within the organization who possess knowledge at an advanced level of continued expertise and who possess proprietary knowledge of the organization's new service products and technology, research equipment and techniques or management. Additional specialists or experts may be allowed subject to market test and the training of Malaysians through an acceptable training.

Provided that such persons are employees of the foreign service supplier and have been in employment of that foreign service supplier for a period of not less than one year immediately preceding the date of their application for a work permit and he is to serve in at least a similar capacity.

continued on next page

APPENDIX 1 — *cont'd*

Limitations on Market Access	Limitations on National Treatment
Mode	*Mode*

2. Others

a) Specialists or experts being persons who possess knowledge at an advanced level of continued expertise and who possess proprietary knowledge of the organization's products and services subject to market test and the employment of Malaysians as counterparts and/or training of Malaysians through acceptable training programmes in the relevant services sector or subsector

b) Professionals being persons who possess necessary academic credentials, professional qualifications, experience and/or expertise which have been duly recognized by the professional bodies in Malaysia and registered with those respective professional bodies

c) Business visitors being persons not based within Malaysia, receiving no remuneration from a source located within Malaysia, who have been employed for at least one year by a foreign service supplier, whose entry and temporary stay is for the purposes of negotiating for the sale services for that service supplier and who will not engage in direct sales to the general public

Entry and stay of natural persons defined in categories 1(a) and (b) and 2(a) and (b) shall not exceed a total of five years. For category 2(c), the period of stay shall not exceed a total of 90 days.

Source: Compiled from MITI 2011.

Notes

1. This is likely to be underestimated as the informal sector is not accounted for and its size is unknown.
2. The ninth package has yet to be signed at the time of writing and it is at the *ad referendum* stage.
3. The first to the seventh packages were signed in 1997, 1998, 2001 (*ad referendum*), 2004, 2006, 2007 and 2009 respectively.
4. This excludes financial and air transport services which were negotiated separately by the respective Ministries and will not be discussed in this paper. The twelve broad sectors are: business services; communication services; construction and related engineering services; distribution services; educational services; environmental services; financial services; health related and social services; tourism and travel related services; recreational, cultural, and sporting services; transport services; and other services not included elsewhere.
5. Flexibilities refer to the margin allowed, in scheduling liberalization commitments, for sub-sectors to be totally excluded from liberalization and the sub-sectors in which not all the agreed parameters of liberalization of the modes of supply are met (ASEAN Secretariat 2013). The quantum of flexibility is under review.
6. Details on the AFAS action plan can be obtained from ASEAN Secretariat 2013.
7. This is limited to the movement of skilled workers only.
8. The two sub-sectors not included are construction and related engineering services and other services not included elsewhere.
9. These are: telecommunications (ASP); international schools; technical and vocational schools; technical and vocational schools (special needs); private hospitals; departmental and specialty stores; incineration services; accounting/taxation; skills training centres; courier services; legal services; private universities; medical specialist services; dental specialist services; telecommunications (NSP and NFP); architectural services; engineering services; and quantity surveying services (Arizal Thani Saadun 2014).
10. Note that the horizontal commitments are the same in the Malaysia-Japan Economic Partnership Agreement and the only change introduced in the Malaysia-Pakistan agreement and included in Malaysia's commitments in the ASEAN-Korea bilateral is the cut-off point, which has been raised to RM10 million in the latter two agreements.
11. Lee (2015) interprets merit-based criteria as one that involves selecting more capable *bumiputera* managers, subcontractors and vendors over less capable *bumiputera* managers, subcontractors and vendors.

References

Arizal Thani Saadun. "Liberalization of the Services Sector in Malaysia". Ministry of International Trade and Industry (MITI), 14 February 2014. Available at <www.smecorp.gov.my/vn2/sites/default/files/Presentations_MITI.pdf> (accessed 30 January 2015).

ASEAN Secretariat 2013. *Roadmap for an ASEAN Community, 2009–2015*. Jakarta: ASEAN Secretariat, 2013.

Dee, Philippa. "Does AFAS Have Bite: Comparing Commitments with Actual Practice", 2013. Available at <https://crawford.anu.edu.au/pdf/staff/... dee/2013/does-afas-have-bite.pdf> (accessed 30 January 2015).

EPU [Economic Planning Unit] . "The Malaysian Economy in Figures: 2013". Available at <http://www.epu.gov.my/documents/10124/2257e64f-b08d-41b7-bed0-b6e6498c38a3> (accessed 30 January 2015).

HKTDC [Hong Kong Trade Development Council]. "Negotiating Malaaysia's Retail Regulatory Hurdles". HKTDC website, 16 April 2014 <http://research.hktdc.com/> (accessed 30 January 2015).

Jurje, Flavia and Sandra Lavenex. "ASEAN Economic Community: What Model for Labor Mobility?". NCCR Trade Working Paper no. 2015/02. NCCR Trade Regulation (Swiss National Center of Competence in Research). Available at <http://www.wti.org/fileadmin/user_upload/nccr-trade.ch/wp4/NCCR_working_Paper_ASEAN_Jurje_Lavenex__.pdf> (accesed 10 April 2015).

Lee, Hwok-Aun. "Political Preference Crowding out Enterprise in Malaysia". *East Asia Forum*, 14 January 2015.

Mahani, Z.A., Tham Siew Yean and Loke Wai Heng. "Exporting Niches for Services Exports: The Case of Malaysia". In *Exporting Services: A Developing Country Perspective*, edited by Arti Grover Goswami, Aaditya Mattoo and Sebastian Saez. Washington, D.C.: World Bank, 2012.

Malaysian Insider, The [online]. "The Conflict of Interest When Regulators Sit on Company Boards", 10 June 2014. Available at <http://www.themalaysianinsider.com/malaysia/article/the-conflict-of-interest-when-regulators-sit-on-company-boards> (accessed 10 April 2014).

⸻. "GLCs told to provide RM7 billion to develop Bumiputera firms", 17 July 2014. Available at <http://www.themalaysianinsider.com/malaysia/article/glcs-told-to-provide-rm7-billion-to-develop-bumiputera-business#sthash. UiuiTGfv.dpuf> (accessed 30 January 2015).

MCMC. *Industry Performance Report 2013*. Malaysian Communications and Multimedia Commission, 2014. Available at <http://www.skmm.gov.my/skmmgovmy/media/General/pdf/IPR2013_English.pdf> (accessed 30 January 2015).

Menon, Jayant. "Malaysia: Growth without Private Investment". *East Asia Forum*, 17 September 2012.

Ministry of Finance, Malaysia. Economic Report 2014/2015. Kuala Lumpur: National Printing Malaysia Limited, 2014.

MITI. "Liberalization of Services under ASEAN Framework Agreement on Services (AFAS)." Ministry of International Trade and Industry, 2011. Available at <www.mfea.org.my/Data/Sites/1/link/Announcement4/Afas.pdf.> (accessed 30 January 2015).

―――. "Progress in Services Liberalization in ASEAN". Ministry of International Trade and Industry, undated. Available at <www.mip.org.my/doc/paper1.pdf> (accessed 30 January 2015).

Sauvé, Pierre. "Services Trade and the ASEAN Economic Community". Presentation at the Asian Development Bank, Philippines. Mimeographed, 18 July 2013.

Sharifah Mariam. "Malaysia Retail Policies and Procedures: Balancing Needs and Demands". *TIJ's Research Journal of Social Science & Management (RJSSM)* 3, no. 10 (2014): 95–111.

Tan, Nicholas. "Revised Guidelines on Foreign Participation in Distributive Trade Services in Malaysia". *Shearn Delamore & Co Newsletter* 9, no. 3, September 2010. Available at <http://www.shearndelamore.com/assets/templates/images/pdf/2010/SD%20Newsletter%20Sept_2010.pdf> (accessed 30 January 2015).

Tham, Siew Yean. "Negotiating for a Malaysia-EU FTA: Contesting Interests from Malaysia's Perspective". *Asie.Visions* 57, November 2012.

―――. "Malaysia". In *Asia Rising*, edited by Hal Hill and Maria Socorro Gochoco-Bautista. Cheltenham: Edward Elgar and Asian Development Bank, 2013.

United Nations. *World Economic Situation and Prospects*. New York: United Nations, 2014.

WTO [World Trade Organization]. "Malaysia Trade Policy Review 2010". Available at <www.wto.org › trade topics › trade policy reviews › list of reviews> (accessed 30 January 2015).

―――. "WTO 2014 Press Releases", 2014*a*. Available at <http://www.wto.org/english/news_e/pres14_e/pr721_e.htm> (accessed 30 January 2015).

―――. "Malaysia Trade Policy Review 2014" (2014*b*). Available at <www.wto.org › trade topics › trade policy reviews › list of reviews> (accessed 30 January 2015).

5

THE PHILIPPINES AND
THE AEC BEYOND 2015
Managing Domestic Challenges

Myrna S. Austria

1. INTRODUCTION

Constant pressure to stay competitive built the momentum for ASEAN Leaders to conceptualize the ASEAN Economic Community (AEC) as a vision for deepening and broadening regional economic integration in 2003. The AEC is characterized by four pillars: a single market and production base; a highly competitive economic region; a region of equitable economic development; and a region fully integrated into the global economy (ASEAN Secretariat 2009). While the original timeline for the AEC was 2020, it was subsequently accelerated to the end of 2015 in response to the confluence of regional as well as global challenges that confronted the region (Austria 2015).

As a founding member of ASEAN, the Philippines has embraced the challenge of moving towards attaining the AEC vision because it is consistent with the overarching goal of increasing the country's competitiveness in an era of globalization and regional economic integration. The Philippines has implemented substantial market-oriented reforms covering liberalization, facilitation, privatization and deregulation since the 1980s. These were carried out in various stages involving unilateral, regional as well as multilateral approaches (Austria 2003). Yet despite these policy reforms, the country has been affected by the boom-bust cycle of economic growth, lagging behind its neighbours in the region after more than three decades of reforms. Nevertheless, for the past three years, the country's growth performance was not only higher than its past records, but it was also the highest in the region, after China. However, it remains to be seen if this performance is sustainable.

In fact, the country's expected structural transformation from agriculture to manufacturing did not take place (Aldaba 2014). The contribution of the manufacturing sector to the economy remained at less than a quarter of GDP, in contrast to Thailand's experience where the sector gradually evolved to become the driver of economic growth. The automobile industry was one of the early industries promoted by the Philippines in its bid for industrialization in the 1980s. This was logical as the country participated in the changing landscape of global production networks in East Asia, whereby the labour-intensive segments of technologically complex production processes are separated from the capital- and skill-intensive segments and located in developing countries, linked through international sub-contracting and outsourcing arrangements (Austria 2013; Aldaba 2008; Rosellon and Medalla 2011). The production networks provided an opportunity for countries in the region to accelerate the development of their manufacturing sector. With its support of the automobile industry, the Philippines should have been in a good position to industrialize and participate in the industry's global production networks. Unfortunately, this did not materialize. As with the performance of the overall economy, the automobile industry has remained generally undeveloped and uncompetitive as will be discussed in section 3 of this paper.

Sluggish economic performance has continued to challenge the government. As the deadline for the AEC is fast approaching (December 2015), all ASEAN member economies are preparing themselves for the potential impact of a more integrated region. They are aiming towards the opportunities that a more integrated region may bring about, but at the same time, they are also apprehensive of the uncertainties and concerns that may arise from closer economic integration. Nonetheless, there appears to be some consensus that the strategic actions and measures outlined in the 2007 AEC Blueprint ("the Blueprint") will not be fully implemented by 2015 (Austria 2013).

By the end of 2013, the Philippines complied with 84.1 per cent of the key deliverable targets mentioned under the Blueprint (Esguerra 2014). Nonetheless, it is unlikely that the country can attain full implementation by the end of 2015. Likewise, the positive impact of the measures that have been implemented may not have reached their intended beneficiaries. What might be the reasons for the disparity between commitments and implementation? Tham and Basu Das (2015) in their overview chapter in this book, hypothesize that conflicting economic interests in a country may be one possible reason for the discrepancy. As with any policy reform, there will be winners and losers and, hence, domestic opposition, by lobbying, can delay, if not block, policy implementation. It is also possible that conflicts may arise from the non-alignment of policy reforms with existing domestic policies, thus giving rise to policy objectives that are inconsistent.

The objectives of this chapter are twofold. First, it will examine the country's performance towards the AEC, identifying the gaps between commitments and actual implementation. Second, it will examine the domestic economic conflicts that have hampered the country's policy reform efforts, focusing on the automobile industry. The experience of this industry best illustrates the experience of the country's manufacturing sector. The conflicts may be due to the lack of coherence of government policies thus, limiting, if not negating, progress towards economic integration. They could also be due to conflicting economic interests among industry players themselves.

The chapter is organized as follows: section 2 discusses the progress of the Philippines towards achieving its commitments in the Blueprint, focusing on trade and investment. Section 3 examines domestic economic conflicts arising from trade and investment policies, and other regulations that have shaped the country's automobile industry. Section 4 discusses moving beyond 2015 by identifying policies and programmes to address the domestic conflicts and the country's remaining AEC commitments. Finally, section 5 presents the summary and conclusions.

2. PROGRESS ON THE AEC BLUEPRINT: TRADE AND INVESTMENT

As part of the overarching goal of increasing the country's competitiveness, the Philippine government has, over three decades, implemented substantial market-oriented reforms covering liberalization, trade facilitation, privatization and deregulation. These were carried out in various phases involving unilateral, regional, as well as multilateral approaches (Austria 2003). The country's commitments in the Blueprint are integral to addressing the remaining constraints to being globally competitive. The Blueprint enabled the government to "lock-in" domestic economic policy reforms. It pushed the government to address the bottlenecks that have constrained the private sector's response to the opportunities arising from greater openness and deeper regional integration (Austria 2003; Rosellon and Yap 2010). But what have been the accomplishments thus far? Are these consistent with actual implementation? This section of the paper provides an overview of the country's progress in the implementation of its commitments in the Blueprint, with a focus on the free flow of goods and investment.

2.1 Free Flow of Goods

The Blueprint sets forth the roadmap for achieving the AEC. The roadmap includes initiatives that build upon earlier economic integration initiatives in ASEAN and sets out timelines for their implementation. The progress of implementation is monitored through the AEC Scorecard.

The major initiative for the free flow of goods is the ASEAN Trade in Goods Agreement (ATIGA) which came into effect in 2010. ATIGA consolidates and streamlines all provisions in CEPT-AFTA (Common Effective Preferential Tariff–ASEAN Free Trade Area), and other protocols related to trade in goods into one single legal instrument (Austria 2013). It covers the elimination of tariffs and non-tariff barriers; rules of origin; trade facilitation, which calls for the harmonization and standardization of trade and customs processes and procedures; customs integration; ASEAN National Single Window; and the harmonization of standards, technical regulations and conformity assessment procedures (ASEAN Secretariat 2009).

For its part, the Philippines removed tariffs on imports from ASEAN in 2010 under Executive Order 850,[1] except with respect to the following sensitive list: swine; poultry; cassava; sweet potatoes; corn and sorghum, which still carry a 5 per cent tariff rate; and rice and sugar with tariff rates of 40 per cent and 10 per cent, respectively. Quantitative restrictions continue to remain but mainly concern weapons and arms, and rice and sugar, which cover less than 1 per cent of the total number of Philippine Standard Commodity Classification (PSCC) lines.

Non-tariff measures are imposed for health and safety reasons. However, non-tariff measures considered as barriers to trade (NTBs) still exist for the priority sectors for integration particularly, the agri-based, ICT, electronics and automotive sectors (Austria 2013). These include non-automatic licensing, technical regulations, testing, inspection and quarantine requirements, covering 62 per cent of total imports of the priority sectors.

On standards, the government passed the Republic Act (RA) of 10611, also known as the *Food Safety Act of 2013*, on 5 June 2013.[2] The law aims to strengthen the regulation of food safety standards, inspection and testing. This new regulatory system is expected to ensure a high level of food safety, promote fair trade and advance the global competitiveness of the country's foods and food products. Another law, RA 10462, also known as the *Philippine Lemon Law*, was enacted in July 2014[3] to further enhance standards. The law protects car buyers from business and trade malpractices. Under the law, buyers may demand a refund or replacement if defects remain unresolved after four repair attempts and one final attempt by the car manufacturer, distributor, dealer or retailer.

On trade facilitation, the Philippine customs reform and modernization programme started in the early 1990s primarily to improve revenue collection, intensify the enforcement of customs regulations, combat corruption and improve the trade and investment climate. At the core of the modernization programme is e-customs, where customs-related processes are automated and implemented electronically. According to Medalla (2013), e-customs is now being implemented in major airports and seaports in the country, with 80 per cent of basic customs operations done electronically, covering 95 per cent of imports and at least 25 per cent of exports. Full coverage is targeted for the end of 2015.

Aligned with the customs modernization programme is the establishment of the Philippine National Single Window (PNSW). This is also in response to ASEAN's initiative to create the ASEAN National Single Window (ASW) to facilitate international trade and investment through fast customs clearance in the region. The PNSW will allow exporters, importers and traders to transact with government agencies through a single Internet-based window. ASEAN's goal is a thirty-minute turnaround for customs processing. The first phase of the PNSW was completed in October 2010. Customs-related processes have been automated, allowing for the electronic transfer of data and documents between and among core government agencies in charge of export- and import-related processing.[4] With fewer person-to-person transactions, the system reduces the opportunity for corruption, expedites customs clearance, and reduces transaction time and costs, thus increasing trade efficiency and competitiveness.

Table 5.1 displays the usage status of the PNSW — some agencies have completely or partially used the system while others are still engaged in manual processing. While the PNSW reflects the respective import permits that are granted by different government agencies, a separate system contains the actual import entry and tabulation of duties and taxes, making it difficult, if not impossible, for some agencies to use the PNSW. Thus, a single system is being developed to integrate all processes and agencies. Dubbed the Integrated Enhanced Customs Processing System (IECPS), or the PNSW Phase 2 Project, the system will be a single gateway through which exporters and importers can access all the information they need for complying with customs processes and procedures. It is expected to be completed before the end of 2015.

Additionally, the government is still unable to exchange data with the other ASEAN members. This will also be covered in Phase 2 of the PNSW, which is currently being implemented. Phase 2 covers the remaining processes, including: integration with the ASW; manifest processing; declaration processing; rationalization; simplification; and harmonization (Medalla 2013).

2.2 Free Flow of Investments

As one of the core elements of AEC, a free and open investment regime is key for enhancing the region's competitiveness in attracting foreign direct investment (FDI). ASEAN's investment regime has evolved gradually since the late 1980s. Originally, separate frameworks governed investment protection and investment liberalization. Investment protection was guided by the ASEAN Agreement for the Promotion and Protection of Investment or what is commonly referred to as the ASEAN Investment Guarantee Agreement (IGA), signed in 1987. On the other hand, investment liberalization was driven by the Framework Agreement on the ASEAN Investment Area (AIA), signed in October 1998 and amended in 2001. In response to the emerging competitive global environment for FDI and, hence, the need to enhance the region's competitiveness as an investment destination, the AIA and IGA were revised and merged into a single comprehensive investment agreement, the ASEAN Comprehensive Investment Agreement (ACIA). The agreement was signed in February

TABLE 5.1
Philippine National Single Window as of October 2014

Completed	Partially Completed	Stopped	Not Connected
Bureau of Animal Industry (BAI)	Bureau of Import Service (BIS)	Philippine Economic Zone Authority (PEZA)	Bureau of Customs
Bureau of Fisheries and Aquatic Resources (BFAR)	Bureau of Product Standards (BPS)	Philippine Coconut Authority (PCA)	Bureau of Export Trade Promotion
Bureau of Internal Revenue (BIR)	Forest Management Service (FMS)	National Meat Inspection Service (NMIS)	Philippine Ozone Desk
Board of Investment (BOI)	Sugar Regulatory Administration (SRA	Department of Health (DOH)	Philippine National Police — Criminal Investigation and Detection Group
Bureau of Plant Industry (BPI)	Bureau of Quarantine (BOQ)	Environment Management Bureau (EMB)	Land Transportation Office
Fertilizer and Pesticides Authority (FPA)	Civil Aviation Authority of the Philippines (CAAP)	Food and Drug Administration (FDA)	Philippine Shippers Bureau
Philippine Drug Enforcement Agency (PDEA)	Firearms Explosives Office (FEO)	National Food Authority (NFA)	Bureau of Immigration
Dangerous Drugs Board (DDB)	Maritime Industry Authority (MARINA)		Bangko Sentral ng Pilipinas
Philippine Nuclear Research Institute (PNRI)	Environment Management Bureau		Intellectual Property Office
National Telecommunications Commission (NTC)			Insurance Commission
Optical Media Board (OMB)			One Stop Shop DOF
			Fiber Industry Development Coordinating Agency
			National Intelligence Coordinating Agency
11	**9**	**7**	**13**

Source: Bureau of Customs (BOC).

2009 and took effect three years later on 29 March 2012. In accordance with the Blueprint, the ACIA encompasses all four major aspects of investment namely: liberalization; facilitation; protection; and promotion.[5]

The Philippines has made substantial progress in the liberalization of FDI with the passing of the following laws:

- RA 7042 or the Foreign Investment Act (June 1991) — 100 per cent foreign equity in all areas, except those specified in the Negative Lists A, B and C;
- RA 8179 (March 1996) — Abolished Negative List C;
- RA 7721 (1994) — Foreign bank liberalization;
- RA 879 (2000) — General Banking Law allow-ing foreign banks to own 100 per cent of one locally-incorporated commercial or thrift bank;
- RA 8762 (March 2000) — Retail trade liberalization law allowing 100 per cent foreign equity with minimum US$7.5 million equity.

Urata and Ando (2010), whose study estimated FDI restrictiveness indices, have shown that the Philippines is considered to have a relatively open economy. Nonetheless, FDI restrictions remain in some sectors as mandated in Executive Order 858 (February 2010).[6] This includes the mass media (no foreign equity); land ownership (40 per cent foreign equity); the exploration and development of natural resources, public utilities and BOT (build-operate-transfer) (40 per cent foreign equity).

Investment promotion is implemented through fiscal and non-fiscal incentives, which are granted to preferred industries, under the Omnibus Investment Code, and to export-oriented enterprises in economic zones. The Philippine Export Processing Zone Authority (PEZA), Subic Bay Metropolitan Authority (SMBA) and Clark Development Corporation (CDC) supervise the major economic zones in the country. Incentives for firms located outside of the economic zones are managed by the Board of Investment (BOI).

Investment facilitation is implemented in the following ways. The National Economic Research and Business Action Center under the BOI gathers representatives from various agencies, under one roof, to answer investor queries and process their business registration. PEZA operates a 24/7 "one-stop and non-stop shop" to process export and import permits as well as building and occupancy permits. The One Stop Action Center under the CDC facilitates the evaluation and approval of investment projects within a thirty-day period. Finally, the Philippine Business Registry (PBR) is a one-stop shop for entrepreneurs who need to transact with the Department of Trade and Industry (DTI), Bureau of Internal Revenue (BIR), Social Security System (SSS), Home Development Mutual Fund (HDMF), Philippine Health Insurance Corporation (PhilHealth), or Securities and Exchange Commission (SEC).

3. DOMESTIC CONFLICTS: THE CASE OF THE PHILIPPINE AUTOMOTIVE INDUSTRY

The Philippine automobile industry comprises two major sectors: automobile assemblers; and parts and components manufacturers. The assemblers are dominated by subsidiaries of multinational companies (MNCs) that have established their operations in the country primarily for the domestic market. On the other hand, parts and components manufacturers are composed of three tiers. The first-tier manufacturers, which include the major players of the industry, are MNCs that not only directly supply the needs of the assemblers, but also export their products. The second- and third-tier manufacturers are subcontractors, mostly small and medium enterprises (SMEs) supplying the needs of first-tier manufacturers.

The government has been trying to develop the industry since the 1970s under various auto policies and car development programmes, the most prominent of which were the: Progressive Car and Truck Manufacturing programme (1970s); Car Development programme (late 1980s); People's Car programme (1990s); and the New Motor Vehicle Development programme (2000s). Aldaba (2007, 2008) has extensively discussed these government policies and programmes that have shaped the industry over the past four decades (refer to Appendix for a summary of programmes and policies). Both studies have shown that the industry developed under a system of protection and promotion through high tariffs, import restrictions and a high local content requirements scheme. The outcome is a classic protected industrial regime and an import-dependent industry that has failed to create the expected forward and backward linkages in the economy. Thus, value-added has remained at only 2 per cent of manufacturing value-added and employment generation is less than 1 per cent of total manufacturing employment. To date, the Philippines has lagged behind ASEAN's vehicle manufacturers. Motor vehicle and motorcycle production in the country was the lowest in the region in 2012 and 2013 (Figures 5.1 and 5.2). Motor vehicle production in the Philippines is only 3 per cent of Thailand's, 7 per cent of Indonesia's and 13 per cent of Malaysia's (Figure 5.1). Vietnam overtook the Philippines in 2013. Furthermore, motorcycle production in the Philippines is only 8 per cent and 22 per cent of Indonesia's and Thailand's. Likewise, international trade in vehicles generated more import payments than export receipts (Table 5.2). On the other hand, trade in auto parts and components have been more promising with exports higher than imports.

The rest of this section will present the domestic economic conflicts that have been stumbling blocks to the growth and development of the automobile industry. These obstacles have led to the industry's failure to participate competitively in the global production networks of MNCs, which have made ASEAN their production base and platform for automobile exports to developed countries. The conflicts emanate from two sources: (i) conflict in economic interests among the industry players themselves and (ii) the non-alignment and lack of coherence across government policies and programmes, resulting in inconsistent policy objectives.

3.1 Conflict in Economic Interests Among Industry Players

As was discussed earlier, the industry players comprise MNCs as well as SMEs — herein lies the conflict of economic interests. The MNCs, which have access to capital, technology and networks of export markets from their parent companies, are competitive and support initiatives for greater liberalization and competition for their regional and global operations. On the other hand, SMEs, with their low productivity and old technology and equipment, have lobbied for greater government protection. The policy on local content, which required auto assemblers to increase their domestic content from 10 per cent to 60 per cent, was clear evidence of government protection in favour of local manufacturers over MNCs. As will be discussed subsequently, this policy was eventually eliminated. The winners of govern-ment protection eventually became the losers in the industry. To date, the key players in the industry that have remained competitive, either in assembly manufacturing or part and components manufacturing, are the automobile MNCs (Aldaba 2011).

Another example of conflicting interests among the industry players can be gleaned from an analysis of the ownership structure of the subsidiaries of MNCs. Some of the country's local banks have control over significant

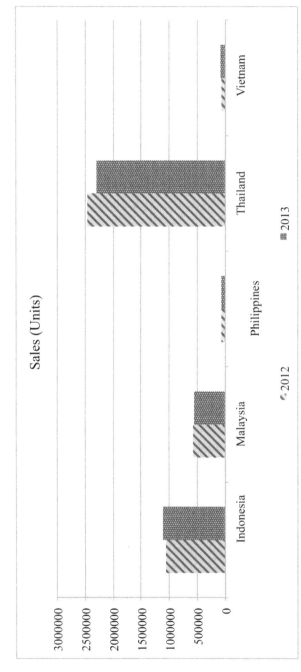

FIGURE 5.1
Motor Vehicle Units of Production, ASEAN, 2012–13 (Units)

Source: ASEAN Automotive Federation (AAF).

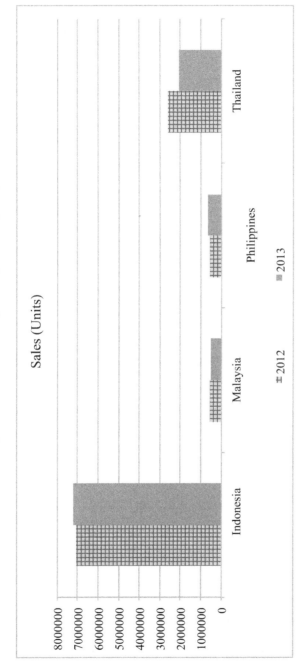

FIGURE 5.2
Motorcycle Units of Production, ASEAN, 2012–13 (Units)

Source: ASEAN Automotive Federation (AAF).

TABLE 5.2
Trade in the Automobile Industry, 2006–12 (US$ million)

Year	CBU Vehicles		Parts and components	
	Imports	Exports	Imports	Exports
2006	666	92	41	2,439
2007	1,011	64	90	2,981
2008	1,256	96	133	3,502
2009	1,270	96	151	2,605
2010	2,000	128	578	3,319
2011	1,769	90	689	3,751
2012	1,940	58	702	3,506

Note: CBU – Completely Built Unit.
Source: Chamber of Automotive Manufacturers of the Philippines, Inc. (CAMPI).

shares of major automobile MNCs in the country (Ecumenical Institute for Labor Education and Research 2011) and, hence, they have influenced the direction of capital in the industry. Capital was not designed to finance auto manufacturing. Instead, these banks have aggressively marketed automobile loans, contributing to the increase in auto sales. The increase in auto sales, however, came largely from imports, evidenced by the increase in the share of completely built unit (CBU) imports in auto sales from only 8 per cent in 2002 to 66 per cent in 2013 (Kabigting 2013). This conflict in objectives may have contributed to low investment in the industry (Table 5.3).

3.2 Lack of Coherence of Government Policies

The implementation of a local content requirements policy and the reduction in tariff rates is clear evidence of the lack of coherence across government policies. As was discussed earlier, the former scheme was meant to support the development of local parts and components manufacturers by requiring auto assemblers to increase their domestic content from 10 per cent to 60 per cent. Yet with the introduction of the tariff reduction programme in the 1990s, the tariff rate of 10 to 35 per cent levied on local parts and components was higher than the 3 per cent

TABLE 5.3
Investments in the Philippine Automobile Industry, 2002–09

Year	No. of New Motor Vehicle Programme Participants	Investments (billion pesos)
2002	3	0.293
2003	1	0.115
2004	1	0.153
2005	2	3.411
2006	3	2.651
2007	8	4.292
2008	3	5.950
2009[a]	2	0.18
Total	23	17.053

Note: a. includes January to August 2009 only
Source: Department of Trade and Industry (DTI).

tariff rate on completely knocked down (CKD) imports. Thus, it became cheaper for local assemblers to import CKD parts and components than source them locally. In general, only 10 to 15 per cent of the total parts and components requirements of local assemblers are locally produced, in contrast to Thailand where domestic suppliers provide 80 to 90 per cent of total requirements (Aldaba 2011). Thailand's supplier base is not only large but it is also competitive, allowing the country's auto assemblers to source their auto parts from local suppliers. The local content requirement was eventually eliminated in 2003 as part of the Philippines's commitment to the World Trade Organization (WTO). Similarly, tariffs within ASEAN were reduced to zero in 2010.

Delays and administrative costs at the border are yet another indicator of the lack of coherence across domestic policies when the country moved towards zero tariffs along with the rest of the ASEAN region. A 2010 study by Wignaraja, Lazaro and de Guzman shows that only 38.9 per cent of the transport sector firms use or have used the AFTA-CEPT scheme. The same study identified impediments to the use of the CEPT scheme such as the lack of information, delays and administrative costs and rent-seeking behaviour arising from the arbitrary classification of products.

With the introduction of the country's customs modernization programme, the time and cost of transactions across the border decreased between 2010 and 2015 (Table 5.4). However, the country's performance still pales in comparison to the other ASEAN-5 countries (World Bank 2014). The cost required to export and import in the Philippines has remained the highest among the ASEAN-5 (Tables 5.4 and 5.5). The country is second to Indonesia in terms of the number of documents and time required to export and import. Overall, the country ranked the lowest (65) among the ASEAN-5 with respect to ease of trading across borders (Figure 5.3). Nonetheless, the distance to frontier score increased from 74.73 in 2010 to 77.23 in 2015 indicating that the country has managed to narrow the gap between its performance and the regulatory frontier.[7]

The lack of coherence across government policies is also evident among its trade and investment policies. EO 156 prohibits the importation of all types of second-hand motor vehicles and parts and components except those imported by returning residents and members of the diplomatic corps. Yet, policies in the SEZs meant to promote FDI run counter to the objectives of EO 156. Traders have been using free port zones and SEZs as entry points for bringing duty-free used vehicles into the country. Car dealers locate their companies in the free port zones to take advantage of the duty-free privileges on second-hand vehicles from countries such as South Korea and Japan (Aldaba 2013). As a consequence, industry groups have lobbied against EO 156. Although the enforcement of this EO has been put on hold by restraining orders from the Olongapo City Regional Trial Court and the Court of Appeals in 2005 — which declared the EO to be unconstitutional and illegal — the Supreme Court affirmed its validity in 2013. Nonetheless, smuggling of used vehicles through the free port zones and special economic zones has become rampant in recent years. The smuggled cars find their way into the local market with prices 30 to 50 per cent cheaper than brand new vehicles, creating strong competition for local assemblers.

4. MANAGING DOMESTIC CONFLICTS BEYOND 2015: THE WAY FORWARD

The Philippines needs to enhance its competitiveness, as it will have to cope with greater competition from the AEC. Fortunately, several positive developments have been taking place in the domestic front in recent years. The country has consistently improved its World Economic Forum's Global Competitiveness Index (GCI) ranking;[8] it moved up thirty-

TABLE 5.4
Transactions Across Borders, ASEAN-5, 2010 and 2015

Indicators	Measure	Indonesia		Malaysia		Philippines		Thailand		Singapore	
		2010	2015	2010	2015	2010	2015	2010	2015	2010	2015
Documents to export	Number	4	4	4	4	6	6	5	5	3	3
Time to export	Days	18	17	13	11	16	15	14	14	6	6
Cost to export	Deflated US$ per container	888.6	571.8	467.8	525	892.7	596.6	709.3	595	435.7	460
Documents to import	Number	8	8	4	3	8	7	5	5	3	3
Time to import	Days	27	26	8	4	16	15	13	13	4	4
Cost to import	Deflated US$ per container	910.7	646.8	484.6	419.5	948.3	915	902.2	760	419.5	440

Source: World Bank (2009, 2014).

TABLE 5.5
Summary of Predetermined Stages and Documents for Trading Across Borders, ASEAN-5, 2015

Indicators	Time (days)					Cost (US$)				
	Indonesia	Malaysia	Philippines	Thailand	Singapore	Indonesia	Malaysia	Philippines	Thailand	Singapore
A. Stages to exports										
Customs clearance & inspection	1	1	2	1	1	125	60	85	50	50
Documents preparation	11	5	8	8	2	135	85	105	175	120
Inland transportation & handling	3	3	2	2	2	160	260	340	210	140
Ports & terminal handling	2	2	3	3	1	165	120	225	160	150
Total	**17**	**11**	**15**	**14**	**6**	**585**	**525**	**755**	**595**	**460**
B. Stages to imports										
Customs clearance & inspection	4	1	2	2	1	125	60	185	255	50
Documents preparation	13	3	8	8	1	210	120	90	135	100
Inland transportation & handling	2	2	2	1	1	160	260	340	210	140
Ports & terminal handling	7	2	3	2	1	165	120	300	160	150
Total	**26**	**8**	**15**	**13**	**4**	**660**	**560**	**915**	**760**	**440**

Source: World Bank (2014).

FIGURE 5.3
Ease of Trading Across Borders, Distance to Frontier, ASEAN-5, 2010 and 2015

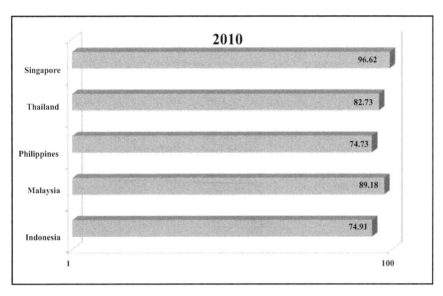

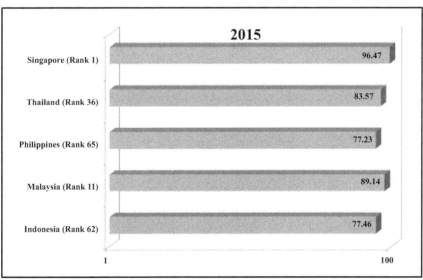

Source: World Bank (2009, 2014).

five spots since 2009 (Table 5.6). Sovereign credit ratings for the country have been positive. The Philippines earned its first ever investment grade credit rating in March 2013 when Fitch Ratings raised the country's rating from BBB– to BB+ in March 2013. In October 2013, Moody's Investment Service upgraded its rating from Ba1 to Baa3. In May 2013, Standard & Poor's Ratings Services upgraded the country's rating to BBB– and further upgraded it to BBB in May 2014. The Philippines has consistently recorded higher economic growth, making it one of the fastest growing economies in Asia. The economy grew from 3.72 per cent in 2011 to 6.6 per cent in 2012, 7.2 per cent in 2013 and 6.1 per cent in 2014. Likewise, auto sales have been growing and hit a record high in 2014 growing at 29.5 per cent (Figure 5.4).[9] The industry appears poised to benefit from high economic growth as this is expected to translate to increased sales arising from higher domestic income.

However, the above indicators are not sufficient to spur the much-needed growth for the country needs to make it an attractive production base for auto MNCs. The country should address the above-mentioned domestic conflicts, especially as the region is now at the tail end of the Blueprint implementation process.

To achieve domestic consensus on how the country should move towards achieving its AEC commitments, the government should level the playing field by compensating the potential losers under a more integrated region, thereby, improving their capability to compete and withstand competition from imports. This should come in the form of government assistance in terms of testing facilities and access to cheaper credit for local

TABLE 5.6
Global Competitiveness Ranking, Philippines

Year	Ranking
2009–2010	87
2010–2011	85
2011–2012	75
2012–2013	65
2013–2014	59
2014–2015	52

Source: Schwab (2009, 2010, 2011, 2012, 2013, 2014).

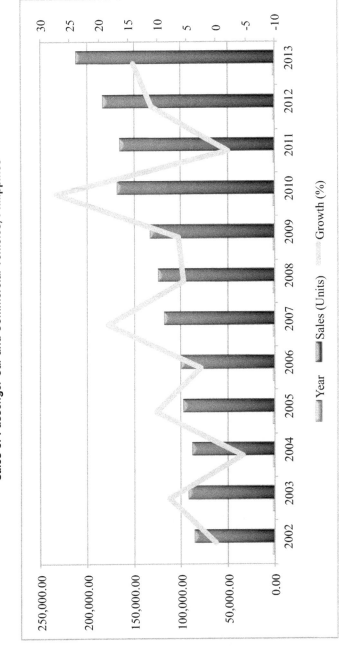

FIGURE 5.4
Sales of Passenger Car and Commercial Vehicles, Philippines

Source: Chamber of Automotive Manufacturers of the Philippines, Inc. (CAMPI).

assemblers as well as parts and components manufacturers. Testing facilities are very expensive and are often unaffordable to local parts manufacturers. However, these facilities are critical in ensuring the quality and safety of local parts and components. Access to credit in terms of lower interest rates will allow local manufacturers to expand and build their manufacturing capabilities as well as their research and development facilities.

At the same time, coherence and alignment of the different policy reforms is crucial. With zero tariffs under the AEC, competitiveness will be defined in terms of cost and quality. Fundamental to lowering costs and cutting administrative delays in production and trade is the completion of the PNSW and its eventual integration with the ASW. By limiting human intervention at customs transactions, the PNSW and ASW will push the government to make port operations transparent and efficient and thereby reduce costs. However, full implementation of the PNSW requires harmonization and standardization of all trade-related data, and integration among all the agencies involved. Unless all partner agencies keep pace with the move towards customs modernization by using ICT and e-commerce in handling the processing of all applications related to exports and imports such as licences, permits, clearances and certificates, the country will not realize the full benefits of the PNSW and ASW.

In terms of quality, the country should harmonize its standards and technical regulations with the rest of the region to enable companies to consolidate their regional and global production. This is the best way of dealing with non-tariff barriers to trade, not only for the automobile industry but for other industries as well.

To avoid conflict in trade and investment policies, investment incentives should be harmonized. Investment incentives given to investors differ across the government agencies in charge of promoting investments such as the BOI, PEZA, SBMA and CDC resulting in competition among these agencies. For example, the BOI and PEZA grant four to eight years of income tax holidays as an investment incentive, while the SBMA and CDC do not. Also, the BOI provides tax credit for raw materials and supplies while the PEZA, SBMA and CDC grant tax and duty exemption for the same. The absence of uniform legislation on the granting of incentives may create legal issues and affect investment inflows.

Moreover, harmonization will be ensured if investment promotion and facilitation are centralized under one agency. The absence of an overall integrated investment promotion and facilitation strategy by the abovementioned agencies has created a complex system of investment promotion at both the local and national level (Aldaba 2013). Such an environment has affected the certainty of investment in the country. Therefore, there is a need to establish a one-stop lead agency for investment promotion and facilitation activities.

Finally, the Philippines should find niche products and markets for the automobile industry. With zero tariffs, a small domestic market, the lack of a strong local supplier base and imports of vehicles expected to increase further, becoming an export platform for automobile companies, as in the case of Thailand, may not be feasible in the short run. Thus, the country's automobile industry should specialize in products in which it can compete — niche products that are complementary to the global production networks based in the region. Aldaba (2014) has identified parts of tractors and motor vehicles as one of the emerging champions in the Philippine manufacturing industry roadmap. Emerging champions are products with increasing levels of competitiveness, indicating the need to build on such product discoveries. The industry is anticipating the release of the Comprehensive Automotive Resurgence Strategy (CARS), the government's automotive industry roadmap, within the year. It is hoped that the roadmap will include the abovementioned policy reforms.

5. SUMMARY AND CONCLUDING REMARKS

Given the growth limitations experienced in other parts of the world, the ASEAN region remains an attractive market. The removal of tariffs and other trade restrictions under the AEC has created a regional market of over 600 million people that is of sufficient size to allow for economies of scale in production. As the market expands, however, regional competition from exports also increases. For the automobile industry, competition is created not only among industry players but also within the network of subsidiaries of MNCs as well as among assemblers and parts manufacturers that are located in other countries.

As the deadline for the AEC approaches, the Philippines has yet to complete the implementation of its commitments under the Blueprint. While it is true that the government has implemented most of its commitments, the effects of policy reforms have yet to make a significant impact on the economy. As the country faces stronger competition from a more integrated AEC, the government should focus its efforts by addressing the economic conflicts created by the lack of coherence across legislation, policies and programmes. It is also necessary to enhance the competitiveness of weak industry players to help them withstand competition just as much as key industry players, which have benefitted from greater openness. The experience of the country's automobile industry further shows that coherence and well-coordinated policies indeed matter.

APPENDIX
Government Programmes and Policies on the Philippine Automotive Industry

Year	Programme/Policy	Objectives
1973	• Progressive Car Manufacturing Program (PCMP) • Progressive Truck Manufacturing Program (PTMP)	– increase local assemblers' domestic content from 10 per cent in 1973 to 60 per cent in 1976 – promote horizontal integration in the industry through subcontracting and transfer of technology – build up exports of manufactured products in a regional (ASEAN) automotive complementation programme
1987	• Car Development Program (CDP)	– increase local assemblers' domestic content from 32.26 per cent in 1988 to 40 per cent in 1990 – develop a viable automotive parts manufacturing industry – facilitate technology transfer and development – generate employment, make available reasonably priced passenger cars, and earn and save foreign exchange for the country
1990	• People's Car Program (PCP)	– include the assembly of smaller cars, named as people's cars, or passenger cars with gasoline engine displacement of not more than 1200 cc – meet the minimum local content usage from 35 per cent in 1991 to 51 per cent in 1993
1992	• Luxury Car Program	– allow the entry of high-end passenger cars defined as passenger cars with engine displacement greater than 2800 cc
1994	• ASEAN Industrial Joint Venture (AIJV) Scheme	– allow the entry of new assemblers under the ASEAN Industrial Joint Venture (AIJV) Scheme
1996	• Memorandum Order Number 346 • Car Development Program (CDV) • Commercial Vehicle Development Program (CVDP)	– open up the closed vehicle categories to new participants and remove restrictions on the number of models and variants – terminate the foreign exchange and local content requirements under the CDP and CVDP in the year 2000

continued on next page

APPENDIX — *cont'd*

Year	Programme/Policy	Objectives
2002	• New Motor Vehicle Development Program (EO 156)	– ban the importation of all types of used motor vehicles, and parts and components, except those that may be allowed under certain conditions – restructure the Most Favoured Nation (MFN) tariff rates for motor vehicles and their new materials and parts and components at such rates that will encourage the development of the Philippine motor vehicle industry. – restructure the current excise tax system for motor vehicles with the end view of creating a simple, fair and stable tax structure – continue the application of AICO scheme as may be adopted by ASEAN – give incentives to assemblers and parts and components makers for the export of CBUs and parts and components
2003	• EO 262 • EO244	– modify the tariff rates on motor vehicle parts and components – provide special incentives to certain CBU exports
2004	• EO 312	– modify EO 244 to expand coverage of CBU exports and provide special incentives for the export of certain CBUs

Source: Aldaba (2007).

Notes

The author would like to acknowledge the excellent research assistance provided by Inalyn Lapating.

1. Executive Order No. 850, s. 2009: Modifying the Rates of Duty on Certain Imported Articles as Provided for Under the Tariff and Customs Code of 1978, as Amended in Order to Implement the Commitment to Eliminate the Tariff Rates on the Remaining Products in the Inclusion List in year 2010 under the Common Effective Preferential Tariff (CEPT) scheme for the ASEAN Free Trade Area (AFTA)/ASEAN Trade in Goods Agreement (ATIGA).

2. Republic Act 10611, "An Act To Strengthen The Food Safety Regulatory System In The Country To Protect Consumer Health And Facilitate Market Access Of Local Foods And Food Products, And For Other Purposes" is known as the *Food Safety Act of 2013*.

3. RA 10642 or "An Act Strengthening Consumer Protection in the Purchase of Brand New Motor Vehicles". The law's implementing rules and regulations (IRR) were released in November 2014 with the Department of Trade and Industry (DTI) as the sole implementing agency.

4. Among others, the functions included in the PNSW include: registration of importers/exporters via the Internet; application for and issuance of permits, licences and clearances for exports and imports; e-payment for traders to pay agency fees; digital signatures; and so on.

5. This paragraph was taken from Austria (2015).

6. Executive Order No. 858, s. 2010: Promulgating the Eighth Regular Foreign Investment Negative List.

7. The distance to frontier score is indicated by a scale of 0 to 100, where 0 represents the worst performance and 100 the frontier. The score in any given year measures how far an economy is from the best performance in that year. On the other hand, the difference in score between any period indicates the extent to which an economy has closed the gap to the regulatory frontier overtime (World Bank 2014).

8. The GCI measures microeconomic and macroeconomic foundations of national competitiveness.

9. Sales went up from 181,283 units in 2013 to 234,747 units in 2014 (CAMPI).

References

Aldaba, Rafaelita. "Assessing the Competitiveness of the Philippine Auto Parts Industry". Discussion Paper Series No. 2007-14. Makati: Philippine Institute for Development Studies (PIDS), 2007.

———. "Globalization and the Need for Strategic Government-Industry

Cooperation in the Philippine Automotive Industry". Discussion Paper Series No. 2008-21. Makati: PIDS, 2008.

————. "Getting ready for the ASEAN Economic Community 2015: Philippine Investment Liberalization and Facilitation". Discussion Paper Series No. 2013-13. Makati: PIDS, 2013.

————. "The Philippine Manufacturing Industry Roadmap: Agenda for New Industrial Policy, High Productivity Jobs, and Inclusive Growth". Discussion Paper Series No. 2014-32. Makati: PIDS, 2014.

————, Roehlano Briones, Danilo Israel, Gilbert M. Llanto, Erlinda Medalla and Melanie Milo. "The ASEAN Economic Community and the Philippines: Implementation, Outcomes, Impacts, and the Way Forward". Discussion Paper Series No. 2013-01. Makati: PIDS, 2013.

ASEAN Secretariat. *Roadmap for an ASEAN Community 2009–2015.* Jakarta: The ASEAN Secretariat, 2009.

Austria, Myrna. *The Philippines in the Global Trading Environment.* Makati: PIDS, 2003.

————. "Non-tariff barriers: A Challenge to Achieving the ASEAN Economic Community". In *The ASEAN Economic Community: A Work in Progress,* edited by Sanchita Basu Das, Jayant Menon, Omkar L. Shrestha and Rodolfo Severino. Singapore: Institute of Southeast Asian Studies, 2013.

————. "Towards a Free Flow of Investment: Is the ASEAN Making Progress?". In *The Regionalization of International Investment Agreements,* edited by N. Jansen Calamita and Mavluda Sattorva. London: British Institute of International and Comparative Law, 2015.

Ecumenical Institute for Labor Education and Research. "Capital Mobility in the Philippine Automotive Industry and its Impact on Workers". Capital Mobility Research Paper Series No. 2. Hong Kong: Asia Monitor Resource Center, 2011.

Esguerra, Emmanuel. *Overview of the Philippines' Action Plan for AEC 2015.* National Economic and Development Authority (NEDA), 2014.

Kabigting, Ramon Vicente. "The Use of Statistics in the Philippine Automotive Industry Roadmap". Paper presented at the 12th National Convention on Statistics, Mandaluyong City, Philippines, 2013.

Medalla, Erlinda. "Trade Facilitation: NSW and ASW". In *The ASEAN Economic Community and the Philippines: Implementation, Outcomes, Impacts, and Ways Forward (Full Report),* edited by Rafaelita Aldaba, Roehlano Briones, Danilo Israel, Gilbert M. Llanto, Erlinda Medalla and Melanie Milo. Discussion Paper Series No. 2013-01. Makati: PIDS, 2013.

Rosellon, Maureen and Erlinda Medalla. "ASEAN+1 FTAs and Global Value Chains in East Asia: The Case of the Philippine Automotive and Electronics Sectors". In *ASEAN+1 FTAs and Global Value Chains in East Asia,* edited by Christopher Findlay. ERIA Research Project Report 2010-29, Jakarta: ERIA, 2011.

Schwab, Klaus, ed. *The Global Competitiveness Report 2009–2010*. Geneva: World Economic Forum, 2009.

————. *The Global Competitiveness Report 2010–2011*. Geneva: World Economic Forum, 2010.

————. *The Global Competitiveness Report 2011–2012*. Geneva: World Economic Forum, 2011.

————. *The Global Competitiveness Report 2012–2013*. Geneva: World Economic Forum, 2012.

————. *The Global Competitiveness Report 2013–2014*. Geneva: World Economic Forum, 2013.

———— *The Global Competitiveness Report 2014–2015*. Geneva: World Economic Forum, 2014.

Urata, Shujiro and Mitsuyo Ando. "Investment Climate Study on ASEAN Member Countries". ERIA Research Project Report 2009, no. 3. Jakarta: ERIA, 2010.

Wignaraja, Ganesh, Dorothea Lazaro and Genevieve DeGuzman. "FTAs and the Philippine Business: Evidence from Transport, Food and Electronics Firms". ADB Working Paper 185. Tokyo: Asian Development Bank, 2010.

World Bank. *Doing Business 2010, Reforming Through Difficult Times*. Washington, D.C.: International Bank for Reconstruction and Development/The World Bank, 2009.

————. *Doing Business 2015, Going Beyond Efficiency*. Washington, D.C.: International Bank for Reconstruction and Development/World Bank, 2014.

6

THE AEC BEYOND 2015
Implementation and Challenges
for Singapore

Chia Siow Yue and Sanchita Basu Das

1. INTRODUCTION

Given its small-size and dearth of natural resources, Singapore's development strategy was to create an open economy, with the world and the region as its hinterland. This has enabled Singapore to progress from a third world city-state, at the beginning of its political independence in 1965, into a first world economy. Decades of growth have transformed a regional entrepot into an export-manufacturing platform, a services hub and a knowledge-based economy. The government played a crucial role in this process, initially to jump-start industrialization and increasingly to facilitate economic restructuring. Policy orientation is towards a free-trade and liberal foreign direct investment (FDI) regime, heavy investments in physical infrastructure, human capital to ease supply constraints and achieve competitiveness, a pro-business environment with an efficient and non-corrupt bureaucracy, a stable macroeconomic and industrial relations environment, efficient regulations and a minimal fiscal burden.

Singapore's participation in ASEAN and the ASEAN Economic Community (AEC) is for both strategic and economic reasons. On strategic grounds, ASEAN helps Singapore to achieve its goals of regional peace and stability, and regional cooperation in handling trans-boundary problems of environmental pollution, pandemic outbreaks, security issues and financial contagion. On the economic front, ASEAN economic integration facilitates Singapore's exports and outward investment flows to neighbouring countries and helps anchor Singapore as a key node in regional production networks and as a regional services hub.

For many economies, opening up to globalization and regionalization — with their attendant winners and losers — have engendered strong domestic political economy responses. In the AEC, this is a key reason for the slow and weak implementation of many initiatives. Fortunately for Singapore, the domestic lobbies and pressures hindering implementation of liberalization commitments have been weak. This is in part due to the small size of the city-state and its long exposure to the competitive forces of globalization and regionalization. In part, it may also be attributed to the high trust of Singaporeans in their political and economic leadership, high employment rates and a low incidence of poverty. Hence, as the case studies on the electronics and aviation sectors illustrate, there is very little domestic pressure in Singapore, particularly against the AEC's liberalization process. Instead, pressure comes mostly from Singapore's general approach of adopting non-protectionist measures to manage global competition.

The following section (section 2) discusses the determinants of Singapore's economic and trade strategies. Section 3 discusses Singapore's progress and challenges in implementing AEC initiatives. Sections 4 and 5 examine two case studies, the electronic and aviation sectors, to identify how they address global and regional challenges, including the AEC. Section 6 concludes this chapter.

2. SINGAPORE'S ECONOMIC AND TRADE STRATEGIES

This section underlines the distinctiveness of Singapore's economic and trade strategies, which contributes to its efforts in the AEC.

2.1 Economic Strategy

As the Singapore economy grew rapidly in the 1970s and 1980s, a variety of factors — competition from regional low-cost producers, Singapore's labour shortage and labour costs — led to economic restructuring away from labour-intensive towards capital-intensive, high value-added and knowledge-based activities. In the electronics sector, high value-added segments have replaced low value-added segments. In the chemicals and petrochemicals sector, Jurong Island has been developed into a dedicated and vertically integrated chemicals complex. The government facilitates restructuring through the creation of supporting physical and institutional infrastructures, provision of human capital resources, provision of financial incentives for research and development (R&D), innovation and creativity. There are also parallel efforts to reduce input costs, including increased labour market flexibility (particularly through the adoption of a flexible wage system), and continuing liberalization of the services and utilities sectors.

Since 1991, Singapore's economic strategy has been to develop manufacturing and services as twin pillars of the economy. The *1991 Strategic Economic Plan* (MTI 1991) outlined the promotion and development of Singapore as a total business centre, and the development of high-tech and high value-added manufacturing and services as twin engines of growth. In manufacturing, the emphasis has been on industry clusters, such as chemicals and petro-chemicals, shipbuilding and ship repair, electronics and biomedical sciences; as well as strengthening innovation, through linkages between industry, R&D and intellectual property protection, and bridging the gap between the research and commercialization of products and processes. Liberalization and facilitation measures ensure Singapore remains a key node in the global value chain. This strategy can clearly be observed in Singapore's electronics industry, described later, as the city-state is positioning itself as a hub for the high value-added activities of capital-intensive manufacturing, assembly, R&D, and headquarter activities.

In services, the focus has been on the development of Singapore as a services hub in: commerce and logistics; maritime and air transport; information and communications technology (ICT); finance; and professional services. For example, to maintain its international maritime and air hub status amidst intensifying regional competition, the government has adopted measures to strengthen the competitiveness of Singapore as a one-stop shop for all port, shipping and maritime activities. In the air transport sector, it has further opened up air services bilaterally and within the ASEAN framework. This is, once again, observed in the case study of the aviation industry described later in this paper.

2.2 Trade Strategy

Singapore has a very high trade/GDP ratio of over 300 per cent, reflecting its position as a major transhipment hub. Entrepot exports (also known as re-exports) comprise half of Singapore's total exports and have shifted from traditional Southeast Asian primary commodities to machinery and equipment, reflecting the growing industrialization of the region and the establishment of regional production networks. They are now mainly in electronics, petroleum and products, and chemicals and products. Domestic exports have been increasingly capital- and technology-intensive. These, in turn, have pushed Singapore to practice free trade in goods for a long time, save for the six tariff lines imposed on alcoholic beverages.[1]

As for services sector liberalization, it has accelerated in recent years, in line with the objective of consolidating and enhancing Singapore as a regional services hub, although government-linked companies (GLCs) continue to dominate essential services.

Singapore pursues a three-tier trade strategy, simultaneously supporting multilateralism via the World Trade Organization (WTO), as well as regionalism and bilateralism via free trade agreements (FTAs). At the WTO, Singapore participates in the Information Technology Agreement (ITA) and Plurilateral Agreement on Government Procurement and is a signatory to the GATS protocols on telecommunications and financial services. Singapore's GATS commitments, and although they cover a wide range of services sub-sectors, could be categorized as limited liberalization, especially when compared to its goods economy. Under its Schedule of Commitments, market access for natural persons are unbound, except for the temporary movement of intra-corporate transferees. Commercial presence restrictions apply to foreigners registering their companies or businesses in Singapore.

In East Asia, Singapore is one of the most active economies in forging regional and bilateral FTAs. Currently, it is participating in twenty FTAs that are at different stages of negotiation and implementation.[2] The city-state views FTAs as a way to consolidate its political and economic relations with selected countries.

These have implications for a regional agreement like the AEC, as Singapore already has advanced trade liberalization policies for goods. AEC measures such as tariff elimination, trade facilitation through a National Single Window or investment facilitation were carried out by Singapore long before the AEC initiatives. However, it is the limited liberalization of services under GATS that enables Singapore to offer its services markets on a preferential basis to ASEAN countries in exchange for greater market access for Singapore manufactures.

The beneficiaries of the city-state's trade policies are the Singapore-based domestic and foreign companies, goods exporters and service providers and investors. Singapore consumers benefit little since imports already enter Singapore duty-free, except for alcoholic beverages, which enjoy zero preferential tariffs under FTAs. However, the liberalization of trade in services leads to an inflow of foreign service providers, therefore, improving the quality of services available to Singapore consumers. There are also indirect benefits, as the expansion of trade and investment also leads to job creation. In particular, FTAs are expected to draw more FDI into Singapore, creating jobs and spin-offs for domestic industries. Singapore's FTAs give the country a competitive advantage in attracting foreign companies to use Singapore as a headquarters for their regional activities and as a gateway to explore opportunities in FTA partner-countries. They can form partnerships with Singapore companies to enter third countries, or set up operations in Singapore and help stimulate local enterprises. As the city-state increasingly seeks outward direct investments, national and preferential treatment and investment protection measures in FTAs encourages more Singapore enterprises to venture abroad.

3. SINGAPORE IN THE AEC: PROGRESS AND CHALLENGES IN IMPLEMENTATION

Chia (2014) notes that there are two ways of interpreting progress in AEC implementation. The first is to measure progress against the actions listed in the 2007 AEC Blueprint, while the second is to assess current AEC commitments against its four main objectives of: (1) a single market and production base; (2) a competitive economic region; (3) equitable economic development; and (4) integration into the global economy. The second interpretation is difficult to achieve as the AEC is still far from achieving its stated objectives. The first interpretation also appears difficult to achieve by the deadline (the end of 2015). The AEC Scorecard indicates that up to March 2013 only 82.1 per cent of the targeted measures in the Blueprint have been implemented.[3] Although the Blueprint did not reveal the implementation performance of individual ASEAN countries, Singapore is one of the countries that has achieved a high level of implementation.[4]

On the free flow of goods, Singapore has had zero tariffs for all products in the Inclusion List for the Common Effective Preferential Tariff (CEPT) under the ASEAN Free Trade Area (AFTA) long before the stipulated deadline of 1 January 2010. However, Singapore has not fully eliminated all non-tariff measures (NTMs) because some of them are not non-tariff barriers (NTBs) to intra-ASEAN trade.[5] Ando and Obashi (2010) have found that almost half of all tariff lines in ASEAN are linked to at least one NTM, with Singapore below the ASEAN average. In addition, Austria (2013) has found that Singapore's few NTMs do not affect any tariff lines.[6] Removing NTMs remains one of the biggest challenges to ASEAN's economic integration. Another is the establishment of the ASEAN Single Window (ASW) as a network of National Single Windows. In this respect, Singapore is a pioneer, with its TradeNet having been in operation since 1989.

On services, Singapore has completed nine packages of commitments to liberalize services trade under the ASEAN Framework Agreement on Services (AFAS), and the government is presently consulting relevant domestic agencies for the tenth package. ASEAN-wide, negotiations under AFAS have resulted only in marginal services liberalization, mainly because services is a "sensitive" sector with a very large employment impact and some uncompetitive services demanding national protection (Nikomborirak and Jitdumrong 2013). Among the designated priority integration services sectors, only tourism services have made considerable progress. The ASEAN National Tourism Organizations have developed a vision statement for developing ASEAN as a quality tourism destination by 2025 (ASEAN Secretariat 2015). There is no visa requirement for ASEAN tourists, except for Myanmar. Of Singapore's 15.6 million international travellers in 2013, around 40 per cent were from the ASEAN region.

On investment flows, an enhanced ASEAN Comprehensive Investment Agreement (ACIA) has been in place since April 2012. Table 6.1 shows Singapore ranks highly in the Logistics Performance Index, Ease of Doing Business Index and Global Competitiveness Index. While FDI inflows into ASEAN have increased from US$21.8 billion in 2000 to US$110.3 billion in 2012, the predominant share has gone to Singapore.

Singapore, under the AEC, allows for flows of skilled professionals (mode 4) to facilitate flows of services and investments. It has concluded

TABLE 6.1
Attractiveness of ASEAN Member Countries and Inward FDI Flows

	Ranking in Logistics Performance Index, 2014[a]	Ranking in Ease of Doing Business, 2012[b]	Ranking in Global Competitiveness Index, 2012–13[c]	Value of FDI, US$ billion (Share in ASEAN FDI Flows, %), 2010–12
Brunei	—	83	28	9.1 (1.2)
Cambodia	83	138	85	6.9 (0.9)
Indonesia	53	129	50	81.1 (11.0)
Laos	131	165	—	2.1 (0.3)
Malaysia	25	18	25	72.5 (9.8)
Myanmar	145	—	—	9.9 (1.3)
Philippines	57	136	65	22.3 (3.0)
Singapore	5	1	2	382.5 (51.7)
Thailand	35	17	38	93.9 (12.7)
Vietnam	48	98	75	59.1 (8.0)
Total ASEAN	—	—	—	739.5 (100.0)

Note: a. out of 160 countries; b. out of 183 economies; c. out of 144 countries.
Source: Logistics Performance Index 2014, *Doing Business 2012*, World Bank; World Competitiveness Index, 2012–2013; *The ASEAN Statistical Yearbook, 2013*, The ASEAN Secretariat.

eight Mutual Recognition Arrangements (MRAs)[7] with other ASEAN members. But it is only the architectural and engineering services that provide standardized recognitions of the skill level of registered ASEAN architects and engineers. As noted by Chia (2011*a*), MRAs only provide frameworks to promote the mobility of professionals between member states and do not guarantee market access, as most countries impose rules and restrictions on the employment of foreigners, including constitutional prohibitions and requirements for employment visas and passes.

Free trade, investments and the movement of people in ASEAN have to be supported by improved physical connectivity. The 2010 Master Plan on ASEAN Connectivity (MPAC) aims to reduce transportation and logistics costs. For Singapore, its regional connectivity remains a work-in-progress. Singapore has ratified all protocols under key transport facilitation agreements such as the ASEAN Framework Agreement on the Facilitation of Inter-State Transport (AFAFIST) and the ASEAN Framework Agreement on Multimodal Transport (AFAMT). However, it has yet to ratify all the protocols of the ASEAN Framework Agreement on the Facilitation of Goods in Transit (AFAFGIT).

On the ASEAN objective of equitable economic development, infrastructure availability helps to narrow the development gap among countries, and between core and peripheral areas. ASEAN also has the Initiative for ASEAN Integration (IAI), in which more developed ASEAN members help those that are less developed. Singapore, as the most developed member of ASEAN, has spent around US$135 million cumulatively on various initiatives during 2001–15. Most of Singapore's contribution goes into human resource development and related training projects.[8]

ASEAN's open regionalism is seen in its FTAs with various major trading and investment partners, including China, Japan, South Korea, India and Australia-New Zealand, which have become the basis for the Regional Comprehensive Economic Partnership (RCEP) Agreement currently under negotiation. Except for the ASEAN-China FTA, Singapore has played a pathfinder role for ASEAN by having first established bilateral FTAs with Japan, South Korea, India, Australia and New Zealand. Its bilateral FTAs with the United States (US) and with the European Union (EU) could also eventually lead to ASEAN FTAs with these two countries.

In sum, Singapore is one of the lead countries in AEC implementation. A key point to note is that the city-state has been liberalizing its real economy long before it embarked on the journey of establishing an AEC. By having an "open economy" as its key strategy and being a part of several bilateral FTAs, that are both wider and deeper in scope vis-à-vis the AEC, the city-state has already exposed itself to the competitive forces of globalization and regionalization. Hence, the current domestic challenges for Singapore cannot be solely attributed to the AEC.

Nonetheless, there are both proponents and opponents of globalization, including ASEAN economic integration. While the winners are businesses and workers in expanding export-oriented sectors, the losers are businesses and workers in uncompetitive sectors facing increasing import and inward FDI challenges, as well as Singaporean professionals facing competition from inflows of ASEAN professionals.[9] However, the Singapore policy response to these competitive challenges is not to slow down implementation. Instead, it is facilitating the necessary restructuring of the economy through measures that help businesses to be more competitive, and retrenched workers more marketable through retraining. The fact that the Singapore labour market remains tight has helped retrenched workers to find alternative employment, particularly as the government has tightened the inflow of foreign workers since 2011.[10]

The subsequent sections present case studies from the manufacturing and services sector that showcase Singapore's challenges from increased competition and its policy response.

4. CASE STUDY OF MANUFACTURING PRODUCTION NETWORK: THE SINGAPORE ELECTRONIC SECTOR

With regard to the Singapore manufacturing sector, the AEC aims to increase intra-regional trade, connect it with global supply chains and attract more investment. Merchandise imports to Singapore have always enjoyed free trade. Similarly, exports have close to free trade as tariffs have been reduced to zero for most of the manufacturing products across all ASEAN countries. However, most of the benefits for the manufacturing sector arise from economies of scale, harmonization of technical regulations, customs modernization and MRAs, which allow companies to produce standardized products, thereby avoiding duplicative testing and pool skilled labour, mainly through intra-corporate transfers. The electronics sector is one of the industries that will significantly benefit from ASEAN integration (McKinsey 2014).

4.1 Singapore's Electronics Sector

Singapore is a prominent location in ASEAN for electronics manufacturing. It currently hosts: fourteen silicon wafer fabrication plants, including the world's top three wafer foundries; twenty semiconductor assembly and test operations, including three of the world's top six outsourced semiconductor assembly and test companies; fifteen fabless semiconductor companies; and forty integrated circuit (IC) design centres. The city-state is a leading manufacturer of hard disk drives and is a major hard disk media manufacturing location, accounting for about 40 per cent of the world's hard disk media volume.[11]

Singapore's electronics industry comprises: subsidiaries of multinational corporations (MNCs; such as Broadcom Singapore); several large indigenous firms (Chartered Semiconductor, Creative Technology and Venture Corp.); and a range of small-cap firms supplying components to major producers. Singapore GLCs have started a number of joint ventures with foreign MNCs, such as Texas Instruments and Hewlett-Packard of the United States, and Canon of Japan. The number of electronics-related establishments increased from 270 in 1999 to 310 in 2010, accounting for more than 3 per cent of total establishments in the manufacturing sector (Toh 2014).

Table 6.2 shows selected performance indicators of the electronics sector. The sector appeared to be on a downward trend since early 2000. From 1991 to 2013, output expanded from S$42 billion to S$83 billion, but the share in total manufacturing declined from 45.1 per cent to 28.1 per cent. The electronic sector's share of total manufacturing value-added, employment and direct exports also declined.

One reason for the decline is the rapid growth of other manufacturing activities in Singapore's domestic economy, like pharmaceuticals. Moreover, the electronics sector has been facing rapid changes in technology and intense competition since the late 1990s, leading to cost-cutting measures by leading firms and difficulties in funding R&D. These developments have affected some Singaporean firms too, such as Chartered Semiconductors.[12] In addition, the drop in the absolute number of workers in the sector can be attributed to the sector's shift from labour-intensive to technology-intensive, and higher value-added activities (Toh 2014). Indeed, the labour productivity of the electronic sector was at 205 during 2011–13, higher than the manufacturing sector average of 140.4 over the same period.

TABLE 6.2
Selected Performance Indicators for Singapore Electronics Sector

	1991–95	1996–2000	2001–05	2006–10	2011–13
Output (S$ billion)	41.8 (45.1)	67.9 (50.1)	68.1 (40.0)	78.8 (31.5)	83.0[a] (28.1)
Value-Added (S$ billion)	7.6 (35.0)	12.5 (40.4)	13.4 (33.2)	15.5 (29.6)	16.2[a] (27.5)
Employment ('000)	122.2 (33.8)	114.4 (32.3)	93.1 (26.1)	87.6 (21.3)	79.4[a] (18.9)
Yearly Av. Fixed Asset Investment (S$ billion)	–	3.6 (30.6)	4.5 (52.8)	4.6 (37.4)	5.6 (50.5)
Domestic Export at the end of the period (S$ billion)	59.3 (60.3)	74.4 (54.7)	75.4 (36.3)	65.0 (26.1)	48.8 (17.8)
Productivity					
VA per Worker ($'000 per worker)	32.5	82.2	130.2	207.2	205.0

Note: The figures in brackets denote % share of total manufacturing; a- the numbers for the year 2013 are predicted.
Source: Ministry of Trade and Industry Singapore, *Economic Survey of Singapore*, various issues; Department of Statistics, *Yearbook of Statistics* (various issues), Singapore.

4.2 Trade Patterns of the Electronics Sector

Appendix 1 shows that the average annual growth rate of electronics exports slowed down from 9 per cent in the 1998–2005 period to around 1 per cent recently, while growth rates of re-exports also slowed down from 16.2 per cent to 1.7 per cent, respectively, over the same period. The downward trend is also evident for domestic exports. While some of the downward trend can be attributed to upswings and downswings in the global electronics industry, the loss of competitiveness of some segments of the Singapore electronics sector is also another contributing factor. Positive growth during 2005–13 was recorded for integrated circuits (IC), personal computers (PC), parts of IC, while negative growth was recorded for parts of PC, disk drives, telecoms equipment and consumer electronics. In recent years, increased demand for digital technology (such as TV and cameras) helped to maintain the growth of the electronics sector.

A key global trend affecting Singapore's electronics sector since the late 1980s and early 1990s was the development of multi-stage production networks across national boundaries (Athukorala and Kohpaiboon 2015). Singapore embarked on the development of this sector in assembly activities that were labour-intensive. With the rise in wages, these activities were re-located to lower cost production sites such as Malaysia, Thailand and the Philippines.[13] The entrance of China in these activities further accelerated the relocation of assembly activities to China due to its comparative cost advantage in these activities then. This pushed domestic policy-makers to think of strategies to restructure the industry. The government facilitated restructuring activities to move up the value chain by providing supporting incentives, including fiscal incentives, R&D grants, providing physical infrastructure and training human resources. The government also carried out parallel efforts to reduce input costs by introducing labour market flexibility, in terms of adopting flexible wage systems and easing policies for the temporary movement of professionals.

Thus, over the years, Singapore's electronics industry, as part of the regional production network, moved from low-skill component assembly and testing to component design and fabrication, R&D, capital-intensive production processes and, assem-bly for original equipment manufacturers (OEM). There is also a shift towards the provision of headquarter services for production facilities located among its neighbours. This restructuring of Singapore's electronics industry and its role in production networks is also reflected in its trade pattern, as trade in parts and components experienced a declining share of total electronics trade (Appendix 1). However, the shift to services is not captured in merchandise trade data (Wong 2007).

As for the geographical distribution of Singapore's electronics trade, shown in Appendix 2, ASEAN is important for both exports and imports, with Malaysia as the biggest trading partner. Intra-industry dominated the trade between ASEAN states and other northeast Asian countries such as China and Taiwan. For Singapore exports, while ASEAN's share fell from 25 to 21 per cent during the 2003–13 period (mainly due to the declining share of Malaysia) and that of the United States from 19.4 per cent to 6.3 per cent, the converse happened with China, Japan and Korea, whose collective share rose from 18 to 30 per cent. For Singapore imports, ASEAN's share dropped from 42 per cent in 2003 to 23 per cent in 2013. Likewise, the shares of Japan and the United States also declined, while the share of China, Korea and other Asia (including Taiwan) rose.

This change in the structure of electronics trade in East Asia is mainly attributed to the rise of China in the regional production network. As China emerged as a final assembly location, it created demand for parts and components (P&C) from ASEAN countries. Singapore moved to high-value tasks while low-value activities were relocated to late industrializers such as Vietnam. Another factor that has contributed to the East Asian electronics trade is the liberalization of the industry, under the WTO's plurilateral Information Technology Agreement (ITA) (Baldwin 2006). This agreement eliminates tariff duties on imports of ICT products and includes six ASEAN countries — Indonesia, Malaysia, Philippines, Singapore, Thailand and Vietnam — and China, Japan and Korea.

In summary, Singapore's electronics sector is part of the regional production network, although its importance has changed over the years. It faced severe competition from rapid technological change and price competition from new emerging markets, which made it harder for domestic firms (such as Chartered Semiconductor, Venture Corp and Creative Technology) to keep pace with rich foreign MNCs and fund the required R&D.

With China and Korea emerging as important production locations for the electronics industry, intra-regional trade for the city-state is more significant with ASEAN+3 countries, rather than with ASEAN alone. This is where regional economic cooperation initiatives like the AEC and its ASEAN+1 FTAs assume importance. While the tariff rates have already been lowered, it is the other cooperation measures like physical and institutional connectivity, harmonization of technical regulations and MRAs of products that are needed to reduce the transaction costs arising from transnational economic activities (Kimura and Obashi 2011). An arrangement like AEC and its initiatives on intellectual property rights (IPR) and competition law also prepare the export-oriented domestic industries to become competitive in the world market, eventually facilitating their participation at a multilateral level.

4.3 Singapore Electronics Sector and the Labour Force

The alignment of Singapore's electronics sector to the changing production structure in the region coincided with changing employment patterns. Much of the public anxiety about this trend is related to job losses in the electronic sector due to closures, relocations and technological change.[14] Some critics of globalization and trade agreements argue that Singapore's PMET (professionals, managers, engineers and technicians) jobs have been taken away from local citizens. This is because as Singapore is continuously upgrading, it adopts a flexible foreign manpower policy to meet the new skill sets demanded by emerging industries and activities. While this helps to address the domestic skill-gap in the short-run, it also generates a fear of the crowding out of local professionals, even though policy-makers have argued that these measures will eventually lead to high-paying job opportunities for locals in the future.[15] As shown in Table 6.3, employment in the electronics sector fell from 106,000 in December 2008 to 90,000 in December 2013,[16] with the largest percentage of redundancy found in the professional category in the manufacturing sector.

Thus, the relationship between globalization and job anxiety is complicated. There could be many factors contributing to job loss, but trade gets most of the blame due to its visibility. In particular, contemporary trade agreements, which include the movement of natural persons as is the case with the AEC, is perceived to contribute to the loss of professional jobs in Singapore.[17]

The Singapore government has adopted various measures to meet the problem. For the workforce, these include adjustment assistance (conducting job fairs and job counselling) and education (which includes training to upgrade workforce skills). The question of whether these measures are adequate to allay the anxieties of workers regarding retrenchment and

TABLE 6.3
Selected Employment Indicators of Singapore Electronics Sector

	2008		2009		2010		2011		2012		2013	
	E	M	E	M	E	M	E	M	E	M	E	M
Employment ('000)	106	565	95	521	100	520	96	524	92	535	90	540
Redundancy (number)	5,440	10,430	6,610	13,640	1,750	4,490	2,060	4,460	1,820	4,050	2,490	5,000
Incidence of Redundancy (per '000 workers)	51.9	24.7	76.7	35.1	19.1	11.5	22.6	11.4	20.4	10.2	28.9	12.5

Note: E — Electronics; M — Manufacturing.
Source: Singapore Yearbook of Manpower Statistics, 2014.

job security is moot. For the corporate sector, the government offers cost reduction or tax packages (such as a variable wage component or lowering employer CPF contribution rates). A slew of measures have also been introduced to help business start-ups and small and medium-sized enterprises (SMEs) become competitive and export-oriented. Above all, the government tries to create new jobs by keeping its economy open, with strict corporate governance, increased R&D support, as well as other investment friendly measures in order to attract higher value-added FDI.

4.4 AEC's Relevance to Singapore's Electronics Sector

From the above discussion, it is clear that in the case of Singapore's electronics sector, the regional arrangements created by the AEC and ASEAN+1 formula are key to supporting its participation in the regional production network. The benefits are derived from the trade and investment facilitation measures, rather than from the tariff preferences offered under the AEC ATIGA provisions.[18]

Tariff elimination under the AEC may not be useful for the electronics industry in Singapore, given that the WTO Information Technology Agreement (ITA) has eliminated tariffs on ICT goods among its signatory members. Moreover, much of the electronics trade happens in ASEAN's export processing zones that are also duty free for electronics and the industry's relevant inputs. Hence, it is not a surprise that Singapore firms' utilization of ATIGA preferential tariffs is low. In a survey of seventy-five firms in Singapore by Chia (2011b), the overall FTA preferential tariff utilization (including AFTA) is low at 17.3 per cent, with the highest utilization rates reported for pharmaceuticals and chemicals (22.2 per cent), followed by electronics (18 per cent), and textiles and garments (12.5 per cent).

However, the importance of the AEC is derived from its facilitation measures. First, the various AFTA/ATIGA and ASEAN FTAs with China, Japan and South Korea promote and consolidate regional production networks and help anchor Singapore's position in regional production and trade (including the location of regional headquarter activities). Second, AFTA/ATIGA facilitate Singapore's electronics exports to other ASEAN countries through the removal of tariffs and NTBs in partner countries. The latter include: MRAs for goods that obviate the need for multiple product testing when they cross borders; trade facilitation measures such as more transparent, simplified and speedier customs procedures (including advance rulings); the operation of national single windows towards an ASW; improved physical and IT connectivity; and services and investment liberalization (although limited to date). The electronics trade is highly time sensitive and heavily dependent on "just-in-time" manufacturing. Hence, measures that minimize the need for duplicative testing, simplify and reduce cost of customs, and ensure that speedy delivery will benefit all Singapore manufacturers and traders, but particularly the electronics sector. According to a Mckinsey report (2014), the biggest impact on electronics manufacturing is likely to come from economies of scale and inventory cost savings (derived from trade facilitation measures), with the total impact accounting for between 11 and 21 per cent of the cost base.

5. CASE STUDY OF THE ASEAN OPEN SKIES POLICY AND ITS IMPACT ON SINGAPORE'S AVIATION HUB AND AIRLINES

5.1 ASEAN Open Skies Policy: Developments, Opportunities and Challenges

With the AEC deadline fast approaching, air services are one of the remaining key ASEAN services to be liberalized. ASEAN officials are pushing for the full implementation of the ASEAN Open Sky or Single Aviation Market (OS/SAM) agreement, which addresses connectivity issues in a geographically fragmented region.

Common provisions of Open Skies agreements include the following:

(a) Free market competition with no restriction on international route rights, number of designated airlines, the capacity, frequency and types of aircraft; pricing is determined by market forces.

(b) Fair and equal opportunity to compete — all carriers may establish sales offices in the partner country, and convert earnings and remit them in hard currency promptly and without restrictions; designated carriers are free to provide their own ground handling services or choose among competing providers; airlines and cargo consolidators may arrange ground transport of air cargo and are guaranteed access to customer services; user charges are non-discriminatory and based on costs; computer reservations system displays are transparent and non-discriminatory.

(c) Cooperative marketing arrangements — designated airlines may enter into code-sharing or leasing arrangements with airlines of partner country, subject to usual regulations; an optional provision authorizes code sharing between airlines and surface transportation companies.

(d) Provision for dispute settlement and consultation.

Rationale and Developments in ASEAN OS/SAM. OS/SAM is ASEAN's major aviation policy to liberalize the region's air transport industry and transform it into a single aviation market by the end of 2015. It entails a phased and progressive approach to liberalizing scheduled passenger services, non-scheduled passenger services and air freight services. OS/SAM is intended to increase regional and domestic connectivity, integrate production networks and enhance regional trade by allowing airlines from ASEAN countries to fly freely throughout the region. It encourages the growth of air traffic and tourism. It will also push down fares and increase pressure on airlines to be more cost competitive, which will benefit consumers. However, less competitive airlines will lose their market share, hence the resistance to aviation liberalization in some ASEAN countries.

The November 2004 Action Plan for ASEAN Air Transport Integration and Liberalization 2005–2015 established certain strategic actions to further liberalize air services towards a single aviation market. Together with the Roadmap for Integration of Air Travel Sector (RIATS), it laid down the target date of 2015 for achieving an effective ASEAN Open Skies policy. RIATS identified the following specific goals and target dates:

(a) For scheduled passenger services: unlimited third and fourth freedom flights for all designated points within ASEAN subregions by 2005, and for at least two designated points in each country between the ASEAN subregions by 2006; unlimited fifth freedom traffic between designated points within the ASEAN subregions by 2006 and at least two designated points in each country between the ASEAN subregions by 2008; unlimited third and fourth freedom flights between capital cities by 2008; and unlimited fifth freedom flights for capital cities by 2010.[19]

(b) For airfreight services: significant liberalization by 2006 and full liberalization by 2008.

RIATS for passenger services are incorporated in two agreements, namely the 2009 ASEAN Multilateral Agreement on Air Services (MAAS), which allows ASEAN airlines to exercise unlimited third, fourth and fifth freedoms between member state capitals, and the 2010 Multilateral Agreement for the Full Liberalization of Passenger Air Services (MAFLPAS) that allows airlines to exercise the same rights between ASEAN's non-capital cities. The removal of restrictions on the third and fourth freedoms between ASEAN capital cities for air passenger services took effect from December 2008, and full liberalization on the fifth freedom between ASEAN capital cities took effect from January 2011. All ASEAN member states need to ratify MAAS and MAFLPAS[20] before proceeding to the seventh, eighth and ninth freedoms. Air freight is covered by the 2009 ASEAN Multilateral Agreement on Full Liberalization of Air Freight Services (MAFLAFS).

In the meantime, some ASEAN states had gone ahead to adopt limited agreements among themselves to liberalize market access. For example, in December 2004, Brunei-Singapore-Thailand concluded an agreement in line with the ASEAN 2+X principle that facilitated early liberalization among like-minded countries, with other ASEAN countries following suit when they are ready; in 2003, Cambodia, Laos, Myanmar and Vietnam adopted a multilateral agreement; and in December 2008, Malaysia and Singapore fully liberalized third and fourth freedom access between their respective points.

ASEAN SAM/OS Implementation. There are several hurdles to overcome before OS/SAM achieves full implementation by the end of 2015.[21] The first issue is whether existing airport infrastructures can handle the expected surge in air traffic, as major regional hubs in Singapore, Bangkok and Kuala Lumpur are already operating at near full capacity, while secondary non-capital airports have not been designed to cope with large air traffic volumes. The second issue is whether some domestic carriers will be able to survive in a more competitive regional environment, as cheaper airfares, predatory pricing or collusion may weed out weaker carriers. Third, safety and security issues need urgent attention with the expected boom in air traffic.[22] There are concerns over the shortage of trained pilots and personnel to fly and maintain the planes, and the adequacy of air traffic control and airport infrastructure. There is also a need for better information sharing on airport security practices, and developing and coordinating a timely and efficient regional response to aviation disasters.

Unlike the legal requirements of Europe's Open Skies agreement, ASEAN's market access liberalization is pursued through voluntary agreements among its member states. The most important aspect of aviation market liberalization is the guarantee of third, fourth, fifth and seventh freedoms of the air. While the third and fourth freedoms are already commonly practised in ASEAN, OS/SAM would grant fifth freedom rights, which involves an airline flying to an airport in country A and, from there, to country B before heading back, without the need for inter-governmental approval. The Multilateral Agreement on Air Services (MAAS) frees up third, fourth and fifth freedom operations between ASEAN capital cities only. Both Indonesia and the Philippines initially opposed MAAS to protect domestic aviation sectors, and because Jakarta's and Manila's airports are already operating far over capacity, Indonesia finally accepted MAAS, giving carriers from other ASEAN countries unlimited rights to fly into Jakarta from their own capitals, subject to the availability of airport landing slots, but the Philippines has yet to do so. The Multilateral Agreement for the Full Liberalization of Passenger Air Services (MAFLPAS) provides for complete third, fourth and fifth freedom relaxations for all ASEAN non-capital cities and, in this instance, the Filipino and Indonesian positions are reversed — while the Philippines has accepted MAFLPAS, Indonesia has not.

To be effective, market access liberalization under OS/SAM must be accompanied by adequate aviation infrastructure: airlines need to secure landing slots; air traffic controllers need to be able to cope with growing air traffic; and passenger terminals need to be able to accommodate increased arrivals and departures. With the projected high growth in air travel demand, there will be massive delays and congestion for consumers, and flights will be endangered if air traffic systems are not upgraded. Preparations are underway in several ASEAN countries to accommodate the anticipated growth in air traffic. A number of airlines, especially budget carriers, have stepped up expansion plans and there is a battle over acquiring dominance over ASEAN skies. In Singapore, Changi Airport's Terminal 4 will be ready by 2017, and Terminal 5 will be ready by 2025 to handle up to 50 million passengers a year. This will increase the airport's total capacity to 135 million passengers a year. In addition, a third runway will be operational by end of this decade.

Alan Tan (2013) argues that the challenge for ASEAN states is to fully implement their AEC commitments by the end of 2015, and for ASEAN to devise a post-2015 plan for greater liberalization and harmonization. The latter includes seventh freedom rights, domestic cabotage rights, ownership and control rules, competition law regimes, consumer protection policies, and safety and technical requirements. However, reaching such an agreement (as with the other ASEAN services agreements) is difficult in view of the diverse levels of development among ASEAN states, as well as concerns over sovereignty issue. Tan argues that the most significant pending issue is the seventh freedom right, that is, the ability of an ASEAN carrier to connect to other international points within ASEAN without commencing or ending in its home point. The lack of seventh freedom rights accorded by ASEAN states to each other will seriously disadvantage ASEAN when implementing its ASEAN+1 FTAs. For example, the ASEAN-China agreement provides unlimited third and fourth freedom operations for ASEAN and China. This allows ASEAN carriers to operate to all points in China but their flights must begin and end in their respective home states. In contrast, because China is a unified aviation market, a China carrier can use similar rights and operate to all points in ASEAN from all points in China, so that its network penetration will be larger than any individual ASEAN country. To neutralize this advantage, a carrier from ASEAN must be able to connect to any other ASEAN point with any point in China, but this cannot be done without each of the ASEAN states according each other seventh freedom rights. ASEAN budget airlines such as AirAsia, Tigerair and Lion Air have managed to skirt this problem by forming minority-owned subsidiaries in other ASEAN states.

5.2 OS/SAM and Opportunities and Challenges for the Singapore Aviation Sector

Singapore has built up its aviation sector to be a key driver of its economy. Superior air connectivity is vital to its competitiveness as a global manufacturing base, information business centre, and travel and tourism destination. Through its liberal air services policy and superior airport infrastructure, Singapore has become a leading air hub. It adopts a liberal aviation policy and has concluded air services agreements with more than 100 countries, including about forty open sky agreements. In addition to RIATS (see above) Singapore is a signatory to the Multilateral Agreement for the Liberalization of Air Transport (MALIAT).

Changi Airport Connecting the World. Singapore welcomes foreign airlines to operate in Singapore, promoting its airport as a hub for the world and the region. Changi Airport serves over ninety airlines that operate more than 4,500 weekly flights that serve 200 cities in sixty countries regionally and globally. The airport is also a leading air cargo hub, with transshipment cargo accounting for half of its total throughput.

However, Changi is currently facing multiple challenges. Its position as a hub is being increasingly challenged by the rise of new air hubs such as Dubai, which has recently overtaken even Heathrow as the world's leading international hub, and in the region by Bangkok's Suvarnabhumi Airport. Both Changi and Suvarnabhumi are strategically located to capture European and Northeast Asian air traffic and interregional connections, and both have invested heavily in airport infrastructure to enhance competitiveness as regional air hubs. Changi completed a S$240 million upgrade of its Terminal 2 just before Suvarnabhumi opened in 2006. Additionally, Changi opened its S$1.75 billion Terminal 3 in January 2008, increasing its capacity to 64 million. Terminal 4 will be ready by 2017 and Terminal 5 by 2025. By then, Singapore will be able to handle over 136 million passengers a year. To boost air traffic, Changi also has an incentive package to encourage airlines to use it as a transfer hub. Scoot and Tigerair, Singapore budget carriers, could also play a special role in boosting Changi's attractiveness as a transfer hub.

Singapore Airlines and Its Affiliates. Singapore Airlines (SIA) is a publicly listed national carrier with government majority ownership. There are no competing privately owned airlines based in Singapore. SIA has been noted for its excellent service and spends more than rival airlines in key areas: buying new aircrafts; replacing its fleet more frequently than competitors do; depreciating aircrafts over fifteen years versus the industry standard of twenty-five years; and investing heavily in inducting and retraining employees.

However, SIA's core business has been facing headwinds in recent years from three directions. First, is the competition from the new Middle East airlines — Emirates, Etihad Airways and Qatar Airways — which have established modern fleets with luxurious facilities and services, successfully attracting premium-class passengers on the Asia-Europe routes that were SIA's traditional strengths. Second, closer to home, established carriers in the region — Japanese, Korean, Hong Kong and Thai — are improving their air services, such that the high quality of SIA's services are no longer unique. Third, the proliferation of budget carriers has challenged SIA's economy class segment. Hence, SIA's load factors and profit levels are falling.

SIA's corporate responses to the various challenges have taken many directions, without resorting to government protection and special privileges. First, in late 2015 it launched a premium economy class service for medium- and long-haul routes to further differentiate itself from budget carriers by catering to passengers willing to pay more for better than economy-class service. For business class and first class, it is upgrading aircraft cabins and services. Second, it is expanding its partnerships with other airlines. These include: a new standard carrier, Vistara based in New Delhi (in 2015), together with the Indian Tata Group to penetrate the Indian market; increased investment in Virgin Australia Holdings with code-sharing flights and marketing to compete with Australian flag carrier Qantas (in November 2014); a non-equity alliance with Air New Zealand with code-sharing flights (in September 2014); in the last couple of years at least sixteen alliances or tie-ups with other airlines; trying to entice more budget airlines to operate from and through Singapore. With lower oil prices in 2015–16 pushing down fuel costs, SIA's competitiveness vis-à-vis Middle Eastern airlines should improve.

Singapore's Transport Minister, Lui Tuck Yew,[23] has argued that SIA should work more closely with its affiliate airlines (SilkAir, Scoot, and Tigerair) to improve convenience and service offerings and, therefore, competitiveness. SilkAir is a regional carrier of SIA, while Scoot is a fully owned budget carrier of SIA, and Tigerair is an SIA majority-owned budget carrier. However, SIA's budget carriers face fierce competition from AirAsia, Indonesian budget carriers and Qantas-subsidiary, Jetstar Asia.

Among ASEAN countries, Singapore appears the most prepared to fully implement ASEAN OS/SAM as it has been a pioneer in advocating liberal skies, and has the competitive and highly reputable Changi Airport and Singapore Airlines. OS/SAM will enhance the importance of hub airports such as Changi, which will benefit from feeder traffic connecting with other flights to a wider region. Also, OS/SAM is beneficial for airlines that can quickly move their resources where they are needed and those with extensive networks. SIA and its affiliates will benefit from the growing importance of the Changi air hub. However, Singapore's competitive advantages may have contributed to some ASEAN countries' reluctance to participate in the ASEAN OS/SAM. For example, for some years, Singapore carriers had reached their limits and could not launch new flights into Indonesia until recently.

SIA's concern with OS/SAM relates mainly to sixth freedom rights, which is critical for the Changi air hub. This is because it enables SIA to carry passengers, for example, from Jakarta to Singapore and then onwards, on connecting flights, to elsewhere and everywhere. By avoiding ASEAN agreements, Indonesia can limit the third and fourth freedom rights that form the backbone of other carriers' sixth freedom operations. Also, OS/SAM does not encompass seventh freedom rights and domestic flights. In the absence of seventh freedom rights, SIA cannot take advantage of the China market by operating from Singapore and other ASEAN countries. In the ASEAN Open Skies policy/agreement, domestic operations are still reserved exclusively for domestic players; Singapore is handicapped in this aspect as a city-state.

At the political economy level, there are no domestic conflicts obstructing the country's stance of advocating full implementation of the ASEAN Open Skies policy. As was noted at the outset, businesses and workers in Singapore have been accustomed to competing in a free market environment. An established and competitive Changi air hub benefits not only Singapore carriers but all other ASEAN and foreign carriers that use the air hub. Competition between Changi, Suvarnabhumi and other ASEAN air hub aspirants, and between ASEAN national carriers will have to be determined by market forces unleashed by the ASEAN Open Skies agreement. Both Changi and SIA and its affiliates expect Singapore policy-makers to implement aviation agreements as it will not disadvantage them. Any conflicts between promoting the Changi air hub and SIA and its affiliates are resolved at the intra-governmental level, since both are government-owned.

6. CONCLUSION

Singapore is a highly trade- and FDI-dependent economy. Thus, it is in its national economic interest to promote global free trade and FDI flows. As such it remains a strong supporter of the multilateral trading system under the WTO. Singapore has also taken regional and bilateral FTA routes to achieve its trade and investment objectives. Of its various FTAs, the AEC is the most important — politically, strategically and economically.

Singapore is constantly restructuring itself to meet the challenges of globalization and economic integration, whether via market-driven production networks, or policy-driven FTAs. As a small city-state with long and established policy regimes of free trade and FDI, it is not surprising that Singapore is one of the leading implementers of the AEC commitments.

Having said that, there are nevertheless concerns with implementing the AEC, as with any liberalization process. There are both benefits and costs and, hence, winners and losers. However, Singapore is characterized by its non-protectionist approach to resolving concerns and problems. The electronics sector has undergone dramatic restructuring in response to changing cost advantages and the emergence of competitive facilities in other ASEAN countries and in China. The Singapore policy response has been to fully support trade in goods liberalization in the AEC, and to help affected businesses and workers to upgrade and move resources into more competitive sectors and activities. Likewise, the aviation sector is undergoing tremendous pressure, with challenges to Changi's air hub status and SIA's premier airline status. The government's policy response is to develop and upgrade Changi into a more competitive air hub, and SIA and its affiliates into more competitive airlines.

APPENDIX 1
Exports of Electronics Products and Components, 1998–2013

	Value in S$ billion			% Share of Electronics Sector			Av Annual Growth Rate (%)	
	1998	2005	2013	1998	2005	2013	1998–05	2005–13
Electronics								
Total Exports	96.0	174.1	161.6	100.0	100.0	100.0	8.9	-0.93
Re-exports	34.6	98.7	112.7	100.0	100.0	100.0	16.2	1.67
Domestic Exports	63.6	75.3	48.9	100.0	100.0	100.0	2.4	-5.25
Imports	62.0	128.7	119.5	100.0	100.0	100.0	11.0	-0.92
Integrated Circuits								
Total Exports	25.0	75.0	96.3	26.0	43.1	59.6	17.0	3.17
Re-exports	13.2	53.1	73.8	38.2	53.8	65.5	22.0	4.20
Domestic Exports	11.8	21.9	22.5	18.6	29.1	46.0	9.2	0.34
Imports	23.9	59.1	69.9	38.5	45.9	58.5	13.8	2.12
Parts of PC								
Total Exports	15.9	26.5	15.9	16.6	15.2	9.8	7.6	-6.19
Re-exports	3.6	10.4	8.8	10.4	10.5	7.8	16.4	-2.07
Domestic Exports	12.3	16.1	7.1	19.3	21.4	14.5	3.9	-9.73
Imports	12.5	22.3	9.8	20.2	17.3	8.2	8.6	-9.77
Disk Drives								
Total Exports	22.2	16.4	4.5	23.1	9.4	2.8	-4.2	-14.9
Re-exports	3.6	3.0	2.1	10.4	3.0	1.9	-2.6	-4.4
Domestic Exports	18.7	13.5	2.4	29.4	17.9	4.9	-4.5	-19.4
Imports	5.9	3.6	2.4	9.5	2.8	2.0	-6.8	-4.9
Telecom Equipment[a]								
Total Exports	2.9	14.9	10.0	3.0	8.6	6.2	26.3	-4.9
Re-exports	1.2	9.7	8.5	3.5	9.8	7.5	34.8	-1.6
Domestic Exports	1.8	5.2	1.5	2.8	6.9	3.1	16.4	-14.4
Imports	2.6	10.8	11.9	4.2	8.4	10.0	22.6	1.2

continued on next page

Appendix 1 — cont'd

	Value in S$ billion			% Share of Electronics Sector			Av Annual Growth Rate (%)	
	1998	2005	2013	1998	2005	2013	1998–05	2005–13
Consumer Electronics[b]								
Total Exports	9.3	11	4.3	9.7	6.3	2.7	2.4	−11.1
Re-exports	5.6	6.4	3.1	16.2	6.5	2.8	1.9	−8.7
Domestic Exports	3.8	4.6	1.2	6.0	6.1	2.5	2.8	−15.5
Imports	6.3	10.9	4.2	10.2	8.5	3.5	8.1	−11.2
Personal Computers (PC)								
Total Exports	5.4	2.5	6.6	5.6	1.4	4.1	−10.4	12.9
Re-Exports	1.4	1.2	2.9	4.0	1.2	2.6	−2.2	11.7
Domestic Exports	4.0	1.3	3.7	6.3	1.7	7.6	−14.8	14.0
Imports	1.1	2.7	4.7	1.8	2.1	3.9	13.7	7.2
Parts of IC								
Total Exports	—	5.8	7.6	—	3.3	4.7	—	3.4
Re-Exports	—	2.0	3.4	—	2.0	3.0	—	6.9
Domestic Exports	—	3.9	4.3	—	5.2	8.8	—	1.2
Imports	—	2.5	4.4	—	1.9	3.7	—	7.3
Diodes and Transistors								
Total Exports	—	8.2	8.5	—	4.7	5.3	—	0.5
Re-Exports	—	6.1	5.3	—	6.2	4.7	—	−1.7
Domestic Exports	—	2.1	3.3	—	2.8	6.7	—	5.8
Imports	—	7.6	5.8	—	5.9	4.9	—	−3.3

Notes:
a. Includes pagers, cellular phones, TV & video cameras and recorders, radar & navigational equipment, radio remote controls, satellite discs and parts of these products.
b. Includes TV receivers, radio broadcast receivers, video & sound recorders, microphones, loudspeakers, headphones, earphones, TV camera, still image video cameras and parts of these products.
Source: Singapore Yearbook of Statistics (various issues); authors' calculations.

Notes

1. For further reading, refer to *Trade Policy Review of Singapore* (2012).
2. For a full list of regional and bilateral FTAs that Singapore has signed on to and enforced as well as those still under negotiation, consult this website: <http://www.fta.gov.sg/>.
3. *9th ASEAN Economic Community Council Meeting*, 15 April 2013.
4. Ong Keng Yong quoted a 93 per cent implementation rate for the period 2008–09 (Ong 2012).
5. Non-tariff measures (NTMs) should not be confused with non-tariff barriers (NTBs). Not all NTMs are NTBs, as some of them may have been introduced to meet various regulatory requirements related to health, social, safety and environmental reasons; moreover, some of them have no trade impact and are, therefore, not NTBs.
6. Although there are seven measures discriminating against foreign commercial interests, they do not affect any tariff lines. This is because the NTMs fall mostly under migration measures.
7. Engineering and architecture, nursing, accountancy services, surveying services, medical and dental professionals and tourism professionals.
8. Refer to the Singapore Cooperation Programme (SCP) website at <www.scp.gov.sg>. The currency conversion rate used is SG$1 = US$0.80.
9. See Iswaran (2014).
10. Uncharacteristically, Singaporeans in recent years have reacted negatively to the surge in foreign worker inflow, blaming them and their families for the overcrowding of transport, housing, education and recreational facilities, and crowding out in the job market. The government has taken heed of their concerns and improved the supply of public facilities as well as imposed restrictions on the growth of the foreign workforce.
11. For more information, refer to the Singapore Economic Development Board webpage on the electronics industry at <https://www.edb.gov.sg/content/edb/en/industries/industries/electronics.html>.
12. According to experts, although Singapore is trying hard to develop high-level capabilities in product innovation and design, the local industries have yet to catch up with the speed of innovation achieved by industry leaders. See Embassy of the United States Singapore (2004).
13. While Singapore's electronics sector's real wage went up from US$19,151 to US$31,700 during 2000–01 to 2007–08, the same for Malaysia went up from US$5,753 to US$6,033, and for the Philippines, it went up from US$2,590 to US$2,638 (Athukorala and Kohpaiboon 2015).
14. For example, Hitachi Chemical Singapore is introducing robots to make Singapore the most automated printed wire board plant in the world. And

Texas Instruments has implemented a fully automated warehousing system, improving productivity by 40 per cent and space utilization fourfold. (See Lim, 6 September 2014.)

15. See MTI (n.d.).

16. This is the period when the industries were classified based on the SSIC 2010, and when electronics and computer industries were combined with optical products.

17. For example, in the AEC, under MRAs of professionals, Singapore is committed to allowing intra-corporate transfers of PMETs. This implies that overseas companies can send foreign professionals to fill up managerial positions in their companies based in Singapore. However, Singapore has limited it by stating that transferees must come on a two-year contract with the option to extend their stay for three years afterwards up to a total of eight years. According to the policy-makers, as Singapore has a low unemployment rate, this movement of labour is beneficial and is not likely to hurt local professionals (Iswaran 2014).

18. Under the ATIGA preferences, tariff has been eliminated for ASEAN-6 countries and Laos, while the deadline for Cambodia, Myanmar and Vietnam is 2018.

19. Under the 1941 Convention on International Aviation, nine freedoms of the air have been enshrined. These are: (First freedom) fly over a foreign country without landing; (Second freedom) land in a foreign country for refuelling or maintenance, without loading/unloading cargo or passenger; (Third freedom): fly from home country to a foreign country; (Fourth freedom) fly from a foreign country to home country; (Fifth freedom) fly to a foreign country, allowing loading/unloading of cargo and passengers in a second foreign country, on a flight originating or ending in home country; (Sixth freedom) fly from a foreign country to another, with an intermediary stop in home country for reasons other than maintenance or refuelling; (Seventh freedom) fly from a foreign country to another, without a stop in the home country; (Eighth freedom) fly between two or more points in the same foreign country, beginning from or continuing into home country; and (Ninth freedom) fly between two or more points in a foreign country, without home country point, also known as "stand alone cabotage".

20. The EU Open Skies agreement allows any EU airline to fly any route within the boundaries of EU member countries, with unlimited seventh, eighth, and ninth freedoms, however, the ASEAN OS/SAM Agreement in its current form is far more limited.

21. *Asia Weekly*, 25 July 2014.

22. The issue of air safety is gaining prominence, particularly with the hundreds of lives lost in three accidents in 2014 involving Malaysian Airlines and AirAsia Indonesia.

23. See Saifulbahri Ismail, 20 December 2014.

References

9th ASEAN Economic Community Council Meeting. Hanoi: Ministry of Industry and Trade of the Socialist Republic of Vietnam, 15 April 2013. Available at <http://www.moit.gov.vn/en/News/252/9th-asean-economic-community-council-meeting.aspx> (accessed 6 February 2015).

Ando, Mitsuyo and Ayako Obashi. "The Pervasiveness of Non-Tariff Measures in ASEAN — Evidences from the Inventory Approach". In *Rising Non-Tariff Protectionism and Crisis Recovery*, edited by Mia Mikic and Martin Wermelinger. A Study by the Asia-Pacific Research and Training Network on Trade (ARTNeT). Bangkok: United Nations, 2010.

ASEAN Secretariat. "ASEAN Develops Tourism Strategic Vision 2016–2025", 13 January 2015. Available at <http://www.asean.org/news/asean-secretariat-news/item/asean-develops-tourism-strategic-vision-2016-2025> (accessed 8 May 2015).

ASEAN Secretariat. *Declaration of ASEAN Concord II (Bali Concord II).* Bali: ASEAN Secretariat, 7 October 2003. Available at <http://www.asean.org/news/item/declaration-of-asean-concord-ii-bali-concord-ii> (accessed 8 May 2015).

ASEAN Secretariat. *The ASEAN Statistical Yearbook.* Jakarta: ASEAN Secretariat, 2013.

Athukorala, Prema-Chandra and Archanun Kohpaiboon. "Global Production Sharing, Trade Patterns and Industrialization in Southeast Asia". In *The Routledge Handbook of Southeast Asian Economics*, edited by Ian Coxhead. U.K.: Routledge, 2015.

Austria, Myrna. "Non-tariff Barriers: A Challenge to Achieving the ASEAN Economic Community". In *The ASEAN Economic Community: A Work in Progress*, edited by Sanchita Basu Das, Jayant Menon, Omkar L. Shrestha and Rodolfo Severino. Singapore: Institute of Southeast Asian Studies, 2013.

Chia, Siow Yue. "Free Flow of Skilled Labour in the AEC". In *Toward a Competitive ASEAN Single Market; Sectoral Analysis*, edited by Shujiro Urata and Misa Okabe. ERIA Research Project Report 2010-01. Jakarta: ERIA, 2011*a*.

————. "Singapore". In *Asia's Free Trade Agreements: How is Business Responding?*, edited by Masahiro Kawai and Ganeshan Wignaraja. Cheltenham, U.K.: Edward Elgar, 2011*b*.

————. "Modalities for ASEAN Economic Integration: Retrospect and Going Forward". Paper prepared for the conference on "ASEAN's Long Term Economic Potential and Vision", RSIS-NTU (Economic Growth Centre), Singapore, 20–21 November 2014 *(forthcoming)*.

Department of Statistics. *Yearbook of Statistics.* Singapore: Department of Statistics, various issues.

Embassy of the United States Singapore. "Singapore's Electronics Industry — Facing Challenges, but First Mover Advantages". 20 February 2004. <http://singapore.usembassy.gov/uploads/images/kT16tWH8gc2pmfpb1PPV7g/ElectronicsInd_04.pdf> (accessed 1 February 2015).

Initiative for ASEAN Integration. Singapore Cooperation Programme (SCP) website. <http://www.scp.gov.sg/content/scp/iai_programmes/about.html> (accessed 8 May 2015).

Iswaran, S. "Second Minister S Iswaran's Reply to Parliament Question on ASEAN Economic Community Goal of Movement of Natural Persons". Singapore: Ministry of Trade and Industry, 14 April 2014. Available at <http://www.mti.gov.sg/NewsRoom/Pages/Second-Minister-S-Iswaran%27s-reply-to-Parliament-Questions-on-ASEAN-Economic-Community-goal-of-movement-of-natural-persons.aspx> (accessed 8 May 2015).

Lim, Kok Kiang. "Electronics Industry Remains Competitive". *Straits Times* Forum, 7 September 2014. Available at <http://www.straitstimes.com/premium/forum-letters/story/electronics-industry-remains-competitive-20140906> (accessed 8 May 2015).

McKinsey Global Institute. *Southeast Asia at the Crossroads: Three Paths to Prosperity.* McKinsey and Company, 2014.

MTI. *Economic Survey of Singapore.* Singapore: Ministry of Trade and Industry, various issues.

————. *The Strategic Economic Plan: Towards a Developed Nation.* Singapore: Ministry of Trade and Industry, 1991.

————. *MTI Occasional Paper on Population and Economy.* <http://www.mti.gov.sg/MTIInsights/Documents/MTI%20Occasional%20Paper%20on%20Population%20and%20Economy.pdf> (accessed 6 February 2015). Singapore: Ministry of Trade and Industry, undated.

Nikomborirak, Deunden and Supunnavadee Jitdumrong. "ASEAN Trade in Services". In *The ASEAN Economic Community: A Work in Progress,* edited by Sanchita Basu Das, Jayant Menon, Omkar L. Shrestha and Rodolfo Severino. Singapore: Institute of Southeast Asian Studies, 2013.

Ong, Keng Yong. "ASEAN Economic Integration: Perspective from Singapore". In *Achieving the ASEAN Economic Community 2015: Challenges for Member Countries and Businesses,* edited by Sanchita Basu Das. Singapore: Institute of Southeast Asian Studies, 2012.

Saifulbahri Ismail. "Closer Integration Between SIA, Scoot, Tigerair is a Natural Evolution". *Today,* 20 December 2014.

Singapore Economic Development Board [SEDB]. *Electronics Industry in Singapore.* Available at <https://www.edb.gov.sg/content/edb/en/industries/industries/electronics.html> (accessed 1 February 2015).

Singapore Yearbook of Manpower Statistics. Singapore: Ministry of Manpower, 2014.

Tan, Alan Khee-Jin. *Toward a Single Aviation Market in ASEAN: Regulatory Reform and Industry Challenges.* Discussion Paper 2013-22. Jakarta: ERIA, October 2013.

Toh, Mun Heng. "The Development of Singapore's Electronic Sector". In *Architects of Growth? Subnational Governments and Industrialization in Asia,* edited by Francis E. Hutchinson. Singapore: Institute of Southeast Asian Studies, 2014.

Wilson, Karl. "Cracks show in ASEAN's Aviation Sector". *China Daily Asia* [online], 25 July 2014 <http://www.chinadailyasia.com/asiaweekly/2014-07/25/content_15152109.html> (accessed 8 May 2015).

Wong, H. K. "The Remaking of Singapore's High-Tech Enterprise System". In *Making IT: The Rise of Asian in High Tech*, edited by Henry S. Rowen, Marguerite G. Hancock and Lilliam F. Miller. Stanford: Stanford University Press, 2007.

World Bank. *Logistics Performance Index 2014*. Washington, D.C.: World Bank, 2014.

———. *Doing Business 2012*. Washington, D.C.: World Bank, 2012.

World Economic Forum. *World Competitiveness Index, 2012–2013*. Geneva: World Economic Forum, 2012.

WTO. *Trade Policy Review of Singapore*. Geneva: World Trade Organization, 2012.

7

MOVING THE AEC BEYOND 2015
Managing Domestic Economic Interests in Thailand

Sineenat Sermcheep and Suthiphand Chirathivat

1. INTRODUCTION

ASEAN achieved a milestone with the launch of the ASEAN Free Trade Area (AFTA) Agreement in 1992. Establishing an ASEAN Economic Community (AEC) in 2015 is the next logical goal after the relatively successful implementation of AFTA. ASEAN has set its objectives of building an AEC that is premised on the free flow of goods, services, investment and skilled labour and freer flow of capital in order to move towards a single market and production base. Creating a competitive economic region, equitable economic development, and integration into the global economy are the other elements of the AEC.

Thailand has recently prioritized the AEC in its national agenda and will continue to do so in the coming years ("Policy Statement of the Council of Ministers" 2014). At the same time, the Thai government has been trying to pursue significant economic and institutional reforms aimed at improving the domestic economic structure for a more integrated ASEAN region. Even though some of the literature indicates that Thailand will benefit from the AEC (Plummer and Chia 2009; Intaravitak, Ongkttikul and Lucksahapanyakul 2012), economic integration in ASEAN has had a different impact on different groups of people in the country. Overall, for example, large firms and multinational corporations (MNCs) are supposed to form the main group that gains from the AEC compared to small and medium-sized enterprises (SMEs). Once liberalization deepens, uncompetitive firms in a more integrated region might have to leave the industry if they are unable to adjust to a borderless AEC. This creates a conflict of interest between winners and losers of the AEC.

Policy-makers and academics (Mayer 1992) like to argue that the toughest bargaining during the negotiation process takes place not between nations but within them. Since the impact from proposed international agreements differs across various stakeholders, the liberalized economy is likely to be divided between losers and winners. Possible losers tend to resist complete implementation of trade agreements, thereby limiting a country from benefiting from an international agreement's full potential. Taking this concept and applying it to the Thai case, the AEC 2015 will certainly divide the domestic economy between winners and losers in the years to come. The question then arises: who represents the winners and losers, and how can Thailand resolve the different impact that these groups in the domestic economy will encounter? As such, the years following 2015 will prove even more difficult for Thailand, as the domestic economy will need to align itself not only with earlier unfinished agendas but also with new agendas for deeper economic integration.

From 1 January 2008 to 31 July 2013, Thailand worked to meet 89.1 per cent of the measures listed in the 2007 AEC Blueprint ("Latest Negotiation Status"; Department of Trade Negotiations (DTN) 2014). However, the remaining measures are difficult to comply with, as they require adjustments to domestic laws and regulations. Therefore, it is highly unlikely that Thailand will be able to completely implement them by the end of 2015. This will have implications for the other ASEAN countries. The purpose of this chapter is to examine conflicting economic interests in Thailand with respect to the implementation of the AEC, and the importance of building domestic consensus in order to move the AEC forward.

This chapter is organized as follows. Section 2 examines Thailand's current progress under the Blueprint commitments. Section 3 discusses the role and interests of institutions in policy formulation and implementation.

Section 4 presents the effects of conflicting domestic economic interests on Thailand's continued progress towards implementing its AEC commitments. Three case studies from the agricultural sector, logistics industry and medical profession are used to put forth a picture of potential winners and losers of the AEC as well as how their conflicting economic interests might impede full implementation. The question of whether domestic consensus and enhanced community-building awareness are necessary for moving the AEC beyond 2015 will also be addressed in these sections. Section 5 concludes and offers some policy recommendations on how to achieve domestic consensus in Thailand.

2. CURRENT PROGRESS ON THAILAND'S AEC COMMITMENTS

Since the adoption of the AEC in 2007, Thailand has been trying to align its domestic economy to the regional initiative. However, unlike AFTA, which focuses only on tariff liberalization, the formation of an AEC involves a wider and deeper level of economic integration among the ASEAN countries. Even though the government has been preparing for the AEC, its scope goes beyond the government and includes other stakeholders from the domestic economy. With the AEC 2015 deadline drawing nearer, Thailand's progress in meeting its commitments needs to be examined.

2.1 Pillar 1: Single Market and Production Base

Developing ASEAN into a single market and production base is a priority target for all member economies. This includes mainly, the free flow of goods, services, investment, skilled labour and freer flow of capital.

Free Flow of Goods. By 2010, Thailand had eliminated tariffs on all products from the inclusion list and, by 2011,[1] it had removed the third tranche of non-tariff barriers (NTBs) that resulted in the elimination of quotas on twenty-three agricultural products (ASEAN Secretariat 2012, p. 3). Currently, Thailand is working on preparing and updating the country's non-tariff measures (NTMs) database to support the ASEAN NTMs database.

The country's Minister of Commerce launched the National Trade Repository (NTR)[2] on 27 November 2014 to enhance transparency as well as to act as a one-stop service centre for rules and regulations relating to the ASEAN Trade in Goods Agreement (ATIGA). Thailand, along with Brunei, Malaysia and Singapore, participated in the first pilot project for the self-certification of rules of origin (ROOs); the Philippines and Indonesia joined the second pilot project. This self-certification system is expected to reduce costs to exporters and the workload of government staff.

Moreover, Thailand established a National Single Window (NSW) in 2011, a necessary step towards achieving the ASEAN Single Window (ASW). The Customs Department, which falls under the Ministry of Finance, has been assigned as the lead agency for this; it will coordinate with thirty-seven other government units to establish the Thai NSW. This move will help to improve the operations of government agencies and reduce time and costs for international trade transactions (Thai Customs Department 2010). As the various ASEAN countries are still at different stages of NSW operation, the ASW will most likely not be operational by the end of 2015 (Chia 2013, p. 18).

Free Flow of Services and Skilled Labour. Thailand included services sub-sectors such as consultancy, accounting, maritime transport and online data services for liberalization under the ninth package of the ASEAN Framework Agreement in Services (AFAS), which was completed in 2014.

However, the country's performance with respect to liberalizing services is still limited for three reasons. First, member countries are allowed flexibility in complying with commitments in services (Nikomborirak and Jitdumrong 2013, p. 108). This results in slow progress as countries utilize the flexibility to delay their compliance. Second, services liberalization in the Blueprint does not cover other pertinent issues such as foreign land ownership and licensing requirements, which are also important for establishing a foreign presence. Third, Thailand's commitments in services liberalization do not go beyond current allowances in domestic laws and regulations.

In terms of skilled labour mobility, Thailand has signed MRAs for the travel and tourism sector as well as seven professions (engineering, nursing, architecture, surveying, accountancy, and medical and dental practitioners). These MRAs are expected to facilitate the movement of professionals to Thailand. For the movement of natural persons, Thailand only allows intra-corporate transferees at the managerial or executive level (or specialists in some sub-sectors) and grants business travellers a temporary visit. General medical and dental services, as well as services provided by nurses, have to comply with current domestic laws and regulations.

Free Flow of Investment. Thailand ratified the ASEAN Comprehensive Investment Agreement (ACIA), effective on 28 March 2013, offered initiatives for investment liberalization, facilitation, protection and promotion. With this agreement, ASEAN aims to have a community with free and open investment under more transparent, consistent and predictable investment rules. Thailand has agreed to liberalize investments in agriculture, fishery, forestry, mining, manufacturing and services related to these five sectors. However, some reservations have been imposed on sub-sectors such as rice and animal farming where foreign ownership cannot be greater than 50 per cent. This is in line with the Foreign Business Act (1999), which prohibits foreign ownership in some sub-sectors. Currently, Thailand has liberalized investment in three sub-sectors — the cultivation, propagation or development of onion seeds, tuna aquaculture and spiny lobster aquaculture. According to the International Institute for Trade and Development (ITD), investment liberalization is not a major threat to Thailand because foreign investors will still need to abide by other domestic regulations such as licensing and minimum capital requirements (ITD 2014).

Freer Flow of Capital. The Ministry of Finance, Bank of Thailand (BOT) and the Securities and Exchange Commission (SEC) are the major agencies responsible for negotiating the liberalization and integration of financial and capital markets.

With regard to financial services liberalization, BOT cooperates with the ASEAN Central Banks to exchange data and knowledge on regulating foreign financial intermediaries. This cooperation extends to ensuring that commercial banks in ASEAN meet the standards for Qualified ASEAN Banks (QAB) certification. BOT has allowed foreign commercial banks' full branches to upgrade their licences to subsidiary status. Licences for new foreign commercial banks have also been issued to ensure that a range of financial services are available for more efficient trade and investment.[3] In terms of capital account liberalization, BOT has currently liberalized foreign direct investment (FDI) and the portfolio of investments for both inward and outward flows. This move is aimed at supporting the distribution of investments by Thai investors, encouraging the development of the financial market and creating an environment that facilitates capital flows (Ruengvirayudh 2013).

Moreover, to promote the ASEAN capital market, the Stock Exchange of Thailand (SET) and six other exchanges from ASEAN have collaborated to form the "ASEAN Exchange". In October 2013, SET started trading through the "ASEAN Trading Link" along with the stock exchanges of Malaysia and Singapore. The ASEAN Exchange also provides a list of 180 ASEAN blue-chip stocks in the form of ASEAN Stars in order to facilitate cross-border investment (ASEAN Exchange 2012).

2.2 Pillar 2: Competitive Economic Region

Thailand has aligned itself with the aims of the AEC by creating a competitive economic market. This has been achieved in several stages. The Competition Act was enacted in Thailand in 1999; it is under the purview of the Department of Internal Trade (Ministry of Commerce) and seeks to ensure competition and prevent monopolistic market activities. In addition, the Consumer Protection Act was established in 1979 (and amended in 1998) with the purpose of ensuring the rights of consumers. This is in line with the establishment of the ASEAN Committee on Consumer Protection (ACCP) in 2007.

The law relating to intellectual property rights (IPR) in Thailand is the Patent Act, which has been enforced since 1979; it was amended in 1992 and 1999. The Department of Intellectual Property (Ministry of Commerce) is in charge of implementing this Act. Moreover, in accordance with the ASEAN IPR Action Plan, Thailand is in the process of acceding to The Hague Agreement and the Madrid Protocol (TDRI 2012*a*).

With respect to infrastructure development, the government has partnered with sub-regional groupings such as the Greater Mekong Subregion (GMS), the Indonesia-Malaysia-Thailand Growth Triangle (IMT-GT) and Mekong-Japan cooperation to develop infrastructure in terms of both hardware and software.

2.3 Pillar 3: Equitable Economic Development

The Thai SMEs Promotion Act was enacted in 2000 with the objective of supporting SMEs. This is in line with the ASEAN Policy Blueprint for SME Development (2004–09) and the ASEAN Strategic Action Plan for SME

Development (2010–15). At the ASEAN-level, Thailand has adopted the second phase of the Initiative for ASEAN Integration (IAI) in Narrowing the Development Gap (NDG) and operating the Co-shepherd Mechanism between the ASEAN-6 and the CLMV countries.[4] During 2000–11, Thailand implemented eighteen projects with a value of US$1.33 million under the IAI. With reference to the Co-shepherd Mechanism, Thailand cooperates with Cambodia in transportation and investments (Wuttisorn 2013).

2.4 Pillar 4: Integration into the Global Economy

In order to further connect itself to the global economy, Thailand agreed to establish free trade agreements (FTAs) along with the other ASEAN members and external partners: China; Japan; South Korea; Australia; New Zealand; and India. The country's cooperation with the Gulf Cooperation Council (GCC) and the Common Market of the Southern Cone (MERCOSUR) is also a work-in-progress in this direction.

Furthermore, in November 2012, ASEAN agreed to establish the Regional Comprehensive Economic Partnership (RCEP) with the six FTA partners of ASEAN. Pupphavesa (2012) analysed the potential impact of the RCEP and found that the partnership/agreement will contribute to an increase in Thailand's GDP by 4.03 per cent and a rise in exports in many products such as vegetables, processed food, electrical appliances, auto parts, and rubbers and plastics. Thailand has also integrated itself into the global economy by participating in global value chains, and by gradually adapting international practices and standards to its production and distribution processes.

3. ROLE AND INTERESTS OF INSTITUTIONS IN POLICY FORMULATION AND IMPLEMENTATION

In order to explain the conflicting interests that emerge while formulating and implementing the AEC commitments, one has to understand the nature of the institutions and domestic politics that underpin the Thai political system. This section of the chapter starts by offering some initial insights on policy formulation in ASEAN before the advent of the AEC. Subsequently, it will outline the context of domestic politics and its importance to policy formulation and the country's implementation of the AEC.

3.1 Evolution of Policy Formulation

Long before Thailand fully embraced the Blueprint measures, adopting them into national policies and strategies, the country, like many other ASEAN member states, adhered to the association's norms — known widely as the ASEAN way of decision-making. The latter is defined as an experiment in constructing regional affairs by consensus and consultation, allowing member states to focus on and devote their resources to region-building tasks (Sukma 2014, p. 5).

Throughout ASEAN's existence and the gradual evolution of its institutional structures, Thailand participated in various ASEAN meetings including the ASEAN Ministerial Meeting (AMM), the ASEAN Economic Ministers Meeting (AEMM) and other ministry meetings on labour, welfare, energy, health, science and technology, and the environment. The Thai public sector, therefore, was increasingly drawn into formulating different policy responses on ASEAN issues.

Up to the emergence of AFTA in 1993, Thailand's policies on ASEAN-related economic issues mainly engaged two key ministries and their respective departments — the Ministry of Foreign Affairs and the Ministry of Commerce. The former acts as the main coordinator for Thailand's participation in ASEAN affairs, while the latter acts on behalf of Thailand to formulate policies on trade issues (Chirathivat, Pachusanond and Wongboonsin 1999).

In the late 1980s and early 1990s, however, there was a shift in Thailand's approach as the country needed to respond to the changing global and regional environment. Competent and knowledgeable technocrats who could represent the private sector and the general public, such as former Prime Minister Anand Panyarachun, were appointed to the economic ministries. This initial engagement of the private sector was seen as a positive development as their interests are directly affected by regional and global changes. The country's response to the AFTA project was pertinent for their businesses; therefore, ASEAN policy discussions during that time actively involved the participation of private sector institutions such as the Thai Chamber of Commerce, Federation of Thai Industries and Thai Bankers Association. The country's modified approach helped the private sector witness their interests being considered with respect to ASEAN policy formulation.

Despite these changes, ASEAN economic matters continued to primarily engage the interests of a few key players, such as private and public sector elites involved in policy-making, right up till the 1990s. Since the impact of any trade agreement takes time to materialize, the conflicting interests among domestic stakeholders were not very apparent during the initial days of AFTA. The 1997–98 Asian Financial Crisis (AFC) further diverted attention from domestic conflicts because ASEAN initiatives were treated with less priority during the crisis. Thailand started to discuss the importance of regional trade liberalization and embarked on new FTAs both at the country- and ASEAN-level only after the shock of the AFC subsided in the early 2000s.

3.2 The Impact of Domestic Politics on AEC Formulation and Implementation

The proliferation of bilateral and regional FTAs created a new policy environment in response to trade liberalization, well before the advent of the AEC (Chirathivat and Srisangnam 2013). Thailand appeared to be competing with Malaysia and Singapore for FTAs as both these countries had concluded numerous bilateral FTAs with other trade partners. Numerous studies have examined the rationales behind the pursuit of FTAs in different countries (Chirathivat and Mallikamas 2004) but, more importantly, each FTA has created a policy debate about their respective impact within individual countries. Policy debates on FTAs span a broad range of issues including their sectoral impact, impact on employment, the environment and on a large group of diverse stakeholders. This leads to the possibility of conflicts arising between various affected stakeholders.

Greater liberalization in the 2000s also created new stakeholders (in addition to the few traditional private and public sector players in 1990s). They include SMEs, foreign companies, non-governmental organizations (NGOs) and the general public. Their participation in these earlier FTAs helped old and new stakeholders weigh the potential impact of the AEC. In a sense, the development of the AEC has been greatly facilitated by previous developments in trade liberalization, beginning with AFTA in the 1990s and progressing to the proliferation of FTAs in the 2000s.

However, Thailand's FTA policy was subsequently derailed again by developments in domestic politics following the fall of former Prime Minister Thaksin Shinawatra in 2006 and the subsequent take over of power by the military. This turn in the domestic political situation delayed

Thailand's FTA negotiations and implementation as well as the country's ratification of the ASEAN Charter and the AEC measures. Even with the return to democracy after the 2007 elections, former Prime Minister Abhisit Vejjajiva continued to face difficulties in dealing with divisive domestic politics. Hence, FTA policy formulation remained a low priority agenda item. Only after the Cha-am Hua Hin ASEAN Summit, held at the end of 2009, was the Abhisit government finally able to redeem the importance of ASEAN and its policies.

Once the Yingluck government took over the Abhisit government, Thailand started, once again, to seriously discuss gains and losses resulting from further delays in implementing the AEC. There was a general consensus among the public as well as stakeholders that AEC implementation had to become a national agenda item. Indeed, the changing policy environment with respect to emerging bilateral and regional FTAs had been favourable to policy-makers, allowing them to fully turn their attention to the implementation of the AEC.

3.3 Thailand's Implementation of the AEC Blueprint

Following the formation of the Yingluck government and the major flooding crisis of 2011–12, Thailand became more active in the implementation of the Blueprint as the country found itself lagging behind its ASEAN neighbours. The government agencies responsible for the three pillars are: the Ministry of Foreign Affairs for the ASEAN Political-Security Community (APSC); the Ministry of Commerce for the AEC; and the Ministry of Social Development and Human Security for the ASEAN Socio-Cultural Community (ASCC). The Ministry of Foreign Affairs, together with its Department of ASEAN Affairs, plays an important role in coordinating Thailand's implementation of the Blueprint.

By the time the Prayut military government took over, discussions on the AEC had been taken up in all quarters of the country. This is the first time a trade policy has captured so much attention in the media and society. However, success in promoting discussions on the AEC does not reflect a similar success with its implementation. One has to carefully distinguish between the dissemination of news on the AEC and the extent to which Thai citizens understand this initiative or see eye-to-eye on it. The following paragraphs further discuss conflicting interests among various stakeholders.

A lack of integration at the policy-level in Thailand may hinder the realization of the full potential benefits of the AEC. Sound integration within Thailand would require resolving discrepancies between national laws and the AEC commitments, and working in tandem with various stakeholders such as non-government organizations (NGOs), import-competing small producers, farmers and consumers.

Close observers of Thailand will be familiar with the country's bureaucracy and inefficient policy coordination. Within the context of the AEC, the Department of ASEAN Affairs faces a difficult task in coordinating preparation for its implementation. The Ministry of Commerce, which is in-charge of the economic pillar, also appears to lack coherence with other government agencies. Without proper bureaucratic understanding of the AEC and its policies, leaders within the Yingluck government were not able to steer the implementation of the AEC targets in the right direction. Cabinet meetings have not appeared to improve coordination among agencies as discussions have been lacking in substance, depth and coherence.

As a result, it is evident that Thailand still lacks institutional reforms in terms of its efforts at coordination. Government agencies tend to maintain the status quo unless they are pressed by affected stakeholders. The private sector, major Thai and foreign firms in particular, have taken the AEC framework seriously for their future business plans. However, they understand the weakness of the country's bureaucracy and political system. So instead of waiting for things to happen, these firms tend to anticipate AEC implementation by studying and seeking the best strategy to cope with liberalization measures. SMEs in Thailand, on the other hand, are much less prepared and still lack in-depth understanding of the AEC and its impact on their businesses. Despite its effort to rectify the problem, the government has yet to find an effective solution. The public sector must find ways to address these challenges, by providing better in-depth information and encouraging firm preparedness for internal changes from within each firm.

4. IMPLICATIONS OF DOMESTIC ECONOMIC INTERESTS ON AEC IMPLEMENTATION: THREE CASE STUDIES

Liberalization affects stakeholders in different ways and this may result in conflicting domestic economic interests — one of the reasons for the slow pace of liberalization (Scheve and Slaughter 2001; Peamsilpakulchorn 2006). Thus, identifying winners and losers of the AEC, and how they will be affected, is a key challenge. Deepening integration post-2015 is another challenge for Thailand. In this section, three case studies — the agricultural, logistics, and medical services sectors — are used to illustrate conflicting domestic economic interests.

4.1 The Case of the Agricultural Sector

The agricultural sector has played an important role in Thailand's economic development. It was the economy's engine of growth during the 1960s and 1970s (Poapongsakorn and Anuchitworawong 2006). It continues to be a key source of employment for many Thais living in rural areas and is a key contributor to food security. More than a third of the Thai population was employed by the agricultural sector in 2012. The sector also serves as a source of exporting income, contributing 1,308,905 million baht to the economy or about 17.89 per cent of total exports in 2014 (Office of Agricultural Economics 2015). Moreover, raw materials from agribusiness create forward linkages, another important aspect of Thai exports.

ASEAN-led agricultural sector liberalization has a potentially large impact on the Thai economy, especially on: agricultural income; the structure of the sector; as well as the lifestyles of small farmers. By 2010, Thailand had removed all tariffs on goods in the inclusion list, except for four goods in the sensitive list — coffee, potato, copra and cut flower plants — which still have tariffs of less than 5 per cent. Liamchamroon (2012) argues that Thailand has too few products in the sensitive list and no products in the highly sensitive list.

In 1999, the Thai government made commitments via the ASEAN Investment Area (AIA) council to liberalize three sub-sectors in the temporary exclusion list (TEL): (i) plant cultivation and propagation, including artificial and transplant propagation and breeding; (ii) fishery, specifically aquaculture and; (iii) forestry from forest plantation in 2009. When the AIA was subsumed and transformed into the ASEAN Comprehensive Investment Agreement (ACIA), this commitment was retained.

A total of 103 non-governmental organizations (NGOs) objected to this action. These groups argued that opening up investment in the agricultural sector will negatively affect Thai businesses. MNCs will invest in seed businesses, drive locals out and subsequently monopolize these businesses. This will also change the way Thai farmers develop their seeds and lead to more competition among plantations for resources that are already in short supply. Replacing forests with agricultural plantations may affect the ecosystem and environment. Even though the government claims that it has prepared measures to cushion the effects of liberalization, many of these measures are not effective and their enforcement is weak (Liamchamroon 2012). Thus, these groups have decided to protect farmers and small agricultural businesses from competition from MNCs and large companies by requesting for a delay of in the liberalization of these sectors. Currently, the three above-mentioned agricultural sub-sectors are on the country's reservation list with a 51 per cent Thai equity participation requirement.

Therefore, agricultural liberalization is controversial, with varying benefits. On the one hand, Thailand will receive benefits from international trade expansion and its spillovers on growth. People who will gain from the AEC are large exporters, large processing food companies and high productivity farmers (SCB Economic Intelligence Center 2012). These companies have the capabilities to adjust themselves and compete in the ASEAN market. The AEC provides greater opportunities to Thai exporters to expand their agricultural shipments in the region and Thai investors can also discover new investment locations in other ASEAN member states. Data from the Office of Agricultural Economics shows that, from 2003 to 2012, the share of agricultural exports from Thailand to ASEAN increased from 16 to 21 per cent respectively. Liamchamroon (2012) further argues that MNCs will gain from the AEC with the opportunities to enter and take advantage of the Thai market.

On the other hand, small and unproductive Thai farmers are the potential losers of the AEC's liberalization measures (*PostToday*, 26 May 2012; SCB EIC 2012; Changpinyo and Cherdchoochai 2013). First, the survey findings from the SCB EIC (2012) show that most Thai farmers do not understand the AEC. This observation is important since Thai farmers form the majority of stakeholders in this sector and need to be prepared for changes from the AEC as soon as possible. Secondly, greater competition and more imports of agricultural products from other ASEAN member states may threaten the livelihood of these small farmers (Changpinyo and Cherdchoochai 2013). Third, even though Thai farmers are the main players in agricultural production, they have been marginalized from the benefits of trade liberalization (Zamroni 2006). For example, the Center for

International Trade Studies (CITS 2011) analyses the distribution of rice farmers' incomes under the AEC's liberalization measures and argues that only 15.12 per cent of the total increase in income will go to Thai farmers, with the rest going to non-farmers involved in the rice industry. Therefore, small farmers will benefit from the protection of the agricultural sector.

The Thai government has prepared FTA funds to remedy these adverse effects and to enhance the competitiveness of affected groups.[5] The agricultural sector is a key group asking for support from these funds. Even though the implementation of these funds have been consistent with their objectives, they are inefficient. The funds are insufficient to cover everyone affected by FTAs or the entire value chain; additionally, the approval process takes a long time and it is difficult to apply for these funds (ITD 2013).

There are several implications of these different economic interests on the pace of AEC implementation vis-à-vis the Thai agricultural sector. First, different views between winners and losers, coupled with restrictions on foreign ownership from the Foreign Business Act (1999), have resulted in slow progress in opening up the agricultural sector. Even though trade in agricultural products has already been liberalized and FTA funds have been set up, the affected groups and NGOs may not view these measures as effective. This may lead to greater public wariness of further agricultural liberalization. Secondly, it is necessary to have greater consultation with all stakeholders of the entire value chain, including representatives of small farmers and NGOs and consider, not only the potential economic effects, but also the social and environmental effects to obtain domestic consensus. Third, government agencies should work towards creating greater awareness about the AEC, especially by providing information on how to prepare for it. Fourth, although the Thai government has prepared FTA funds to mitigate the negative effects of FTAs and improve farmers' competitiveness, the funds need to be managed more efficiently. In preparation for the AEC, they should be consolidated into one fund and operated as a single public entity in order to increase flexibility in responding to requests from applicants (ITD 2013).

4.2 The Case of the Logistics Industry

Logistics plays an important role in enhancing a country's competitiveness and economic growth. In Thailand, the logistics services sector is a huge industry with the potential to generate about 300 billion baht of value-added each year (NESDB 2013; Solidiance 2014). The government has recognized the significance of the logistics sector and adopted the First Logistics Development Plan during 2007–11 to improve the competitiveness of local logistics firms. As a result, Thailand's share of logistics cost to GDP dropped from 17 per cent of GDP in 2007 to 14.7 per cent in 2011 and the sector created jobs for 3.5 million people during 2000–10 (NESDB 2013). However, the country's logistics cost to GDP is still relatively high when compared to Singapore and Malaysia. According to the World Bank's Logistic Performance Index (World Bank 2014), out of 160 countries, Thailand ranks 35 in logistics competency after Singapore (rank 5) and Malaysia (rank 25).

The government has continued to develop this industry by including logistics development in the Eleventh National Economic and Social Development Plan (2012–16) and implementing the Second Logistics Development Plan (2013–17) in order to increase capacity in supply chain management and enhance trade facilitation and capacity building (NESDB 2013, p. 8).

Most of the firms in the Thai logistics industry are small local firms while a majority of the large firms are MNCs such as DHL, Linfox, DB Schenker and Eternity. Because of their size, the large firms will be the potential winners of a more liberalized logistics sector. Opening up the logistic market will provide an opportunity for MNCs and other large logistics companies to expand their networks and investments in the Thai market, and in turn, further enhance their bargaining power (Kasikorn Research Center 2010). Moreover, Thailand is aiming to increase connectivity with neighbouring countries such as China and India and to become ASEAN's logistics hub. ASEAN's expansion into a single market and production base will increase regional demand for logistics services (Solidiance 2014, p. 68). Customers of the industry can also benefit from lower logistics costs and greater options once this sector is fully liberalized (Tantraporn 2012).

Nevertheless there are signs that Thai logistics service providers may face difficulties and lose out from AEC-led liberalization. Most of the Thai logistics service providers are small and medium businesses, operated by single owners as family businesses, with a registered capital of less than 5 million baht. Usually they work as sub-contractors of logistics firms, which may be partially foreign-owned, and they serve only as logistic service providers (LSPs). They have a lower capacity and are less competitive than subsidiaries of MNCs which operate as Third Party Logistics Providers (3PL) with integrated services (INSAPS 2010; DTN 2012b). Moreover, small, local logistics firms do not have access to financial support, more advanced technology, management systems and marketing strategies (DTN 2012b, p. 23).

As the deadline for the AEC approaches, losers may not be able to adjust and compete with foreign firms. Solidiance (2014) suggests that in order to survive the scheduled liberalization, local firms have to adapt in several ways. First, they have to coordinate among themselves to form a larger network. Secondly, they have to become the outsourced business units of global logistics companies. If they cannot adjust themselves, they might be driven out of the market or acquired. A committee on logistics services has been established to oversee the development of the logistics industry. This is a joint committee formed by representatives of the Ministry of Commerce and the private sector (Thai Federation on Logistics, Thai Logistics Service Provider Federation, Thai Chamber of Commerce, Federation of Thai Industry and Thai National Shippers' Council). This is one government mechanism aimed at assisting potential losers of the AEC.

Under the Ninth Package of AFAS, the Thai government has allowed for more ASEAN foreign equity participation, not exceeding 70 per cent, in some logistics services sub-sectors such as international sea cruises, and storage and warehousing services for frozen or refrigerated goods. However, most of the key logistics sub-sectors still require majority Thai ownership.

Therefore, even though the government has made progress in liberalizing the sector, its pace remains slow. There are two key reasons for this. First, since the Thai government is aware of the potential adverse effects on local firms, it is trying to improve their competitiveness and readiness by slowing down implementation. Secondly, liberalizing logistics services involves not only negotiations under the AEC framework, but also implementing appropriate domestic laws and regulations, i.e., beyond-the-border measures. Thirteen major laws and regulations govern the logistics industry including the Foreign Business Act (1999), Working of Alien Act (2008) and Multimodal Transport Act (2007) (DTN 2010). These laws have some restrictions on how Thai logistics services should be operated, hence, contributing to slow pace in implementation.

At the same time, both the government and private sector are aware that they cannot hold off opening up the industry indefinitely. Hence, this chapter identifies some suggestions to enhance the preparatory measures that have thus far been taken to face the challenges of liberalization. First, even though the stakeholders in the logistics services are aware of the AEC and the liberalization that will take place within their industry, they need more information on the details of such liberalization. For example, to prepare for the AEC, DTN (2010) argues that it is necessary to also liberalize some sub-sectors related to logistics services infrastructure in order to improve the competitiveness of the entire value chain. Second, to mitigate the negative impact of the AEC on potential losers, local logistics firms themselves need to improve their competitiveness. In this regard, firms have to anticipate the impact of liberalization on the entire value chain; not just on the firm alone. This will require greater consolidation among local small players to create larger local players. Together with the expansion of the logistics network within the Thai market, the aforementioned are some of the ways of resolving the uneven distributive impact of the AEC liberalization measures. The Second Development Plan for Logistics has contributed to the competitiveness of Thai logistics firms by improving local capabilities in supply chain management (NESDB 2013). Third, it has also been suggested that the government should accelerate structural reform and enhance the competitiveness of the industry by adjusting the domestic laws and regulations to facilitate fair competition between local small players and MNCs (DTN 2010; INSAPS 2010).

4.3 The Movement of Natural Persons (MNPs) within the Medical Profession

The movement of natural persons (MNPs) is an important contributor to the success of trade in services (Tullao and Cortez 2006; Chia 2011). However, liberalization has been slow because of different economic interests in the domestic economy and limitations from domestic laws and regulations.

As with all of the other ASEAN countries, the movement of natural persons is a sensitive issue because the liberalization of professional mobility may affect the domestic labour market and social welfare. Concerns revolve around greater competition in the labour market and the quality of foreign professionals' work on the health, safety and living standards of Thai citizens. This section considers the mobility of professionals in medical services as an example.

The significant milestones arising from the AEC are the Mutual Recognition Agreements (MRAs) on nursing services (signed 8 December

2006), medical practitioners (signed 26 February 2009) and dental practitioners (signed 26 February 2009). Thailand has committed to the temporary movement of the natural persons in the following categories: (i) business visitor; and (ii) intra-corporate transferee (with the requirement that the person who will be responsible for operating the outpatient clinic must have a licence to operate not more than one such clinic, and has obtained a licence to practise in Thailand). Thus doctors, dentists and nurses from other ASEAN countries must comply with these domestic regulations in order to work in the country. The Medical Council of Thailand, the Dental Council and the Nursing and Midwife Council awards relevant medical licences to professionals who have passed examinations that are conducted in Thai. While some argue that the language requirement is a barrier to professional mobility, others have pointed out that knowledge of the Thai language is necessary because the doctors, nurses and dentists have to communicate with their patients.

When Thailand moves towards more liberalized movement of professionals, the potential winners will be the Thai people and the country's hospitals. First of all, Thailand is currently facing a shortage of medical staff. The density of physicians, nurses and midwives is 24.7 per 10,000 people, just barely above the minimum 23 per 10,000 target recommended by the World Health Organization (WHO). Allowing for the entry of more medical professionals may help to meet this shortage in the industry.

Secondly, since 2003, the government has positioned the country as Asia's medical hub. This is a result of the transformation of medical services in Thailand from a weak local market into a facility for international patients after the 1997–98 Asian Financial Crisis (AFC) (Chokedamrongsuk 2010). The country, now one of the world's largest medical tourism markets, has attracted a large number of patients with its availability of traditional and alternative medicines. Moreover, Thailand is promoted as a place for retirement homes and care centres as well as dedicated health centres with advanced technological devices and facilities (BOI 2014). As the medical market has grown fairly strongly, more doctors and nurses are required. With greater professional mobility, hospitals and medical businesses can hire more staff to fulfill the expansion needs of their businesses. Third, some experts in medical services also perceive that liberalization is necessary to facilitate the movement of medical staff in ASEAN countries for an exchange of experiences and to update practitioner knowledge.

However, some Thai medical staff are more concerned about the potential negative effects of the AEC. First, some professionals, such as nurses, may view the inflow of medical professionals from other ASEAN countries as a threat to the domestic labour market. Although the inflow of nurses, for example, may help to solve a manpower shortage in Thailand, it may also create greater competition among some segments of the industry, such as the private hospitals. Thai professionals fear that with more international patients coming to Thailand, nurses and dentists from other ASEAN countries with better English skills will more hireable (Ariyasajjakorn and Manprasert 2015). This could also apply to hospitals located at the Thai border. Nurses from other ASEAN countries have some advantages over Thai professionals when communicating with patients from neighbouring countries. Secondly, greater liberalization increases the opportunities for Thai hospitals to expand their businesses to these neighbouring countries. This may further add to the shortage of Thai medical staff as some may relocate out of Thailand.

5. CONCLUSION

Thailand has come a long way in implementing the AEC measures. Currently, the AEC is Thailand's priority and its Blueprint is being progressively implemented in the domestic economy. However, deeper and broader economic integration under the AEC, coupled with increasing participation from a broader and more diverse group of stakeholders, each with different economic interests, has contributed to the slow pace of integration in Thailand. To move the AEC beyond 2015, a measure of domestic consensus needs to be achieved.

Three case studies were used in this chapter to examine the implications of conflicting domestic economic interests. In the agricultural sector, Thai farmers may end up being marginalized, while large exporters in the processed food industry and farmers with high productivity can expand their market base and gain from regional liberalization. Similarly, large logistics companies and MNCs are likely to gain from greater regional market and investment expansion. Local and smaller Thai logistics firms would then have to either consider domestic consolidation measures or become outsourced business units for MNCs. In an extreme scenario, they may be driven out of the market. Finally, although medical professionals have played an important role in the Thai economy, they have always been protected by domestic regulatory measures such as licensing requirements. Thai citizens and hospitals stand to gain as the country moves towards a more liberalized environment for medical professionals. However, nurses may face stiff competition in the domestic labour market.

It is, therefore, important for Thailand to consider putting greater efforts into developing domestic consensus among the different stakeholders so that the country may more effectively participate in ASEAN's liberalization and community building process. In this regard, some of the key policy recommendations are put forth in the following paragraphs.

First, although the stakeholders in each business sector are aware of the AEC, Thai government officials should convey detailed information on the liberalization and facilitation measures to be undertaken. Any misunderstanding can result in misinterpretation and, subsequently, resistance towards liberalization efforts. In this regard, more research on the impact of the AEC on particular sectors should be encouraged and disseminated to the public (TDRI 2012*a*).

Second, the government agencies responsible for the AEC, in particular the Department of Trade Negotiations, should regularly consult the representatives of professional bodies and the private sector. A well-structured and integrated working relationship between each of the relevant ministries and the business community will help Thailand advance the implementation of its AEC commitments.

Third, in the medium-term, going beyond 2015, Thailand needs to prepare its domestic workforce, including professionals and business leaders, to incorporate AEC commitments into their work strategies. These could be in the form of developing various skills such as language, management and ability to work in a cross-cultural environment. Moreover, in tandem with the implementation of the AEC measures, Thailand should enhance its assistance programmes to mitigate the adverse impact of the AEC on potential losers. This will help the country develop domestic consensus and eventually benefit from its efforts at regional economic integration.

Notes

1. The four products on Thailand's sensitive list are coffee, potato, copra and cut flower plants. They still have tariffs of no more than 5 per cent.
2. Thailand is the third country in ASEAN to succeed in setting up a National Trade Repository (NTR) after Indonesia and Laos.
3. BOT has planned to issue new licences to five foreign banks in Thailand. However, only two banks, ANZ (Australia) and Sumitomo Mitsui Trust Bank

(Japan) have applied for the licences. On 30 April 2014, BOT, together with the Ministry of Finance, agreed to award licences to these two banks (*Thansettaki*, 23 April 2014).

4. CLMV: Cambodia; Laos; Myanmar; and Vietnam. The Co-Shepeherd mechanism is used to improve the competitiveness of the CLMV countries by reducing poverty, improving standards of living and bureaucracies. The ASEAN-6 and CLMV are paired as co-shepherds and coordinators in each of these areas: infrastructure; human resource development; information and communication technology (ICT); investment; tourism; poverty; and quality of life. Projects such as an educational programme to assist CLMV countries in implementing multimodal transport operations and workshops on enhancing the investment climate in these countries have also been implemented (Department of ASEAN Affairs 2012).

5. These are the Ministry of Agriculture's FTA fund (which falls under the supervision of the Office of Agricultural Economics, Ministry of Agriculture and Cooperatives) and the Ministry of Commerce's FTA fund (which falls under the Department of Foreign Trade, Ministry of Commerce).

References

Ariyasajjakorn, Danupon and Somprawin Manprasert. *"Sathanakarn Lae Pholkratop Jakkarn Kleanyai Rang-ngan Seri Nai Phumipak ASEAN"* [Situation and Impact from Free Flow of Labour in ASEAN]. Bangkok: Chulalongkorn University Press, 2015.

ASEAN Exchanges. *"ASEAN: The World's Growth Market"*. 2012. <http://www.set.or.th/th/asean_exchanges/files/AseanExchanges_en.pdf> (accessed 2 April 2015).

ASEAN Secretariat. *ASEAN Economic Community Scorecard 2012*. Jakarta: ASEAN Secretariat, 2012.

BOI [Board of Investment]. "Thailand Region's Top Logistics Hub Leading to AEC Trade Boom". *Thailand Investment Review (TIR)* 22, no. 9 (2012): 5–6.

———. "Industry Focus: Thailand's Medical Industry", February 2014. <http://www.boi.go.th/tir/issue_content.php?issueid=108;page=42> (accessed 6 December 2014).

Bureau of Trade Preference. *Trade Preference Journal*. Bangkok: Bureau of Trade Preference, Department of Foreign Trade, various issues.

Changpinyo, Niti and Supatra Cherdchoochai. *"Kaset Thai Nai Vethi ASEAN"* [Thai Agriculture in ASEAN]. *Journal of Economics and Society* 50, no. 2 (2013): 24–30.

Chia, Siow Yue. "Free Flow of Skilled Labor in the AEC". ERIA Final Report, 2011.

———. "The ASEAN Economic Community: Progress, Challenges, and Prospects",

ADBI Working Paper No. 440. Manila: Asian Development Bank Institute, 2013. <http://www.adbi.org/files/2013.10.25.wp440.asean.economic.community. progress.challenges.pdf> (accessed 15 December 2014).

Chirathivat, Suthiphand and Sothitorn Mallikamas. "Thailand's FTA Strategy: Current Development and Future Challenges". *ASEAN Economic Bulletin* 1, no. 1 (2004): 37–53.

────── and Piti Srisangnam. "The 2030 Architecture of the Association of Southeast Asian Nations Free Trade Agreements". ADBI Working Paper no. 419. Manila: Asian Development Bank Institute, 2013.

──────, Pachusanond, Chumporn and Patcharawalai Wongboonsin. "ASEAN Prospects for Regional Integration and the Implications for the ASEAN Legislative and Institutional Framework". *ASEAN Economic Bulletin* 16, no. 1 (1999): 28–50.

Chokedamrongsuk, Jessada. *"Yudthasart Karnpattana Soonklang Karnpaat"* [Development Strategy for Medical Hub]. Individual Study, Foreign Affairs Executive Programme-Devawongse Vorapakarn: Institute of Foreign Affairs, 2010.

CITS [Center for International Trade Studies]. "The Impact of the ASEAN Economic Community (AEC) on Thai Rice". *Thailand Economic & Business Review* 4, no. 1 (2011): 4–8.

Department of ASEAN Affairs. *Kwarm Rirerm Pue Karnruamtua Kong ASEAN* [Initiative for ASEAN Integration: IAI]. Bangkok: Ministry of Foreign Affairs, 2012.

DTN (Department of Trade Negotiations). *"Karn Perdseri Pak Borikarn Paitai AEC Saka Logistics"* [Service Liberalization under AEC: Logistics]. Bangkok: Department of Trade Negotiations, 2010.

──────. "AEC Fact Book: One Vision, One Identity, One Community", Bangkok: Department of Trade Negotiations, 2012*a*.

──────. *Turakit Borikarn: Logistics* [Logistics Services]. Bangkok: Department of Trade Negotiations, 2012*b*. Available at <http://www.dtn.go.th/filesupload/ aec/images/logis29-05-55.pdf > (accessed 6 December 2014).

──────. "Sathanakarn Jeraja Larsud" [Latest Negotiation Status], 3 February 2014. Available at <http://www.thaifta.com/thaifta/Home/NegoLastestStatus/ tabid/117/Default.aspx> (accessed 20 January 2015).

ERIA. *Mid-Term Review of the Implementation of AEC Blueprint: Executive Summary.* Jakarta: Economic Research Institute for ASEAN and East Asia, 2012. Available at <http://www.eria.org/Mid-Term%20Review%20of%20the%20 Implementation%20of%20AEC%20Blue%20Print-Executive%20Summary.pdf> (accessed 20 November 2014).

INSAPS [International Institute for Asia-Pacific Studies]. *Karn Perd Seri Logistics ASEAN: Okard Pholkratop Lae Karnprabtua Khong Phuprakobkarn Thai* [Logistics

Liberalisation in ASEAN: Opportunity, Impact and Adjustment of Thai Entrepreneurs]. Paper submitted to the Department of Trade Negotiations, Ministry of Commerce, December 2010.

Intarawitak, Chetta, Sumet Ongkittikul and Nuttawut Lucksahapanyakul. *"Karn Kasinka Lae Karn Aumnuykwarmsaduak Tangkarnka"* [Trade in Goods and Trade Facilitation]. Presentation at the Thailand Development Research Institute (TDRI) Annual Seminar on "ASEAN Economic Community: Myths, Reality, Potentials and Challenges", Thailand, 2012.

ITD [International Institute for Trade and Development]. *Kolkai Kwarmchouylea Phudairub Pholkratop Karnperdseri Tangkarnka.* [Assistance Measures for Negative Impacts of FTA]. Bangkok: Kiddee Plus Creation, 2013.

————. *Okard Lae Aubprasuk Karnlongtun Paitai Karnlongtun ASEAN* [Opportunity and Challenge under ACIA]. Bangkok: Onpa Publishing, 2014.

Kasikorn Research Center. "ASEAN Liberalization of Logistics Services: Implications for Thailand". K-Econ Analysis, Business Brief No. 2871, 6 July 2010. Available at <https://www.kasikornresearch.com/en/k-econanalysis/pages/ViewSummary.aspx?docid=25426> (accessed 6 April 2015).

Liamchamroon, Witoon. *Phakkaset Thai Kub AEC Promleaw Jingrue?* [Thai Agricultural Sector and AEC: Are We Really Ready for It?]. Bangkok: FTA Watch, 2012. <http://www.ftawatch.org/sites/default/files/documents/2012_FTA-witoon. pdf> (accessed 29 December 2014).

Mayer, Frederick W. "Managing Domestic Differences in International Negotiations: the Strategic Use of Internal Side-Payments". *International Organization* 46, no. 4 (1992): 793–818.

NESDB (Office of National Economic and Social Development Board). *Phaen Yuttasart Karn Pattana Rabop Logistics Khong Prathed Thai Chabap Thee Song* [Thailand's Logistics Development Strategy Phase 2 (2013–2017)]. Bangkok: Office of the National Economic and Social Development Board, 2013.

Nikomborirak, Deunden and Supunnavadee Jitdumrong. "ASEAN Trade in Services". In *The ASEAN Economic Community: A Work in Progress,* edited by Sanchita Basu Das, Jayant Menon, Omkar L. Shrestha and Rodolfo Severino. Singapore: Institute of Southeast Asian Studies, 2013.

Office of Agricultural Economics. "Export Value of Major Agricultural Products, 2014–2015". 2015. Available at <http://www.oae.go.th/oae_report/export_ import/exp_topten.php?imex=1> (accessed 1 April 2015).

Peamsilpakulchorn, Pajnapa. "The Domestic Politics of Thailand's Bilateral Free Trade Agreement Policy". *International Public Policy Review* 2, no. 1 (2006): 74–120.

Plummer, Michael G. and Chia Siow Yue. *Realizing the ASEAN Economic Community: A Comprehensive Assessment.* Singapore: Institute of Southeast Asian Studies, 2009.

Poapongsakorn, Nipon and Chaiyasit Anuchitworawong. "The Decline and

Recovery of Thai Agriculture: Causes, Responses, Prospects and Challenges". In *Rapid Growth of Selected Asian Economies: Lessons and Implications for Agriculture and Food Security; Republic of Korea, Thailand, and Viet Nam*. FAO Policy Assistance Series 1/3. Bangkok: FAO, 2006.

Policy Statement of the Council of Ministers. Delivered by General Prayut Chan-o-cha, Prime Minister, to the National Legislative Assembly, 12 September 2014.

PostToday [online]. "Anakod Kaset Thai Paitai AEC" [Future of Thai Agriculture under AEC], 26 May 2012. Available at <http://tdri.or.th/archives/download/news/pt2012_05_26a.pdf> (accessed 1 April 2015).

Pupphavesa, Wisarn. *Jub Krasae Jak AEC Soo RCEP: Okard Rue Kubdug Kong Prated Thai* [From AEC to RCEP: Opportunity of Trap for Thailand]. Thailand Development Research Institute (TDRI) Public Seminar, 7 December 2012.

Ruengvirayudh, Pongpen. *Senthang Karn Nguen Su AEC* [Financial Path to AEC]. Bangkok: Bank of Thailand, 2013. Available at <https://www.sasin.edu/pdf/AEC_BOT.pdf > (accessed 15 December 2014).

SCB EIC [Siam Commercial Bank Economic Intelligence Center]. "AEC and Beyond...What's Next to Thai Farm Sector". *EIC Analysis*, October 2012. Available at <https://www.scbeic.com/en/detail/product/957> (accessed 1 April 2015).

Scheve, Kenneth F. and Matthew J. Slaughter. "What Determines Individual Trade-policy Preferences?". *Journal of International Economics* 54 (2001): 267–92.

Solidiance. "Thailand's Logistic Opportunities in the Cross-Border Trades and AEC Development", January 2014. Available at <http://www.solidiance.com/whitepaper/thailands-logistic-opportunities.pdf> (accessed 10 January 2015).

Sukma, Rizal. "ASEAN Beyond 2015: The Imperatives for Further Institutional Changes". ERIA Discussion Paper. Jakarta: Economic Research Institute for ASEAN and East Asia, 2014.

Tantraporn, Apiradi. *Kormoon Cherngluek Perdseri Logistics Rub AEC* [In-depth Information on Logistics Liberalization under the AEC]. Available at <http://www.thai-aec.com/438#ixzz242sm9Mgx> (accessed 27 March 2015).

Thai Customs Department. *Thailand National Single Window*, 2010. Available at <http://www.thainsw.net/INSW/index.jsp?nswLang=E > (accessed 6 January 2015).

Thailand Development Research Institute (TDRI). *Phol Kratop Jakkarn Perd Taladkarnkha Seri Paitai ASEAN+3 Lea ASEAN+6 Lea Naewthang karn Jerajathi Maosoam Samrab Prathed Thai* [Impact of liberalization under ASEAN+3 and ASEAN+6 and Appropriate Negotiation Guideline for Thailand]. Bangkok: Thailand Development Research Institute, 2012*a*.

———. *Thailand Country Study: ASEAN Economic Community (AEC) Blueprint Mid-Term Review*. Bangkok: Thailand Development Research Institute, 2012*b*. Available at <http://tdri.or.th/wp-content/uploads/2012/10/High-level-

dialogue-on-AEC-Blueprint.pdf> (accessed 20 January 2015).

Thansettakij [online] *"Bank Tangchart Koatung Borisatlook Song Rai"* [Two Foreign Banks Apply for the Licenses], 23 April 2014. Available at <http://www. thanonline.com/index.php?option=com_content&view=article&id=227930: 2&catid=101:2009-02-08-11-30-52&Itemid=440#.VUEYMyGqpBc> (accessed 28 April 2015).

Tullao, Jr. Tereso S. and Michael A.A. Cortez. "Enhancing the Movement of Natural Persons in the ASEAN Region: Opportunities and Constraints". Asia-Pacific Research and Training Network on Trade Working Paper No. 23, December 2006. Available at <http://www.unescap.org/sites/default/files/AWP%20 No.%2023.pdf> (accessed 30 January 2015).

World Bank. *Connecting to Compete 2014, Trade Logistics in the Global Economy: The Logistics Performance Index and Its Indicators.* Washington, D.C.: World Bank, 2014.

Wuttisorn, Piyanuch. *Yudthasart Karn Kaosoo Prachakom ASEAN* [Strategy for ASEAN Community]. NESDB [Office of the National Economic and Social Development Board], 2013. Available at <http://www.diw.go.th/hawk/news/ASEAN-Industrial%20Works%20Piyanuch%20full.pdf > (accessed 26 March 2015).

Zamroni, Salim. "Thailand's Agricultural Sector and Free Trade Agreements". *Asia-Pacific Trade and Investment Review* 2, no. 2 (2006): 51–70.

8

MANAGING DOMESTIC CONSENSUS FOR ASEAN COMMUNITY-BUILDING IN VIETNAM

Vo Tri Thanh

1. INTRODUCTION

Until 1986, Vietnam remained an autarky under a central planning regime with some of the following key characteristics: (i) state or collective ownership of all production means, including those in agriculture; (ii) government administered supply of physical input and output; (iii) the absence of factor markets; (iv) and highly regulated goods and services markets.[1] Poor incentives and restricted information flows led to heavy distortions in resource allocation (Vo and Nguyen 2006). While ensuring the contribution of output to the state, cooperatives usually failed to meet half their members' demands.[2] Facing an economic crisis and severe food shortages, Vietnam carried out reforms in the early 1980s, but only at the micro-level.

The year 1986 marked a major breakthrough in economic reforms as the country rejected the rationale of the central planning model, and declared its intention to transform itself into a mixed-market economy.

Since then, various market-oriented reforms have been undertaken, aimed at stabilizing and opening up the economy, and expanding freedom of choice for all economic units. Reforms of goods markets and factors of production took place gradually; legal and policy reforms were undertaken to create a level playing field for all economic entities, irrespective of their nationality or form of ownership.

The reforms brought about remarkable socio-economic success in Vietnam. The pace of economic growth increased steadily, averaging 7.8 per cent per annum during 1990–2010, despite moderating to below 6 per cent per annum during 2012–14. Exports expanded at an average annual rate of 18.8 per cent per annum during 1990 to 2014. GDP per capita improved from US$98 in 1990 to above US$1,910 in 2013, thereby helping Vietnam to become a middle-income country in 2008 (*Vietnam News Daily*, 14 April 2014). The poverty rate dropped sharply from 58.1 per cent in 1993 to just over 12.1 per cent in 2014.[3]

The country's wide-ranging socio-economic success was the outcome of several factors. First, Vietnam had committed itself to bold and comprehensive reforms. After being severely challenged in 1985 by the failures of microeconomic reforms and by food scarcity, it recognized the importance of undertaking more comprehensive and consistent market-oriented reforms. Once they were initiated, these reforms gathered momentum and have now become practically irreversible. Moreover, these domestic reforms were largely inclusive and focused on benefits to people. This ensured sufficient domestic consensus for reforms and related policy adjustments. As Vietnam gradually adapted itself to international trade and investment rules, domestic policy space to support local enterprises progressively contracted — signaling the continued importance of achieving domestic consensus.

This chapter attempts to review the process of regional economic integration undertaken by Vietnam, focusing on the role of domestic consensus. Specifically, it aims to: (i) document Vietnam's progress towards greater regional economic integration under the ASEAN Economic Community (AEC) framework (following section); (ii) discuss issues related to ensuring domestic consensus for regional economic integration; and (iii) draw out key policy recommendations for enhancing consensus as the country continues to implement its AEC commitments. The rest of this chapter is organized as follows: section 3 focuses on the current utilization rates of ASEAN free trade agreements (FTAs) and reasons for the low rates of utilization. Section 4 discusses three key issues for managing domestic consensus: (i) consultation with domestic stakeholders; (ii) raising awareness; and (iii) enhancing or introducing new policies that are able to mitigate the adverse impacts of regional integration. It should be noted, however, that the AEC is one component of several liberalization measures being undertaken in Vietnam. It is, therefore, difficult to attribute any of these reforms solely to the AEC. Finally, section 5 concludes with key policy recommendations.

2. VIETNAM'S PROGRESS IN IMPLEMENTING ITS AEC COMMITMENTS

Since the implementation of the *Doi Moi* reforms, Vietnam has embarked on a process of international economic integration to expand access to foreign markets and critical resources for developing its domestic economy.[4] The country signed a trade agreement with the European Union (EU) in 1992. It joined ASEAN and the ASEAN Free Trade Area (AFTA) in 1995. Subsequently, in 1998, it also became a member of the Asia Pacific Economic Cooperation (APEC) forum. The country has accelerated its integration process since 2000. That year, Vietnam and the United States signed a bilateral trade agreement; this was Vietnam's first comprehensive trade agreement especially because it included the high standard trade and investment rules typically found in an agreement with the United States. The country also prepared itself for accession to the World Trade Organization (WTO) while simultaneously participating in numerous ASEAN-led FTAs. Accession to the WTO in 2007 really consolidated domestic and international optimism surrounding Vietnam's growth prospects.

The country is currently pursuing negotiations on several ambitious FTAs such as the Trans-Pacific Partnership (TPP), the EU-Vietnam FTA and the Regional Comprehensive Economic Partnership (RCEP). Overtime, the depth and scope of FTAs that Vietnam has participated in have continuously expanded, from agreements focusing only on trade in goods and services to more comprehensive agreements capturing trade and investment facilitation, intellectual property rights and so on. With respect to the AEC, Vietnam has been relatively successful in complying with the measures outlined in the 2007 AEC Blueprint ("the Blueprint"); in fact, the country has achieved some of its commitments ahead of their respective deadlines. Many current account items have been liberalized ahead of schedule. In addition, the country's dual exchange rate system was phased out in 1989. Finally, Vietnam's surrender requirement was abolished in 2004, well ahead of the 2011–12 Blueprint target.[5]

Despite these positive examples of compliance, a more comprehensive examination of Vietnam's implementation of its AEC commitments cannot be carried out due to a lack of detailed and timely information. The costs of compiling and collecting more comprehensive data are too high, therefore, Table 8.1 provides an overview of only the first two phases of the Blueprint's Strategic Schedule for implementation (2008–09; 2010–11).[6]

Out of nineteen AEC Scorecard targets,[7] Vietnam has fully achieved only nine and partially achieved (at levels equal to or greater than 50 per cent) ten targets. The country outperformed the regional average with respect to the first two AEC pillars — (i) a single market and production base; and

TABLE 8.1
AEC Scorecard (Vietnam) under Phases I and II, 2008–11

Pillar	Targets	Vietnam	ASEAN
Single market and production base	Free Flow of Goods	>50%	<50%
	Free Flow of Services	>50%	<50%
	Free Flow of Investment	>50%	<50%
	Freer Flow of Capital	100%	100%
	Free Flow of Skilled Labor	100%	100%
	Priority Integration Sectors	>50%	100%
	Food, Agriculture and Forestry	>50%	<50%
Competitive economic region	Competition Policy	100%	100%
	Consumer Protection	>50%	>50%
	Intellectual Property Rights	100%	>50%
	Transport	>50%	>50%
	Energy	>50%	<50%
	Mineral	100%	100%
	ICT	100%	100%
	Taxation	100%	<50%
	E-commerce	100%	100%
Equitable economic development	SME Development	>50%	>50%
	Initiative for ASEAN Integration (IAI)	>50%	>50%
Integration with global economy	External Economic Relations	>50%	>50%

Source: Extracted from EU-MUTRAP (2014).

(ii) a competitive economic region — and matched the regional average with respect to the last two pillars of the AEC. The Scorecard reports that any shortfalls have been caused by delays in ratifying signed ASEAN-wide agreements as well as delays in the implementation of specific initiatives. As was mentioned above, however, it is difficult to determine the exact extent of implementation because the ASEAN Secretariat does not make such detailed information public.

Notwithstanding Vietnam's Scorecard achievements, during 2000 to 2013, the development gap between Vietnam and more advanced ASEAN member countries (and trade partners) was still large. In terms of GDP per capita, Vietnam only outperformed Laos and Cambodia and it lags far behind Singapore. In addition, the gap between Vietnam and China seems to have widened (Table 8.2).

The human development index (HDI) scores and rankings listed in Table 8.3 also indicate sizeable differences in the level of human development between Vietnam and the ASEAN-6.[8] From 2000 to 2005, Vietnam ranked ahead of Indonesia. Since 2007, the reverse has become true. In fact, the country's ranking dropped from 105 in 2005 to 121 in 2013.

As such, it has become even more important to align future community-building efforts with domestic development objectives. Vietnam is also involved in several regional agreements, which are likely to constrain

TABLE 8.2
Gaps in GDP per capita between Asian Countries

	2000	2005	2008	2013
Cambodia	0.6	0.7	0.7	0.6
Indonesia	1.6	1.4	1.4	1.8
Laos	0.8	0.8	0.8	0.9
Malaysia	6.0	5.3	5.1	4.4
Philippines	1.7	1.5	1.4	1.5
Singapore	23.7	19.9	17.8	15.2
Thailand	3.3	3.1	2.2	2.6
Vietnam	1.0	1.0	1.0	1.0
China	1.7	2.0	2.2	2.3

Note: The comparison is based on GDP per capita (international current US$). Vietnam's figure is set at unity.
Source: World Bank (2014a).

TABLE 8.3
Human Development Index (HDI) of ASEAN Countries, 2000–13

		2000	2005	2007	2013
Ranked countries		173	177	182	187
Vietnam	Value	0.688	0.733	0.725	0.638
	Rank	109	105	116	121
Brunei	Value	0.871	0.894	0.920	0.852
	Rank	32	30	30	30
Indonesia	Value	0.684	0.728	0.734	0.684
	Rank	110	107	111	108
Malaysia	Value	0.782	0.811	0.829	0.773
	Rank	59	63	66	62
Singapore	Value	0.885	0.922	0.944	0.901
	Rank	25	25	23	9
Cambodia	Value	0.543	0.598	0.593	0.584
	Rank	130	131	137	136
Laos	Value	0.485	0.601	0.619	0.569
	Rank	143	130	133	139
Myanmar	Value	0.552	0.583	0.586	0.524
	Rank	127	132	138	150
Thailand	Value	0.762	0.781	0.783	0.722
	Rank	70	78	87	89
Philippines	Value	0.754	0.771	0.751	0.660
	Rank	77	90	105	117

Source: Figures for 2000, 2005 and 2007 from Vo Tri Thanh (2012); Figures for 2013 from UNDP (2014).

its ability to fully participate in the AEC. In particular, the country has limited resources for negotiating international trade arrangements. Accordingly, policy-makers and stakeholders cannot give all pending FTAs equal attention. As a consequence, some policy-makers and stakeholders working on ASEAN FTAs tend to know more about the AEC, whilst others are only familiar with broader integration issues. This leads to a lack of uniform awareness; one can then hardly expect all stakeholders to reach a consensus on the AEC.

3. VIETNAM'S UTILIZATION OF ASEAN FTAs

An important objective of the ASEAN FTAs is the reduction of trade barriers (including tariffs) to increase market access. As an export-oriented economy, this objective is of great importance to Vietnam. Accordingly, it makes sense to revisit the utilization of preferential treatments under the ASEAN FTAs.

Table 8.4 summarizes Vietnam's utilization rates of the various FTAs. Notwithstanding two decades of ASEAN membership, the country's utilization of AFTA was rather low. Right up till 2005, only 6.07 per cent of the country's exports to ASEAN members enjoyed preferential treatment under AFTA. Over time, this figure has improved, climbing to almost 9.4 per cent in 2007, 14.1 per cent in 2010 and 20.2 per cent in 2011.

At below 10 per cent, the utilization rate of the ASEAN-China FTA remained rather low during 2006–08, but it then climbed dramatically to 21.7 per cent in 2009, peaking at 25.2 per cent in 2010 before regressing to 23.1 per cent in 2011. Exports to Korea and Japan had higher rates of FTA utilization. The FTA utilization rate of the ASEAN-Japan Comprehensive Economic Partnership agreement (AJCEP) started at 27.8 per cent in 2009 before increasing to 30.5 per cent and 31.2 per cent in 2010 and 2011, respectively. The utilization of preferential treatment under the ASEAN-Korea FTA (AKFTA) by Vietnamese export enterprises stood at an even more impressive 79.0 per cent in 2009, however, this fell to 66.0 per cent in 2010 before jumping to 90.8 per cent in 2011.

Several reasons have been identified for the relatively low levels of utilization of AFTA/ASEAN Trade in Goods Agreement (ATIGA). First, the local and other-ASEAN originated content of export products are

TABLE 8.4
Vietnam's Utilization Rates of ASEAN FTAs, 2005–11 (%)

	2005	2006	2007	2008	2009	2010	2011
AFTA	6.07	7.10	9.41	12.76	11.41	14.11	20.20
AJCEP	n.a.	n.a.	n.a.	n.a.	27.81	30.52	31.23
AKFTA	n.a.	n.a.	n.a.	n.a.	79.05	65.97	90.77
AANZFTA	n.a.	n.a.	n.a.	n.a.	n.a.	8.89	15.91
AIFTA	n.a.	n.a.	n.a.	n.a.	n.a.	2.39	7.37
ACFTA	n.a.	8.89	6.30	9.83	21.70	25.23	23.11

Note: The utilization rate of each FTA is calculated as the value of Vietnam's exports (in US$) enjoying FTA treatment, over the total value of Vietnam's exports to the corresponding FTA partner; n.a.: Not applicable.
Source: Ministry of Industry and Trade (Cited in Tran Ba Cuong 2012).

rather low, preventing Vietnamese enterprises from enjoying preferential treatment as they do not satisfy the rules of origin (ROO). In the case of some products, the most favoured nation (MFN) tariff rate is already low and differs very insignificantly from the preferential FTA rate. Moreover, the ROO procedures and requirements differ across FTAs and other preferential agreements. Given that the ASEAN+1 trade partners (such as Japan, South Korea and China) often have larger markets than the ASEAN market, Vietnamese enterprises prefer to expand their efforts towards meeting the requirements of these "+1" agreements over AFTA or ATIGA.

The lower utilization rates of AFTA/ATIGA have important implications for the process of building consensus on the AEC in Vietnam. Limited utilization makes it harder to justify further integration. Perhaps this indicates that current allocated resources to raise awareness among domestic enterprises and professionals have been insufficient. Allocating more resources, however, imposes a challenge for Vietnam in the current context of budget constraints.[9] As such, there is a lack of clarity on how Vietnam should go about increasing consensus-building efforts for all its integration tracks. Fostering a complete understanding of the need for domestic reforms in order to join the AEC is no easy task. Services liberalization, mutual recognition, and trade facilitation, for instance, are areas that a considered to be overwhelmingly macroeconomic and technical in nature; they hardly attract the attention of domestic enterprises.

Moreover, low compliance and utilization rates appear to indicate that Vietnam's integration efforts under the AEC have thus far merely followed a top-down approach with insufficient engagement of stakeholders. Stakeholder awareness of the AEC and the opportunities it will create are, therefore, also limited. It should also be noted that Vietnam's integration efforts under various frameworks — ASEAN, ASEAN+1, the WTO and bilateral FTAs — necessitates a horizontal approach to making and implementing integration commitments in the country. Domestic reforms in the country over the past fifteen years have mainly focused on broad laws such as the Enterprise Law, Investment Law, and so on; rather than specific AEC-related laws such as competition policy and intellectual property rights. Furthermore, technical details (such as ROOs and investment protection) appear under-harmonized across these integration frameworks. Given their limited capacity, enterprises in Vietnam are not able to conform to each of these different technical details to effectively utilize FTAs.

4. KEY ISSUES FOR MANAGING CONSENSUS DURING THE ASEAN COMMUNITY-BUILDING PROCESS

This section explores three different issues that Vietnam encounters in gathering consensus for the ASEAN community-building process, namely: (i) increasing stakeholder consultation during reforms; (ii) building community awareness of potential changes; and (iii) mitigating the adverse impacts of reforms. These three issues are discussed within the context of the country's trade and investment liberalization efforts at the multilateral (WTO), regional (ASEAN and ASEAN+1 agreements) and bilateral levels.

4.1 Increasing Consultation with Stakeholders During Reforms

Besides multilateral, regional and bilateral efforts to liberalize trade and investment, attracting foreign direct investment (FDI) also constitutes an important pillar in the ongoing domestic economic reform efforts of the country. Vietnam is unilaterally improving its major economic laws in order to reduce discriminatory policies governing foreign enterprises (relative to those that govern domestic ones). These unilateral efforts contribute towards narrowing the gap between Vietnam's domestic enterprise policies and those of the other ASEAN member countries.

Consulting relevant stakeholders, including the business community and foreign investors, is an important component of major economic reforms. Notwithstanding the top-down approach towards formulating reforms in past decades, Vietnam has more recently endeavoured to consult stakeholders as part of the process of implementing its regional economic integration commitments and domestic reforms. The scope of consultation has gradually been expanding. Various workshops and dialogues have been organized to consult the business community about various integration roadmaps and other related issues. Regarding ASEAN integration, the views of stakeholders on such major issues as tariff reductions for sensitive and highly sensitive products, sanitary and phytosanitary measures and trade facilitation were collected. This practice of consultation was formalized in 2010 after the Prime Minister made consultations with stakeholders mandatory when formulating major economic reforms.

In an example of this, a number of major laws and regulations were presented to the public during the drafting process (Enterprise Law, Investment Law, Construction Law, and so on). Foreign business associations (including the Chambers of Commerce of various countries), foreign investors and foreign enterprises were also invited to provide their comments and/or recommendations, subject to their interests. The Law on Promulgating Legal Normative Documents (i.e., the Law on Law) and its amended 2008 version stipulates different types of regulations that must undergo a public consultation process (via a website) within a period of sixty days. In a notable and more recent effort, the revised Constitution was open for feedback from the Vietnamese people, both inside and outside the country, from January 2 to March 31 of 2013. The Ministry of Justice reported that comments from up to 18 million people in sixty-three provinces and cities were collected by May 2013. The contents of the Constitution that were open for consultation were rather wide-ranging, covering not only issues of economic development but also human rights, environmental protection, and so on.

Another example involves drafting, implementing and reviewing the 2005 unified Enterprise Law. The business community, experts and government agencies were consulted prior to the law's promulgation. Through this process of consultation, the drafting team got to know of the needs of enterprises and the difficulties they might face in the implementation process. Feedback on the draft Law was carefully considered so as to subsequently incorporate relevant changes. Notably, this consultation took place even before the Law on Law formalizing the need for consultation was promulgated.

After the Enterprise Law came into effect, the Task Force for Implementing the Enterprise Law maintained an active role in reviewing practical concerns related to its implementation. For instance, administrative reforms related to business registration were accelerated, saving new businesses time with respect to registering themselves, and acquiring seal and tax numbers. The public consultation process is still being promoted with both domestic and foreign investors identifying the practical implications of the Enterprise Law. A positive consequence of regular consultation was that the National Assembly decided to amend the Enterprise Law, and the revised draft version was finalized for the Plenary Meeting of the National Assembly in May 2014. The revised law was approved by November 2014.

Public consultation has also been extended to issues of socio-economic management, as dictated by the country's annual and five-year development plans. Specifically, different stakeholders — including representatives of local government agencies, local enterprises and other groups (farmers, for example) — are identified at the outset. Such stakeholders are then also invited to participate in assessments of the current situation and outcomes from the previous planning period. Development targets and associated policy measures are undertaken on the basis of such stakeholder consultations.

However, the effectiveness of such consultation is somewhat restricted. With regard to international economic integration in general, and ASEAN integration in particular, consultation efforts are often confined to traditional stakeholders such as government agencies, researchers and the business community. Non-governmental organizations have thus far raised concerns on behalf of various social groups only with respect to the AEC and other important FTAs such as the EU-Vietnam FTA and the TPP. Even then, details of FTA negotiations (including the AEC) are often classified as "confidential", and the public can hardly get access to timely information to raise any of their concerns. For example, the AEC Scorecard data were only made publicly available for the first two phases of implementation (2008–09 and 2010–11), even though the third phase (2012–13) is already over.

Even in the case of domestic reforms that were induced by other international FTAs, the consultation process was not more effective. Consultation was only undertaken with care for major laws such as the Constitution, Enterprise Law, Investment Law, and so on, not only because of their importance to people, but because significant resources (time and money) were dedicated to the drafting processes. Less attention has been paid to various measures of ASEAN integration (such as mutual recognition and services liberalization). Possible reasons include the lack of a regulatory framework for sharing confidential information and technical details during the negotiation process. Accordingly, while various Vietnamese stakeholders had no opportunity to make comments during the negotiation and inception of AEC-related measures, they were also not given sufficient information to plan ahead for the implementation of these measures. In addition, stakeholders were hardly consulted on the reduction of the policy space to support domestic economic activities (due to a phasing out of barriers to trade and investment).

4.2 Building Community Awareness of Potential Changes

It is important to raise awareness on the AEC ahead of any potential changes. As was discussed in section 3, Vietnam's utilization of AFTA/ ATIGA has been modest, amounting to just over 20 per cent in 2011. This figure is noticeably unimpressive considering that the country has been a member of ASEAN for sixteen years. Even when they might benefit from AFTA/ATIGA, export enterprises in Vietnam hardly recognize the need to prepare for and comply with related requirements. Although the problem may be due to seemingly innocuous factors such as the small difference between MFN and AFTA/ATIGA tariffs or the costs of complying with ROOs, it may also indicate some indifference towards the AEC. Even with regard to implementing its WTO commitments, Vietnam's awareness-raising activities were regarded as being insufficient for the needs of lawmakers, regulators, officials and the business community (Government of Vietnam 2012). The adverse impact on the economy in the aftermath of the 2007–08 Global Financial Crisis (GFC) raised additional concerns about the readiness of the business community and policy-makers vis-à-vis more drastic or rapid effects of further liberalization.

Similarly, given the scope and depth of commitments under the AEC, significantly greater efforts to raise community awareness are required. Unfortunately, most Vietnamese businesses are still unfamiliar with the AEC, especially the small- and medium-sized enterprises (SMEs). In a 2014 survey by the Faculty of Economics and Business of the Vietnam National University, only 30 per cent of enterprises in Vietnam were found to have some understanding of the AEC. The rest of the enterprises paid no attention to or had virtually no understanding of AEC-related matters. Accordingly, some argue that the AEC will bring about more difficulties than opportunities for businesses (Nguyen Nhung, 29 January 2015) and this may discourage preparation for more effective Vietnamese participation. Without significant improvements to this state-of-affairs, consensus-building for more concrete reforms to support the AEC will be even harder to realize.

Upon reviewing the institutions for international economic integration (including ASEAN integration) in 2007–11, the Central Institute for Economic Management (2013) has argued that among the reasons for Vietnam's failure to take full advantage of and mitigate negative effects of economic integration is the lack of adequate preparation for the management of international economic integration activities. Unless this is resolved, the country will continue to face further difficulties in making trade and investment liberalization work for its domestic economy.

4.3 Policies to Mitigate the Negative Impact of Trade and Investment Liberalization

Since Vietnam's priority is to reduce inequality, preventing and addressing the adverse effects of reforms (including trade and investment liberalization) are essential complementary policies. In fact, the country has been dedicated to improving its social security since the 1990s. Social security is a priority agenda item that has received even more attention during times of economic difficulties. In the aftermath of the GFC, the government implemented some policies to ensure adequate social security and to prevent an economic downturn and maintain growth. These social security measures have been implemented comprehensively, and they include regular as well as contingency measures to assist households and individuals with managing risks and economic shocks. At the same time, these measures help to mitigate the negative effects of AEC-related liberalization measures. These social security programmes are discussed in greater detail below:

(1) Social insurance acts as a preventative tool for workers when they face illness, work accidents, unemployment and retirement. This was an especially important component during the crisis. The number of compulsory participants grew to 10.6 million in 2013, compared to 9 million in 2009, 8.5 million in 2008 and 3 million in 1995. This figure accounted for 20.3 per cent of the total labour force in 2013. In the case of voluntary social insurance, the number of participants has remained modest — 170,600 people in 2013, compared to around 50,000 in 2009 — even though it came into effect on 1 July 2008.

However, beneficiaries of the social insurance fund are those who have been working in organizations/entities that strictly follow the country's regulations; therefore a large number of workers are excluded from this pool. Some enterprises intentionally ignore the rights of employees, and avoid making contributions to the social insurance fund even when the economy is stable. Since the economic downturn in 2008, there has been a growing trend of evasion or late contributions. This has occurred mainly among the labour-intensive enterprises. Approximately 50 per cent of enterprises are reported to have avoided making contributions to the social insurance fund (Nguyen Thang, 2 November 2014).

(2) Unemployment insurance was implemented for the first time in 2009 (taking effect on 1 January 2009). This aims at providing partial compensation for workers if they lose their jobs or have their labour contracts terminated. Participants of the scheme include contract labour, with unspecified contractual terms of between twelve to thirty-six months with enterprises of more than ten labourers. In addition to monetary support (equal to 60 per cent of the average salary/wage of the last six months prior to unemployment), unemployment insurance provides support for vocational training, job searches and health insurance. Financial support for unemployment insurance comprises contributions by three parties: employees; employers; and the state.

(3) Preferential social treatment is aimed at vulnerable people, mainly the poor, the working poor, people who are schooling, job-seekers, and so on. This social support policy mainly comprises *concessional credit* for job creation, hunger alleviation and poverty reduction as well as credit for poor pupils and students. It should be noted that such policies were already implemented during times of economic difficulty. For example, in 2009, the state set aside about VND8,000 billion for a training and capacity-building education programme so that disadvantaged students can have access to low-interest credit (CIEM 2010). During 2005 to 2012, almost 20 million households were granted concessional credit for income-generating activities; commercial banks also provided direct support to 2.4 million poor households (Tran Huong and Quang Canh, 28 April 2014).

Another long-term policy is the provision of vocational training for poor people. Depending on their needs and the availability of resources, poor labourers were trained free-of-charge. In fact, about 60 per cent of these labourers who were trained as part of a pilot project found jobs or are currently self-employed in income-generating activities (Truong Thi Mai, 17 October 2011). This programme has been highly appreciated by the local population, who consider it a sustainable way of reducing poverty. This model has been extended to cover more communities. From 2006 to 2009, it was replicated in 218 communes spanning 35 provinces. This replicated pilot project was carried out by communal People's Committees in 115 communes (from 17 provinces). The government has continued to support poor communes by implementing specific programmes that include credit support, free health insurance for the poor, building infrastructure for ethnic minorities, who usually reside in under-developed, remote and mountainous areas, and so on. In 2009, notwithstanding scarce budget resources due to the government's economic stimulus programmes, the state built 37,600 new and reconstructed houses for the poor, with a total value of VND400 billion. In addition, 5 million people received insurance cards free-of-charge.

Human resource development has been given particular attention. In 2006 to 2009, 140,000 officials were trained; 90 per cent of them were commune officials. In 2006 to 2010, this number expanded to include 180,000 officials (or 105.8 per cent). Three sets of documents were developed to train officials to plan for community participation and development. Manuals on poverty reduction policies were published and provided to localities and grassroots entities. Central and local media also helped popularize policies on poverty reduction. These efforts have greatly contributed towards improving people's living standards and socio-economic development (Vo Tri Thanh 2014).

(4) Social relief is aimed at providing *basic social relief* in-cash and / or in-kind to those who cannot afford a minimum standard of living. Social relief is implemented in two forms: contingent and regular support. Current support policies are considered safety nets.[10] The effects of these policies on the beneficiaries, however, are not significant as the support amount is rather low, and not even equal to the poverty level. More specifically, regular support amounts to only VND180,000/person/month, which is far below the national poverty line of VND400,000/person/month for rural areas and VND500,000/person/month for urban areas. Recipients are from the bottom percentile of the poor. In addition, with such a small subsidy, it is difficult for them to meet a minimum standard of living. The source of funding for contingent subsidies in the event of adverse shocks (e.g. natural calamities) is the state budget (which accounts for two-thirds of available resources). Other resources from individuals, social organizations and non-governmental organizations are relatively modest.

The natural disaster recovery subsidy is another social relief measure. Depending on the severity and scale of a natural disaster, this subsidy helps people to overcome a fallout through cash or in-kind support from the state budget. This contingent support has contributed to the resettlement of people's lives post-natural disasters. Alongside voluntary support from many households and organizations, these policies have helped contain the incidence of hunger and damage to livelihoods from natural disasters.

The government has also broadened support for those who have served during wartime. They receive monthly benefits and other preferential treatment such as healthcare insurance and housing preferences. In addition to physical support, they receive emotional support via the provision of daily newspapers, participation in cultural activities, support with funeral costs, and so on. The annual state budget for this scheme exceeds VND11,000 billion.

(5) Stimulus packages were introduced by the government in 2006, alongside financial and monetary schemes to overcome the negative effects of the GFC. These packages have taken on several forms such as interest rate subsidies and investments in social infrastructure (including health, education, clean water, transport and housing for the poor). By stabilizing the economy, these packages also ensure social security. In addition, besides supporting the purchase of agricultural machines for production, the state also supports the payment of wages and social insurance via subsidized interest rates. Other policies such as tax exemptions/reductions (for enterprises), the rescheduling of tax payments and the encouragement of exports have a direct impact on maintaining jobs and incomes. They also assist enterprises and household businesses in overcoming difficulties, reducing prices and enhancing competitiveness.[11]

Even so, changes in income inequality have been rather ambiguous (Table 8.5). The Gini coefficient rose from 35.8 per cent in 2006 to 39.3 per cent in 2010. That year, the top quintile reaped a 46.2 per cent share of national income, greater than the share in 2006 (43.3 per cent). At the same time, the bottom quintile only accounted for 6.5 per cent of total income, a reduction from the 7.2 per cent recorded in 2006. This trend reversed in 2010–12, with the Gini coefficient as well as the income share of the top quintile falling; the share of the bottom quintile rose slightly. A decrease in the poverty rate, as was mentioned in section 1, should not be accompanied by an increase in the share of the richest people. Community-building efforts are likely to lead to only modest improvements to the incomes of the poorest segment of the population, lifting them just above the national poverty line. At the same time, their vulnerability to adverse shocks may

TABLE 8.5
Changes in Income Inequality and Poverty Levels, 1998–2012 (%)

	1998	2002	2004	2006	2008	2010	2012
Gini	35.5	37.6	36.8	35.8	35.6	39.3	35.6
Income share (top 20%)	44.0	45.6	44.5	43.3	43.4	46.2	43
Income share (bottom 20%)	8.0	7.5	7.2	7.2	7.4	6.5	7.0
Poverty gap							
Poverty ($1.25/day)	14.9	11.2	8.4	5.3	3.7	0.8	0.6
Poverty ($2/day)	34.0	28.0	22.9	16.3	13.5	4.2	2.9
Poverty headcount ratio							
Poverty ($1.25/day)	49.4	40.1	31.4	21.4	16.8	3.9	2.4
Poverty ($2/day)	78.1	68.7	60.4	48.1	43.3	16.8	12.5

Source: World Bank 2014*b*.

cause them to fall back into poverty again. As such, it is essential that future community-building efforts adopt an inclusive stance.

5. CONCLUSION AND POLICY RECOMMENDATIONS

Over the past decades, Vietnam has strived to combine domestic market-oriented reforms and proactive international economic integration. ASEAN has offered the first opportunity for Vietnam to adapt itself to bolder trade and investment liberalization. At this stage, the country is fully committed to a comprehensive community-building process. From the discussions above, it can be safely deduced that looking ahead, Vietnam should aim to increase people's participation in implementing the AEC as well as in the design of future measures. Therefore, building domestic consensus plays an important role in the future of the AEC beyond 2015.

This chapter has emphasized that efforts directed towards building the AEC should not be separated from fundamental institutional and economic reforms needed for the country to shift towards a market economy and attain more inclusive growth (ADB 2014; CIEM 2013). Addressing these aforementioned needs requires the adoption of several measures, which are outlined below.

First, Vietnam should improve its understanding and knowledge of its international economic integration commitments under ASEAN and other frameworks. It should especially bring discussions on related opportunities and challenges to SMEs in rural areas. Vietnam should ensure effective information-sharing between various ministries, authorities, localities and enterprises. This could start with discussions on trade and investment followed by other issues such as the movement of natural persons and the promotion of SMEs. At the same time, Vietnam should consult larger segments of the private sector, sectoral associations, socio-political organizations and the people in implementing its trade commitments.

Secondly, Vietnam should incorporate action plans or programmes for the implementation of its international economic integration commitments (especially under the AEC). These plans should be incorporated into its socio-economic development schemes. It is important to harmonize the liberalization of Vietnam's commitments at all three levels: multilateral; regional; and bilateral. In fact, the limited utilization of AFTA/ATIGA displays the need for more AEC-specific measures in the country. This should be accompanied by publicly available periodic reviews so that urgent issues emerging from liberalization, insofar as they affect various social groups, can be addressed.

Finally, the country should strengthen the universal, but flexible, social security system that is currently in place. The system should incorporate diversified and efficient social security programmes targeted at low-income and adversely affected people. In this regard, ensuring workers' access to social security systems plays an important role. Experience-sharing with other ASEAN member states, particularly in the areas of rural development, agricultural supply chains, and so on, may enhance Vietnam's active participation in the regional community-building process.

Notes

1. For further reference, see Vo Tri Thanh and Nguyen Tu Anh (2006), and Dinh Hien Minh et al. (2010).
2. See MARD (2004) for further details.
3. However, this occurred alongside several changes to the poverty line. From 2011 to 2015, the national poverty line stood at VND400,000/person/month in rural areas and VND500,000 in urban areas. The corresponding figures for the period 2006–10 were VND200,000/person/month and VND260,000/person/month. From 2001 to 2005 they stood at VND100,000/person/month and VND150,000/person/month, respectively.
4. The country signed a trade agreement with the European Union (EU) in 1992.

It joined the Association of South East Asian Nations (ASEAN) and the ASEAN Free Trade Area (AFTA) in 1995. Subsequently, in 1998, it also became a part of the Asia Pacific Economic Cooperation (APEC) forum.
5. The surrender rate refers to the proportion of export proceeds that foreign-invested enterprises have to convert into domestic currency (i.e., the VND). In order to attract FDI, Vietnam gradually relaxed the surrender requirement in the early 2000s. The surrender rate fell over time from 100 per cent in the 1990s to 0 per cent in 2004.
6. In fact, the strategic schedule is divided into four phases: 2008–09; 2010–11; 2012–13; and 2014–15. However, when this chapter was being written, data were only available for the first two phases.
7. ASEAN established the AEC Scorecard as a monitoring mechanism. As a compliance tool, the Scorecard reports progress on the implementation of various AEC measures, identifies implementation gaps and challenges, and tracks the realisation of the AEC by the end of 2015.
8. The ASEAN-6 includes Brunei, Malaysia, Indonesia, Philippines, Singapore, and Thailand.
9. See CIEM (2013).
10. Theoretically, the supporting programmes are divided into three types: safety nets, risk prevention and capacity-building measures.
11. According to the report by the Standing Committee of the XII National Assembly (6th session), interest rate support helps to reduce borrowing costs in Ho Chi Minh City by 36.6 per cent and in Thua Thien Hue by 30 per cent. Furthermore, 45.8 per cent of enterprises in Da Nang with access to loans with interest rate support have reduced the prices of their products.

References

CIEM. *Vietnam's Economy in 2009*. Hanoi: Finance Publishing House and Central Institute for Economic Management, 2010.
———. *Comprehensive Evaluation of Vietnam's Socio-Economic Performance Five Years after the Accession to the World Trade Organization*. Hanoi: Finance Publishing House and Central Institute for Economic Management, 2013.
———. *Macroeconomic Report for Q4 and 2014*. Hanoi: Finance Publishing House and Central Institute for Economic Management, 2015.
Dinh Hien Minh, Trinh Quang Long and Nguyen Anh Duong. "Trade, Growth, Employment, and Wages in Vietnam: Globalization, Adjustment and the Challenge of Inclusive Growth". In *Globalization, Adjustment and the Challenge of Inclusive Growth: Boosting Inclusive Growth and Industrial Upgrading in Indonesia, the Philippines and Vietnam*, edited by Ponciano S. Intal Jr., Miguel Roberto V. Borromeo and Gerardo L. Largoza. Manila: De La Salle University, 2010.

EU-MUTRAP. "Assessing the Impacts of the Regional Comprehensive Economic Partnership on Vietnam's Economy". Technical Report No. ICB-8, Output 3. European Trade Policy and Investment Support Project, 2014.

Government of Vietnam. "Báo cáo tình hình thực hiện Nghị quyết 16/2007/NQ-CP về đẩy mạnh hội nhập kinh tế quốc tế sau khi Việt Nam trở thành thành viên của Tổ chức Thương mại Thế giới" [Report of the Government on Implementation of Resolution 16/2007/NQ-CP on Advancing International Economic Integration after WTO Accession], 2012.

MARD. "Chuyển dịch cơ cấu nông nghiệp và kinh tế nông thôn 20 năm Đổi Mới" [The Development of Agriculture and the Rural Economy in 20 years since *Doi Moi*]. Summary Report. Ministry of Agriculture and Rural Development, October 2004.

Nguyen Nhung. "Vietnamese Businesses to Face Difficulties when Joining AEC". *Sai Gon Giai Phong Daily News* [online], 29 January 2015. Available at <http://www.saigon-gpdaily.com.vn/Business/2015/1/112509/> (accessed 6 February 2015).

Nguyen Thang. "Xử lý tình trạng nợ đọng bảo hiểm xã hội: Cần những giải pháp mạnh, đồng bộ" [Addressing Outstanding Debts of Social Insurance: A Need for Bold and Consistent Measures]. *Quan Doi Nhan Dan* [online], 2 November 2014. Available at <http://www.qdnd.vn/qdndsite/vi-vn/61/43/kinh-te-xa-hoi/xu-ly-tinh-trang-no-dong-bao-hiem-xa-hoi-can-nhung-giai-phap-manh-dong-bo/329643.html> (accessed 6 February 2015).

Tran Ba Cuong. "FTA Utilization and How to Support SMEs". Presentation file. Mimeographed, 2012.

Tran Huong and Quang Canh. "Tín dụng cho người nghèo là điểm sang" [Credit for the Poor is a Remarkable Success]. *Banking Times* [online], 28 April 2014. Available at <http://www.baomoi.com/Tin-dung-cho-nguoi-ngheo-la-diem-sang/126/13679338.epi> (accessed 6 February 2015).

Truong Thi Mai. "Implementation of Policies on Poverty Reduction in Vietnam". *Communist Review* [online], 17 October 2011. Available at <http://english.tapchicongsan.org.vn/Home/Vietnam-on-the-way-of-renovation/2011/260/Implementation-of-policies-on-poverty-reduction-in-Viet-Nam.aspx> (accessed 6 February 2015).

UNDP. "Human Development Report 2014: Sustaining Human Progress: Reducing Vulnerabilities and Building Resilience". United Nations Development Programme, 2014. Available at <http://hdr.undp.org/en/content/human-development-report-2014> (accessed 31 August 2014).

University of Economics and Business, Vietnam National University. "Assessing the Preparedness of Vietnam ahead of the ASEAN Economic Community" [In Vietnamese]. Research Report under the State-level Program. Mimeographed, 2014.

Vietnam News Daily [online]. "Jury Out on Vietnam's Middle Income Trap

Status", 14 April 2014. Available at <http://vietnamnews.vn/opinion/in-the-spotlight/253608/jury-out-on-vns-middle-income-trap-status.html> (accessed 6 February 2015).

Vo Tri Thanh. "Counting Down to 2015: Progress Towards AEC and Perspectives from Vietnam". Paper prepared for International Conference on "Emerging Regionalism: Paradigm Shift of International Relations in East Asia", Hong Kong, 9 March 2012.

———. "Making Growth Inclusive: The Case of Vietnam". Paper Prepared for UNESCAP, December 2014.

——— and Nguyen Anh Duong. "Vietnam after Two Years of WTO Accession: What Lessons Can Be Learnt". *ASEAN Economic Bulletin* 26, no. 1 (2009): 115–35.

——— and Nguyen Tu Anh. "Institutional Changes for Private Sector Development in Vietnam: Experiences and Lessons". Paper presented at the conference on "Advancing East Asian Economic Integration: Microeconomic Foundation of Economic Performance in East Asia", Manila, 23–24 November, 2006.

——— and Pham Chi Quang. "Managing Capital Flows: The Case of Vietnam". ADBI Discussion Paper No. 105. Manila: Asian Development Bank Institute, May 2008.

World Bank. "GDP per capital, PPP (International Current $)". World Development Indicators Database [online]. Washington, D.C.: World Bank, 2014*a*. Available at <http://data.worldbank.org/indicator/NY.GDP.PCAP.PP.CD> (accessed 6 February 2015).

———. World Development Indicators Database [online]. Washington, D.C.: World Bank. Available at <http://data.worldbank.org/data-catalog/world-development-indicators>.

INDEX

Note: Page numbers followed by "n" refer to notes.

Singapore's participation in, 123
trade facilitation measures in
Indonesia, implementation of,
47–59
trade-in-services agreement, 29–30
trading community, 8
Authorized Economic Operators
(AEO), 52
programme, 51
automobile industry, 95
trade in, 103, 106
autonomous services liberalization,
76–80
aviation hub and airlines, ASEAN
open skies policy impact on
Singapore, 138–45
aviation market liberalization, 140–41

B
Badan Koordinasi Penanaman Modal
(BKPM), 56, 57, 61
Badan Standardisasi Nasional (BSN), 53
Bank of Thailand (BOT), 158
bilateral FTAs, 129, 130
proliferation of, 162
Board of Investment (BOI), 101, 114
bonded-warehouse management, 52
Brunei-Singapore-Thailand
agreement, 140
bumiputera, 72, 87
equity, 73, 74, 83
requirements, 73, 81, 82
Bumiputera Commercial and
Industrial Community (BCIC), 85

C
Car Development Program (CDP),
117
Cebu Declaration on the Acceleration
of the Establishment of an
ASEAN Community by 2015, 27

Center for International Trade Studies
(CITS), rice farmers' income
distribution analyses, 166–67
Cha-am Hua Hin ASEAN Summit, 163
Changi Airport, OS/SAM and
opportunities and challenges,
142–43
Chiang Mai Initiative (CMI), 31–32
Chiang Mai Initiative Multi-
lateralization (CMIM), 32–34
China, International Monetary Fund
and, 31
Clark Development Corporation
(CDC), 114
CLMV countries, 174n4
collective economic mechanism for
regional stability, 4
Commercial Vehicle Development
Program (CVDP), 117
Common Effective Preferential Tariff
(CEPT), 127
Common Effective Preferential Tariff–
ASEAN Free Trade Area (CEPT-
AFTA), 26–27, 97
Competition Act, 159
completely knocked down (CKD)
imports, 106–7
Comprehensive Automotive
Resurgence Strategy (CARS), 115
Comprehensive Economic
Partnership (CEP), 29
Comprehensive Economic
Partnership Agreement (CEPA),
between Japan and ASEAN, 30
Comprehensive Economic
Partnership for East Asia
(CEPEA), 31
Consumer Protection Act, 159
contemporary trade agreements, 135
Convention on International Aviation,
150n19

CPSIA information can be obtained
at www.ICGtesting.com
Printed in the USA
LVHW080150180720
660706LV00005B/105